OZ CLA[RKE]

WINE BU[YING]
GUIDE 2007

Oz's 250 Best Wines
130 Best Wine Shops
What to Buy, Where to Buy it

TIME WARNER
BOOKS

WEBSTERS
INTERNATIONAL PUBLISHERS

This edition first published in 2006

Created and designed by
Websters International Publishers Limited
Axe and Bottle Court
70 Newcomen Street
LONDON SE1 1YT
www.websters.co.uk
www.ozclarke.com

Oz Clarke's Wine Buying Guide 2007 edition
Copyright © 2006 Websters International Publishers
Text copyright © 2006 Oz Clarke

A CIP catalogue for this book is available from the
British Library

ISBN-13: 978-0-316-73242-0
ISBN-10: 0-316-73242-7

Printed and bound in the UK by CPI Bath

Time Warner Books
An imprint of
Little, Brown Book Group
Brettenham House
Lancaster Place
LONDON WC2E 7EN
www.littlebrown.co.uk

A member of the Hachette Livre Group of companies
Time Warner Books is a trademark of Time Warner Inc.
or an affiliated company. Used under licence by
Little, Brown Book Group, which is not affiliated with
Time Warner Inc.

The information and prices contained in the Guide were
correct to the best of our knowledge when we went to press.
Although every care has been taken in the preparation of the
Guide, neither the publishers nor the editors can accept any
liability for any consequences arising from the use of
information contained herein.
Oz Clarke's Wine Buying Guide is an annual publication.
We welcome any suggestions you might have for the
next edition.

Editor Maggie Ramsay
Art Director Nigel O'Gorman
Tastings Co-ordinator Julie Ross
Editorial Assistant Sarah Douglas
DTP Keith Bambury, Jayne Clementson
Production Sara Granger, Emily Toogood

ADVERTISING SALES
Tim Bradshaw
112 Highfield Lane
Hemel Hempstead
HERTS HP2 5JG
tel/fax 01442 231131

Contents

Introduction

2006 has been one of those years when you don't know whether to weep or cheer. Wonderful things have happened in the wine world. But some terrible things have happened too. And sometimes wonderful and terrible have collided at the same wine event.

The most obvious example of this is the 2005 vintage in Bordeaux. This is a stellar vintage. It's not the biggest, the ripest, the brashest Bordeaux vintage I've ever tasted, but it does possess something that several of my favourite Bordeaux producers describe as 'aromatic explosion', 'an aroma of emotion', 'a character which moves me'. These were three guys each saying they'd never experienced anything like the style of the 2005 vintage, and they were proud – and emotional – as we tasted their wines. I had to agree. The aromatic intensity of the best of these wines seems to reach far past your nostrils into your very soul.

And into your wallet. Deep, deep into your wallet. This is the most expensive Bordeaux vintage ever. The fabled First Growths – the handful of top reds – finally announced their prices at the end of June. If any of you out there has just won the lottery, you can have a case – one case of 12 bottles – of Latour or Margaux or whatever, for little more than £4,750. If you want St-Émilion superstar Ausone, then £8,000 might secure you a case. These First Growths have increased their prices on average by 300% over the 2004 vintage. They're the worst offenders, but the average price increase for the couple of hundred châteaux at the top of the tree is 95%.

How happy they must be. Happier than the thousands of proprietors of châteaux rather further off the media-beaten track, where the outstanding quality of the vintage has a bitter taste, because they're going bankrupt. Whereas those First Growths can rejoice in getting a price of £350 for each bottle they sell, out in the Entre-Deux-Mers region, where the majority of Bordeaux's wine is made, many producers are waging a losing battle to achieve a price of one euro – yes, one euro – a bottle. Even with all our taxes and duties you'll find Bordeaux in UK supermarkets and discount stores for £2.99 – which is about as low as drinkable reds go.

Drinkable red? Barely. The bottom end of Bordeaux is awash with rubbish just as the top end is flowing with more excellent wine year by year. Some proprietors are delirious. Far more are desperate. Now this is Bordeaux I've been talking about. But we could be having this discussion in many other parts of France too. The Languedoc, in particular, is making the best wines it has ever made, and many individual properties are charging – and getting – the highest prices they've ever achieved for their wines. Yet the bottom end is in as bad a plight as Bordeaux, if not worse. At least almost all Bordeaux qualifies for an Appellation Contrôlée. Substantial parts of the Languedoc produce wine that basically qualifies for nothing, and whatever market it might once have had is shrivelling by the minute, especially since the French, who used to drink most of it, are now drinking millions of litres of wine less every year.

This is creating very serious social problems in France. In the Languedoc and in Bordeaux wine 'terrorists' are smashing the vats of merchants they suspect of dealing in imported wine even cheaper than the muck they produce, motorways are being blocked, government offices attacked. And it's not just France. Every major wine producer in the EU is suffering as their domestic wine consumption dwindles and their exports can't take up the slack. Wine is being sent for emergency distillation at an unprecedented rate. France and Italy committed 750 million bottles of wine to be turned into car fuel, deodorant, insect spray, aftershave – anything that people might want when they don't want cheap wine. Spain and Greece followed with a crisis distillation of 80 million litres of stuff no one wanted.

ALL CHANGE IN THE EU

The trouble is Europe is producing far too much wine and, in the EU at least, they seem to think they have a right to do so. In every serious wine-producing country in the EU, domestic wine consumption is dropping. If there is any bright light in the gloom it is that people are drinking less but better. So, any logical person, any business-oriented person – any New World person – would say, fine, we must produce less to try to balance supply and demand, to be able to ask for a decent price that will allow us – if people really are drinking less but better – to invest it in our wines and produce higher quality.

Yet it hasn't happened because neither any national government nor the EU has had the courage to say enough is enough. The absurd and wasteful agricultural subsidy which sloshes in waves from Brussels to all the wine regions of the EU must stop. It's our money, our billions that are being wasted. We want to spend our money on wine we like, and our taxes on something more worthwhile than subsidising more than a million hectares of sub-standard European vineyards.

Well, perhaps 2006 will prove to have been the year it all started to change. Mariann Fischer Boel, the EU Agriculture Commissioner, has not only demanded a reduction in acreage of 400,000 hectares across Europe – that's more than three times the size of South Africa's total vineyard area – and has offered over two billion euros enticement to get it done, but she's also realized that one of the reasons so many European wines have gone out of fashion is that they are hidebound by regulations that any New World producer would laugh out of court. At the moment, you can't use oak chips to provide a cheap and cheerful vanilla softness to European wines. All those nice easygoing New World cheapos use them, so why can't the Europeans? Commissioner Fischer Boel says she'll change that. Basic 'Table Wines', i.e. the bottom end of the market, can't use a vintage date, and can't say what grapes they've employed – things that might, you know, help to sell the wine. Can you imagine Blossom Hill or Lindemans or Kumala from the New World accepting such strictures? Well, the Commissioner says she'll ensure Europe doesn't have to either. There's a lot of other stuff she says she's going to implement, and you'll see it in the papers during the next year. Encouragingly, she says she's fed up with cosmetic fixes and intends to start enacting change within nine months. By the time of next year's edition of this Guide we should be seeing the start of an overhaul of European wine that is probably at least a decade, if not two, overdue.

And predictably, but accurately, the New World has been blamed for all Europe's troubles. Well, we Brits have been as well. France in particular accuses the New World of taking away her exports and is clearly laying the blame primarily at the UK's door. Well, yes, it's true. That's because the New World gave us something we wanted, while France and the other European heavyweights refused to believe change was necessary. But while they were banging their jingoistic drums and bewailing the fact that 'the barbarians are at the gate' (a direct quote from a French prime time TV show I saw a couple of years ago) – the barbarians being the Australians, Californians, Chileans, anyone who dares to usurp France's (in particular) and Europe's (in general) God-given right to supply all our wine-drinking needs – well, the barbarians were getting on with it.

WORLD WINE LAKE
Now, you might think that only Europe has a wine lake. Not so. The Australians were complaining just before this year's harvest – which was big, by the way, only 4 per cent lower than the previous year's record crop – that they had a whole year's

Making notes at Château La Clotte (how apt), just outside the town of St-Émilion in Bordeaux

vintage in the vats unsold. Some winemakers said there was a lot more than one full vintage sloshing around. But the 2006 vintage brought crisis. Contracts broken. Millions of vines left unpicked. The growers demanded $60 million from their government to help them in their catastrophe of overproduction. The government offered them $50,000 for research into wine marketing. That's the free market. That's the New World. The government view is that if you can't make a go of grape-growing, do something else and don't expect us to bail you out. And the big Australian brand owners will take the opportunity to pay rock-bottom prices for their grapes, which will allow them to spend even more money promoting their mega-brands in our market. I only wish I could say they would take the opportunity to improve the quality of their product, most of which has been slipping for years now, ever since the multinationals and brewers took over the main companies. But they won't. They're doing too well out of bribing all of us to drink their wines with deep discounts and half-price offers.

DRINKING AND THINKING

But are we actually falling into the discount trap so willingly? Are we really falling for the blandishments that the big brands offer us through patently unreal advertising and discounting of such ferocity that surely we know quality cannot hold up at such prices? Well, yes and no. Earlier this year in Paris they held a 'Wine Evolution' forum to see where wine was going. My friend Robert Joseph had done his sums on the UK. Last year, he said, the four leading brands of wine – Hardys, Blossom Hill, Gallo and Jacob's Creek – increased their sales by 48% in what appeared to otherwise be a stagnant market. If you had to look for a vibrant sector, it seemed to be sweet pink blush wine from California. 65% of the wine we buy is on discount, often as deep as half price. And the traditional European wines that take a bit of an effort to understand – French Appellation Contrôlées, Italian DOCs, Spanish DOs – are struggling to hold on to their shelf space because, in the words of one of our biggest supermarkets, 'we are not in the education business'. And yet whenever wine people talk about how to get the general public to trade upwards, they talk of education as being the most effective tool.

Education, certainly: I'm in that business, even if the big supermarkets aren't. But equally important is avoidance of disappointment. Too many times friends of mine have 'traded up' for a special occasion from a good New World wine to supposedly superior – and definitely more expensive – classic French or Italian, and been left feeling disappointed and confused because it simply didn't taste as good as their regular tipple. Didn't taste as good, or wasn't so easy to understand? Without education, they won't be making a repeat purchase, so we'll never know. And if the European classics simply say, well, that's their problem, and don't try to understand my friends' disappointment, we will see fewer European classics on the shelves of our High Streets, and it'll be left to the doughty independents to continue their struggle to offer us wines that may not have such smashmouth fruit and heady alcohol, but which offer endless fascination if we take the time and effort to drink them with our brains in gear.

THE GOOD NEWS IN THE HIGH STREET

And then you see that Tesco have introduced a 'Premium' range of 50 very serious wines into between 90 and 190 stores. Bordeaux, Burgundy, top Champagne – and Grange from Australia at £100 a bottle. Tesco don't do things that they don't think will make money. Nor do Majestic. They've opened 15 Fine Wine Sections, and they're opening 10 more. Their most recent figures show that fine wine sales are up 30%. Somerfield have reduced their under-£4 range and increased their £5–7 range, which now accounts for a third of sales. Sainsbury's have expanded their Taste the Difference range and the greatest activity is between £6 and £10. All of these must think that there's profit in providing better wine and that we want it enough to buy it. If there really is going to be an increasing divide between discount booze and quality wine, if the UK isn't going to become a laughing stock and a dumping ground for the international wine trade, we must stand up and be counted and buy the wine whose flavours will excite us at a price that is fair to us, to the retailer and to the producers.

Wine finder

RED WINES

VdP = Vin de Pays

Under £5

Cabernet Sauvignon, Budavár 103
Cabernet Sauvignon, Fairtrade 95
Cadet de Gascogne, VdP des Côtes de Gascogne, Vasconia 88
Cinsault-Shiraz, Fairtrade 101
Côtes du Rhône-Villages (ASDA) 98
Cuvée Chasseur, VdP de l'Hérault 103
Cuvée de Richard, VdP de l'Aude 101
Garnacha-Tempranillo, Gran López, Campo de Borja 98
Garnacha-Tempranillo, La Riada, Campo de Borja 91, 136
Grenache, Fruits of France, VdP d'Oc 100
Grenache, Lime Tree, Murray-Darling 93
Malbec, Argentine (Co-op) 100
Malbec-Bonarda, St Lucas 101
Merlot, Chilean Organic 87
Merlot, Sunrise, Concha y Toro 136
Pinot Noir, Casablanca Valley (M&S) 94
Primitivo-Merlot, Da Luca 90
Shiraz Reserve, Bushland (Hope Estate) 101
Vieille Fontaine, VdP du Comté Tolosan 103

£5–£10

Alicante, Laderas de El Sequé, Laderas de Pinosa 94
Almansa, Marques de Rojas, Bodegas Piqueras 77
Beaujolais, Dom. Chatelus de la Roche 81, 136
Blaufränkisch, Feiler-Artinger 63
Blaufränkisch, Erwin Tinhof 63
Bordeaux, Ch. Tire-Pé 128
Bordeaux Supérieur, Ch. de l'Abbaye de Sainte-Ferme 122
Bordeaux Supérieur, Ch. Clos Renon 123
Bordeaux Supérieur, Ch. Grand Village 124
Bordeaux Supérieur, Ch. les Grangeaux 124
Bordeaux Supérieur, Ch. Pey la Tour 124
Bordeaux Supérieur, Ch. Pierrail 124
Bordeaux Supérieur, Ch. Ribeyrolles 126
Bordeaux Supérieur, Ch. Villepreux 128
Cabernet Sauvignon, Miru, Beelgara Estate 76
Cabernet Sauvignon Reserve, Casa Leona 80
Cabernet Sauvignon, Casillero del Diablo 88
Cabernet Sauvignon, Coonawarra (M&S) 53
Cabernet Sauvignon, Coonawarra (Katnook) 67
Cabernet Sauvignon, Kangarilla Road 53
Cabernet Sauvignon, Peñalolen 30, 137

Cabernet Sauvignon, Pirque Estate 54
Cabernet Sauvignon, The Society's Chilean (Concha y Toro) 78
Cabernet Sauvignon-Carmenère, Porta Reserve, Maipo Valley 70
Cabernet-Shiraz, Margaret River (Evans & Tate) 73
Calatayud, Papa Luna 59
Carignan, VdP Catalan, Ferrer-Ribière 43
Carmenère Reserva, Mont Gras 70
Carmenère Reserve, Peteroa 74
Carmenère-Shiraz, Doña Dominga Reserva 45
Chianti Classicio, Villa Cafaggio 139
Chiroubles, Georges Duboeuf 50, 136
Cigales Crianza, Museum 59
Corbières, Ch. Pech-Latt 65, 138
Côtes de Castillon, Seigneurs d'Aiguilhe 126, 138
Côtes du Rhône Villages, Plan de Dieu, Dom. de la Meynarde 91
Côtes du Roussillon-Villages, Le Roc des Anges, Dom. Segna de Cor 23
Douro (Quinta do Crasto) 74
The Fergus, Tim Adams 34
Fleurie, Christian Gaidon 54
Fronsac, Ch. Villars 128
Grenache, Peter Lehmann 95
Grenache, Willunga 100 56

Top 20

One of the inspiring things about getting my thoughts together to recommend my top wines of the year is how often Australia – the real Australia – still powers through. It makes a mockery of the flat, tired, big-brand stuff that crowds the High Street shelves. You won't find all that many of these wines *in* the High Street; you'll have to go to independents and mail order companies for most of the really exciting stuff. I could say the same about the truly exciting wines from France or Italy or Spain – you'll need to contact people like Yapp Brothers, or Lea and Sandeman, or Caves de Pyrene. And if you do, you'll be opening your eyes to a whole new world of wine. You couldn't make a better start than with some of our thrilling top 20 wines.

This year I've picked two winning wines: one white, one red

NO O4 left. Have 2003

Tim Adams

2004
SEMILLON
CLARE VALLEY

WINE OF AUSTRALIA
750mL 12.0%Vol.

❶ 2004 Semillon, Tim Adams,
♀ **Clare Valley, South Australia, £8.99, Tesco**
Talk about originality and consistency combined. Year after year we recommend Tim Adams Semillon, yet every year it tastes different from the last. Vintages make a real difference in the Clare Valley, and Tim Adams is such a man of the soil he would hate to get in the way of a vintage expressing itself. This year, Tim Adams climbs the peak and wins the prize for being the most stunningly original, delicious white wine I've tasted this year. The wine seems to mix several excellent styles in one wine. There's a wonderful bright Sunday morning smell of coffee beans, a mouthwatering scent of grilled cashew nuts and the unexpected beauty of fresh polished leather. Take a mouthful and it's as though the wine is a man-child, austere yet come-hither, mature yet unready. That leather aroma runs right through the wine and the coffee bean becomes green beans and green leaf and acts as a freshener along with a lemon acidity so mild it's as though it's been diluted with a drop of milk chocolate. And in the heart of all this is a bone-dry richness like the flesh of a baked apple as it turns fluffy and the skin just before it burns.

Please bear in mind that wine is not made in infinite quantities – some of these may well sell out, but the following year's vintage should then become available.

① 2003 Châteauneuf-du-Pape, Le Vieux Donjon, Rhône Valley, France, £26, Yapp Brothers

The guys in the Barossa and Napa Valleys of Australia and California ought to get on the plane and turn up at Le Vieux Donjon saying 'give us a lesson in ripening our grapes', because this fantastic Rhône red demonstrates how you can totally, completely, utterly ripen your grapes yet not let them overripen and create shrivelled raisiny flavours in your wine. This is powerful, dense, exciting stuff. Châteauneuf-du-Pape is almost as hot as it gets in southern France, and the 90-year-old vines that make up the core of this wine would have baked in their vineyard, which is largely made up of flat, round heat-conserving stones. And 2003 was the drought year, the hottest year on record in France, yet this wine still has acidity – that's 90-year-old vines and sensitive winemaking for you. The fruit is like a thick brilliant sauce made of black plums, cherries and strawberries, with an added richness like sultanas so crystallized that the sugar crackles on your teeth, and the whole experience is overlaid with the dust of hot stones being cracked together under the blazing sun. *Also at Harrods*

③ 2005 Riesling, Polish Hill, Grosset, Clare Valley, South Australia, £15.95, Liberty Wines

Jeffrey Grosset has been hailed as Australia's Riesling king, and maybe even their white wine king, for some years. I think he keeps on getting better. Like Tim Adams, he grows his vines in the Clare Valley north of Adelaide and, like Adams, he cares passionately about his place in the valley and his ability to show its remarkable conditions at their best. I know the haughty, austere Clare Valley Rieslings well, but I don't think I've ever come across one quite like Grosset's 2005. It's the ultimate attraction of opposites. It shouldn't work, but it does – the mark of genius. The wine is almost tannic. It grips you, it twists your lips and your tongue in its aggressive embrace, then loosens its hold and lets the flavour flood through your mouth. But the aggression isn't over. These are the flavours of the sun-withered skins of discarded peaches, apples scoured by lemon juice, the oil scratched from the lemon skin; this is the mineral scrape of pebbles from the Clare River bed – and magically, this is also a coating of cream, the rub of beeswax and a peacock's tail of ripeness conjured out of nothing.

WINE LIKE YOU'VE NEVER TASTED BEFORE!

From his very first vintage, at age 20, Primo Estate's Joe Grilli wanted to create revolutionary wines

"We didn't just want to make a slightly better cabernet or riesling than someone else", said Joe. "We were going all out to dazzle people. Right from the beginning I wanted to put into practice some of the more radical theories of viticulture and winemaking. I really believed this was the role of small wineries: to explore the unconventional – I still do". And for the past 21 years Joe and his wife Dina have been doing exactly that; creating some wonderfully dazzling and unconventional wines under the JOSEPH and Primo Estate labels.

"We want to keep on with what we are doing – producing highly individual wines inspired by the best Australia can do, with an Italian influence. We introduce some rustic traditions from the old world and blend them with our own hi-tech skills; you can end up with some fabulous stuff."

The 'Moda' fruit drying

For over two decades Primo Estate has consistently produced some of Australia's finest wines. Boundaries have been crossed, technical firsts have been notched up, and innovations become second nature. Primo Estate and JOSEPH wines revolve around handcrafting distinct wines of excellence. Revered by wine lovers, journalists and critics around the world, each vintage becomes a concerted effort to produce something unforgettable!

Have you tasted wine like this before?

www.primoestate.com.au

Available through select outlets and Tesco Fine Wine Range

④ 2003 Petit Manseng Sec, Cabidos, Vin de Pays ♀ des Pyrénées-Atlantiques, Comte Philippe de Nazelle, South-West France, £15.50, Friarwood
This white is a massive antidote to much of the commercial pap that's flooding our High Streets. It comes from way down near the Pyrenees. It uses the rare and intense Petit Manseng grape, and it is *not* afraid of oak. It positively laps the oak up – an intense oak style that only works because the fruit is so interesting. The wine is deep gold and not totally dry, and has a fascinating dense golden flavour of stewed quince and pineapple, bruised baked apple and the strange exhausted sweetness of bletted medlars (I've had them: they *are* strange). This fruit is seasoned with spearmint, sage and coriander seed – does anyone know a recipe that uses those three? – and the texture is waxy and smooth. The whole experience is wild – the flavours way past fresh, halfway to brown – and suddenly, after you've swallowed the wine, your mouth fills with a puddingy softness drifting to shortcrust pastry dryness and a lovely fresh reminder of lemon. The Petit Manseng has performed its role of stormtrooper to the senses once again.

⑤ 2001 Cabernet Sauvignon-Merlot, Moda, Joseph, ♦ Primo Estate, McLaren Vale, South Australia, £19.99, Tesco
The trick with this magnificent wine is either to find some which is sufficiently mature or to buy it young and put it under the stairs until it's gained a bit of age, because the wine transforms into something unique with a few extra years. This one is 5½ years old. When I first tasted this vintage of the Aussie version of north-eastern Italy's Valpolicella Amarone a few years ago, it was impressive but blocked in. Time has now provided the key to releasing the thrilling fruits held inside. It's difficult to imagine that a wine could explode with richer, riper blackcurrant and blackberry fruit than this and still remain drinkable. But the genius of this wine is that the richness doesn't overpower you, it exhilarates you. There's even a date and fig thickness that threatens to rise up in the glass, but the fruit powers past, softened by macaroons and almond cream, and the aftertaste is pure, sweet delight.

⑥ 2004 Lirac, La Reine des Bois, Domaine de la Mordorée, Rhône Valley, France, £15.95, Lea and Sandeman

Lirac is a rocky outcrop that gazes rather balefully over the Rhône Valley to Châteauneuf-du-Pape on the other side of the river. The chief reason for its baleful glare is that the guys at Châteauneuf-du-Pape can ask twice as much money for their wine as the Lirac guys. But another reason is that Lirac rarely achieves the exotic heady brilliance of top Châteauneuf; the wines are usually caught in a strong, rocky cage that seems to imprison whatever extra richness the wine might want to offer. But Mordorée are the best growers in Lirac (they also do a very expensive Châteauneuf, which is fantastic), and they've made Lirac's greater reserve into a strength. This wine has a dark, rich weight, but it's marvellously fresh and is scented with jasmine! You won't get that in a Châteauneuf. The fruit is beautifully fresh too, cherries and loganberries swirled together in rosehip syrup that is lush in the mouth and effortlessly coats the stony tannins which try to butt in without any great conviction of their right to be there. *Also at Ballantynes, H&H Bancroft*

⑦ 2004 Crozes-Hermitage, Alain Graillot, Rhône Valley, France, £13.95, Yapp Brothers

Alain Graillot is the undisputed master of Crozes-Hermitage. This is the broad, rather flat spread of vineyards that stretches away to the south and north of the hill of Hermitage. It doesn't make such dense wines as Hermitage, but in the right hands the wines have an unbeatable perfume and fresh richness of fruit. Graillot's vines aren't even on the best land, but he has the best vision of flavour, he reduces his crop, he calmly waits while others rush to pick, and he then expertly creates this gorgeous red, with its heady exotic scent of lilies and lush blackberry and black plum jam fruit and a savouriness like cold boiled new potatoes that tugs at the wine to stop it being too juicy and to demand that you give it a little respect. *Also at Selfridges*

Vacqueyras in the southern Rhône Valley; beyond it lie Châteauneuf-du-Pape and Lirac

BLANC DE BOTES
2003

Priorat
DENOMINACIÓ D'ORIGEN
QUALIFICADA

750 ML   alc 13.5% by vol.

⑧ 2002
♀ Priorat,
Blanc de Botes,
Clos Berenguer,
Cataluña,
Spain, £13.99,
Raeburn Fine
Wines

White Priorat? I'm not sure I've ever tasted this before – in which case trust Raeburn, one of Britain's true originals, to bring it to my attention. I had thought it would be far too hot for white wine on these baking slate slopes, but then these are the ancient white grapes of the far south – Garnacha Blanca, Xarello and Pedro Ximénez – and they can cope with whatever heat you throw at them. Especially if you decide to barrel-ferment the wine. I'd have said this was too much of a good thing, but this is a magnificent beast. It has a creamy, baked richness like custard skin, like the burnt corner of a rice pudding, like the suffocating softness of semolina, which would be altogether excessive without a continuous raw wiry slash of lemon, and a wood influence that is positively resiny, dry and slightly tannic. Fascinating. Like an overcooked Pessac-Léognan white Bordeaux, with nuts and cereal haphazardly scattered over the glass.

⑨ 2002 Cabernet Sauvignon, The Willows Vineyard, 🍷 Barossa Valley, South Australia, £10.99, Australian Wine Club

Sometimes it's the Shiraz, sometimes it's the Semillon, but The Willows always delivers fabulous flavours. This time it's Cabernet Sauvignon, and my first tasting note is 'a bit tannic, but the flavour is heavenly'. Forget the tannin. My notes talk about soaring scents, unashamed, irresistible – hey, hang on. What does this nectar really taste like? Soaring blackcurrant, fabulously ripe but refreshingly dry and backed up by black morello cherries, and peppermint and eucalyptus scent. The tannin will allow you to age this for a while, but plonk a great steak down next to it and you won't notice the tannin. The taste is so good you may not notice the tannin anyway. *Also at Noel Young Wines*

⑩ 2004 Côtes du Roussillon-Villages, Le 🍷 Roc des Anges, Domaine Segna de Cor, Languedoc-Roussillon, France, £8.75, Les Caves de Pyrene

This wine is all about power. It's a deep, dark purple colour which straight away sends a warning shot across your bows, so don't expect an easy ride. As soon as you take a mouthful, you'll be rocked back on your heels by the sledgehammer density of black plum fruit veering towards date and prune overripeness, but thankfully coming up short so that the wine stays fresh. It's quite tannic, and ideally would be aged for another 2–5 years, and its minerality is like rocks strewn down a mountainside. *Also at Green & Blue, Philglas & Swiggot, Wimbledon Wine Cellars*

⑪ 2004 Shiraz-Grenache, DNA, Tim 🍷 Smith Wines, Barossa Valley, South Australia, £10.99, Oz Wines

Tim Smith. Such a short name. It doesn't even hint at the long legacy of pleasure and fun his wines leave. This is sheer happy juice – damson, loganberry and blackcurrant juice, lush, ripe and ... slurpy? Well, the label says this wine is 'slurpy' – as in fresh, super-ripe slurpy, messy, thrilling, laughter slurpy, burps and stumbles, shrieks and, later, dreamy bliss. This is great picnic and party wine. But at 14.5% alcohol, don't let yourself be seduced by its come-hither charms. Oh do, do. Why not? What's it for? What's life for?

**12 2004 Shiraz, Water Wheel Vineyards,
Bendigo, Victoria, Australia, £9.50, Oz Wines**

This wine piles in at 15.5% alcohol. I really don't want my wine to be so strong, because I like drinking reasonable quantities of the stuff. But this one does taste delicious, and I suppose you could always dilute it with, I don't know, one part water, ten parts wine. That would take it down to 14% and I suspect the flavour would still be much the same. And it is some flavour. Rich, yes, but not artificially so, not cloying, not sweet, just fantastic rich blackcurrant, scented with mint and eucalyptus and fattened out with toffee and the bitter depth of black chocolate.

VI DE GUARDA
2001

Priorat
DENOMINACIÓ D'ORIGEN
QUALIFICADA

750 ML   ALC. 14.5% BY VOL.

**13 2001 Priorat, Vi de Guarda, Clos Berenguer,
Cataluña, Spain, £14.99, Raeburn Fine Wines**

I'm not the biggest fan of most Priorats. A few years ago they seemed to fill a gap in the Spanish wine psyche for a new superstar category. They had all the right attributes in these baking Catalonian vineyards – low yields, high alcohol, wild men, rich men, limited availability, silly price – but I still thought a lot of them were a parade of Emperors in their new clothes. Some still are, but luckily there seems to be an increasing number that are delivering, and at prices that are high but not silly. Clos Berenguer is one that delivers, and the flavour truly *is* unique. So many Priorats lack acidity, and are merely stifling and baked. This has acidity, and this means that, despite a brown richness of sultanas, crunchy sweet raisins, muscovado sugar and dried figs, despite an Amarone-type bitter edge to the cherry plum fruit, the final effect is of a wine that seems old and yet amazingly fresh at the same time.

**14 2001 Jasnières, Cuvée Tradition, Bénédicte de Rycke,
Loire Valley, France, £8.70, Irma Fingal-Rock**

This is absolutely *not* a wine for beginners. In fact, I'm not sure who it *is* a wine for, but it might be a start to say it would help if you're already questioning your sanity. This wine could help you make your mind up. It's

wild stuff. It smells of matchsticks, it tastes of raw acid and burnt syrup mixed with the charred fat on barbecued pork chops. Altogether it's magnificently incorrect yet hypnotically attractive – high in acidity, like zest painfully peeled from an unripe lemon, sulphur mine fumes and then a strange richness of ploughed field clay and a woodsman's evening meal turning on the spit.

15 2002 Shiraz, The Willows Vineyard, ♀ Barossa Valley, South Australia, £10.99, D Byrne, Wimbledon Wine Cellars

There's nothing difficult to understand about this Shiraz. It's just a great big beautiful brawny beast, dripping with ladlesful of chocolate sauce and toffee cream, plum syrup and vanilla and a bright flicker of mint. But there's also a savoury streak like beef tea running through the wine, and some appetizing bitterness rather like tree bark. It all makes for a smashing glassful.

16 2004 Shiraz-Grenache, Blueprint, Tim ♀ Smith Wines, Barossa Valley, South Australia, £11.99, Oz Wines

This is dark stuff, rich stuff, carrying serious alcohol (14.5%) but not tasting at all overripe. I wish some of the other Barossa guys would take note. And it's not over-oaked either, it's just a big rich wine packed with pure ripe blackcurrant and black plum fruit, with a bit of tannic bite that tells you the wine would relish aging for another 3–5 years, and the cat's tongue rasp of some dusty herbs. This is much less of a party animal than Tim Smith's DNA blend (wine no. 11, page 23). You could actually sit down to drink this.

For more wine recommendations see Oz Clarke's Wine Style Guide, pages 136–145

HEARTLAND
Directors' Cut

LANGHORNE CREEK - LIMESTONE COAST
SHIRAZ 2004

H

17 2004 Shiraz, Directors' Cut, Heartland, Langhorne Creek-Limestone Coast, South Australia, £12.95, Great Western Wine

Heartland make a smashing regular release Shiraz and then they trump themselves by making an even more exciting Directors' Cut. It's an extra fiver, but you definitely get an extra fiver's worth of flavour. This has an intense purple colour, and the flavour is a rich, exciting mix of super-ripe black plums as viscous as syrup, caramel chocolate gooiness with just a hint of fudge and figs, and a mild whiff of mint and eucalyptus. The Langhorne Creek fruit provides the lush texture and the Limestone Coast provides the denseness and the extreme scents of the Bush. In this vintage, Langhorne Creek just about holds the upper hand. *Also at deFINE, Nidderdale, Oz Wines, Villeneuve, Noel Young*

McLEAN'S FARM
2005
E.V. RIESLING
EDEN VALLEY

18 E.V. Riesling, McLean's Farm, Eden Valley, South Australia, £8.99, Australian Wine Club

Eden Valley and Clare Valley are South Australia's two most famous regions for growing Riesling. Clare is best at ultra-dry styles, as taut as a piano wire. Eden Valley offers more easygoing pleasures, a little more freewheeling delight, less intellect, more heart. And more perfume. This Riesling has the cool breeze-blown scent of lemon blossom, the prickly burst of lemon zest, and the perfumy fruit of a ripe Cox's apple cut in slices with a white peach and served with a sprig of mint.

⑲ 2002 Jurançon Sec, Vitatge Vielh de
♀ Lapeyre, Jean-Bernard Larrieu, South-West
France, £10.25, Les Caves de Pyrene

This challenging mouthful, from the strange but brilliant world of the Pyrenean foothills, is utterly non-chic, old-style, traditional stuff, with flavours mixed in an unexpected but fascinating compote. The core fruit is like a baked Bramley apple – very ripe but still with the greenness of a cooking apple, with its acid flesh and sharp chewy peel lightly bruised as a windfall. This is soused with quince syrup, with the old tired taste of medlars and the almost greasy richness of ghee, or what we used to call in Ireland 'country butter'. Add to this the smell of macaroons and Bakewell tarts and a toffee finish and this is unusual but excellent stuff. *Also at Thameside Wines, Wimbledon Wine Cellars*

⑳ 2003 Pinot Noir, Rippon, Lake Wanaka,
♟ Central Otago, New Zealand, £22.75, Lea
and Sandeman

There are quite a few rivals for the title 'most beautiful vineyard in the world', and Rippon, on the shores of Lake Wanaka and gazing up at the peaks of the Southern Alps, is one of them. In the past, the wines haven't always matched up to the view, but nowadays there's a new mood at Rippon, keen to maximize the vineyard's great potential. Pinot Noir is the red grape New Zealand's South Island does best, but there aren't many examples to top this Rippon for the sheer luxury of its lacy, silky texture, rich yet delicate, a lovely scented strawberry fruit suspended in syrup, an attractive stemmy green scent and the pale dryness of lakeside stones warmed by the toastiness of grilled cashews.

Runners up

Another really exciting pack of wines, every one of them bursting with personality. Australia – the real Australia – gets lots of votes here, but so does France – the real France – and there are fascinating wines from elsewhere in Europe and the New World.

❶ 2004 Chardonnay, Diamond Valley, Yarra Valley, Victoria, Australia, £10.99, Oz Wines

If only more Australian Chardonnay producers put half so much care and thought into their wine as the guys at Diamond Valley, Aussie Chardie wouldn't be losing popularity to such an extent that even good producers are struggling to sell their world-class wines. But I think Diamond Valley continue to sell out because there's something magic about the way they grow and create their Chardonnay. On their high, sloping vineyard at the very edge of the Yarra Valley they produce wine of exquisite ripeness yet always with a cool, soothing texture. The acidity is like a super-ripe grapefruit – if you can imagine such a thing – the fruit is that juicy, dripping pear flesh and honeydew melon, speckled with nutmeg, and the texture is leather polished with beeswax and a rare quality that good Meursault has which the French call *sauvage* – a wild but delicious cross between oatmeal, hazelnuts and, wait for it, sausage meat.

❷ 2001 Cahors, Le Cèdre, Château du Cèdre, South-West France, £22.45, Les Caves de Pyrene

Cahors needs a few saviours: its reputation has slumped due to producing too many rough raw dark reds that nothing but a dish of pork rillettes could ever soften. But Cahors used to be a great wine area, and Le Cèdre shows it can be again. It *is* tannic, but the bitter roughness of tannin has been transformed into something grand and ripe, which allows you to see the vast vista of rolling black plum and blueberry

Please bear in mind that wine is not made in infinite quantities – some of these may well sell out, but the following year's vintage should then become available.

fruit in the rich, dark heart of the wine. It's already 5 years old but will age for 20, and as it does the richness of dates will appear, the scent of dill, the smoothness of leather and – not just because of the name – the classical austerity of cedar.

Australian Shiraz

- **Buckingham Estate**, Western Australia (page 55)
- **Bushland** (Hope Estate), Hunter Valley (page 101)
- **Directors' Cut**, Heartland (page 26)
- **Hazyblur**, Baroota (page 39)
- **Hazyblur**, Barossa Valley (page 30)
- **Heartland** (page 45)
- **Heritage** (page 32)
- **Klauber Block**, Kies Estate (page 46)
- **Pinnacle**, Palandri (page 93)
- **Water Wheel Vineyards** (page 24)
- **The Willows Vineyard** (page 25)
- **Shiraz-Cabernet Sauvignon**, Godolphin, Glaetzer (page 34)
- **Shiraz-Grenache**, Blueprint, Tim Smith Wines (pages 25, 138)
- **Shiraz-Grenache**, DNA, Tim Smith Wines (page 23)
- **Shiraz-Sangiovese Il Briccone**, Primo Estate (page 139)

❸ 🍷 2004 Shiraz, Hazyblur, Barossa Valley, South Australia, £24.99, Oz Wines

Hazyblur is a collection of wines from different South Australian vineyards. This one, from Barossa, is the best, showing all the richness you could want in a Shiraz yet no overripeness. It manages to be classy and appetizing and pulsing with cream and chocolate and dense red and black plums just stopping short of prune; it's beautifully balanced; and there's a lovely arid high summer scent of dust which gives it a real sense of place.

❹ 🍷 2002 Cabernet Sauvignon, Peñalolen, Maipo Valley, Chile, £7.49, Oddbins

A fantastic bargain for a wine this good. It is the supposedly lighter cuvée from one of Chile's great vineyards, clambering up the mountainside above Santiago. It's a cool vineyard in a warm land, and the scent of menthol and eucalyptus is so fiery it could banish the ague from a Bleak House consumptive. But mix that medicine with wonderfully focused cool blackcurrant fruit and a light evening trail of coalsmoke and you have a really beautiful, balanced mountain red.

For more wine recommendations see Oz Clarke's Wine Style Guide, pages 136–145

⑤ 2002 Riesling, Hand Picked, ♀ Rockford, Eden Valley, South Australia, £10.99, Australian Wine Club

This is 4½ years old – about the moment when a Riesling loses its bright, breezy floral scent and starts a journey into flavours and perfumes altogether different. The lighter, diaphanous scents of youth are long gone here, and the wine has settled into a rich dry mature syrup style, halfway to the dense petrol and toast it will achieve in 5 years' time, but already lovely, showing an evening glow of glycerine and lemon zest and the challenging texture and scent of hot dry stones as the sun fades and the heat remains.

⑥ 2003 Crozes-Hermitage, Cuvée ♂ Albéric Bouvet, Domaine Gilles Robin, Rhône Valley, France, £12.95, Great Western Wine

2003 was *very* hot in the northern Rhône and these guys have done a brilliant job of preserving the freshness in their wine when I suspect their neighbours' grapes were dropping like flies into lifeless prune juice. This has a bright lily scent, rich loganberry and plum fruit and some oak seasoning that doesn't dominate but just offers a few perfumed slivers of cedar as this beautifully weighted red finishes with lingering flavours of red berry fruit and flowers.

Other Australian reds

- **Cabernet Sauvignon**, Coonawarra (Katnook Estate) (pages 67, 137)
- **Cabernet Sauvignon**, Coonawarra (M&S) (page 53)
- **Cabernet Sauvignon**, Kangarilla Road, McLaren Vale (page 53)
- **Cabernet Sauvignon**, Miru, Beelgara Estate, Coonawarra (page 76)
- **Cabernet Sauvignon**, The Willows Vineyard (pages 23, 138)
- **Cabernet Sauvignon-Merlot**, Moda, Joseph (page 19)
- **Cabernet-Shiraz**, Margaret River, (Evans & Tate) (page 73)
- **The Fergus**, Tim Adams (page 34)
- **Grenache**, Lime Tree, Murray-Darling (page 93)
- **Grenache**, Peter Lehmann, Barossa (page 95)
- **Grenache**, Willunga 100, McLaren Vale (page 56)
- **Pinot Noir**, Yering Frog, Yering Station (page 81)
- **Petit Verdot, Vat 4**, De Bortoli (page 83)
- **Petit Verdot-Shiraz**, Inkwell, Salena Estate (page 73)
- **Seven Sleepers/Siebenschlafer**, Kurtz Family (page 54)
- **Tryst**, Cabernet-Tempranillo-Zinfandel, Nepenthe (page 73)
- **Zinfandel**, Lowe, Mudgee, New South Wales (page 40)

❼ 2003 Saumur-Champigny, La Marginale, Thierry Germain, Domaine des Roches Neuves, Loire Valley, France, £16.65, Les Caves de Pyrene

2003 really suited these cool, northerly Loire vineyards where, frankly, reds usually struggle to ripen and even the whites are often so acid they're turned into fizz. And then along comes 2003. This wine is almost purple red – an unheard-of colour in Saumur – and brilliantly mixes typical cool-climate perfume with something much more brawny. It has a delightful scent of coffee bean and blackcurrant leaf that seems to sit very happily with the chocolaty oak and the deep ripe blueberry and blackcurrant fruit. One legacy of the hot vintage is that the wine is quite tannic – and ideally it needs 2–5 years' cellaring, but the flavours are so delicious, why wait?

❽ 2005 Riesling, Inghams, Skilly Ridge, Clare Valley, South Australia, £10.99, Oz Wines

Wine writers have been trying to persuade us to drink Riesling for years now, with very patchy results. Well, the number of Rieslings I've adored this year, I feel like a one-man Riesling booster band. But they're so good. They crackle with freshness and they have a transparent beauty that makes you feel you really can taste the soil and rocks of wherever they came from. This is sheer delight. Citrus zest and lemon flower mingled with honeysuckle, a strong streak of stony minerality coiling with the orchard juiciness of a ripe green apple and softened by the dust of crunched cashew nuts.

❾ 2004 Shiraz, Heritage Wines, Barossa Valley, South Australia, £11.99, Australian Wine Club

This is verging on the OTT but it just manages to pull itself back from the abyss. But then the guys at Heritage are great, big, verging on the OTT guys too, so this 14.5% gentle giant matches its makers. It's got a deep, smoky, chocolate, plum and prune richness, but this is perfumed with mint and leather and the acid juiciness of plum skins dusted with cocoa powder – and although it is burly it's not unwashed or ill-mannered.

⑩ 2003 Cahors, Le Prestige, Château du Cèdre,
❢ South-West France, £10.95, Great Western Wine
Technically Le Prestige is the lighter cuvée of Château du Cèdre. It's a big, beautiful beast, but perhaps it's just a little less dense and complex than Le Cèdre (wine no. 2, page 28). Well, that's okay, because it allows the delicious rich ripe Malbec flavours of sweet damson and oiled leather to shine through, and though there is some tannin and oak here, it's the deep black cherry, plum and damson fruit, softened by cream, that has the lasting effect.

Australian whites

- **Chardonnay**, Allandale, Hunter Valley (page 53)
- **Chardonnay**, Diamond Valley (page 28)
- **Chardonnay**, Kangarilla Road, McLaren Vale (page 58)
- **Chardonnay**, McLaren Vale, (Asda) (page 78)
- **Chardonnay**, McLean's Farm, Barossa Valley (page 34)
- **Chardonnay**, Twin Wells, Hunter Valley, New South Wales (page 55)
- **Chardonnay**, Windy Peak, De Bortoli, Victoria (pages 72, 141)
- **Chardonnay**, Bushland (Hope Estate), Hunter Valley (page 98)
- **Chenin Blanc**, Peter Lehmann, Barossa Valley (pages 74, 140)
- **Pinot Gris**, Tim Adams (page 50)
- **E.V. Riesling**, McLean's Farm (page 26)
- **Riesling**, Hand Picked, Rockford, Eden Valley (page 31)
- **Riesling**, Inghams, Skilly Ridge, Clare Valley (page 32)
- **Riesling Polish Hill** (page 17)
- **Sauvignon Blanc-Semillon** (Capel Vale) (page 76)
- **Semillon**, Ashbrook, Margaret River (page 40)

- **Semillon**, Denman Vineyard Estate Reserve, Hunter Valley, New South Wales (page 141)
- **Semillon**, Tim Adams (page 16)
- **Semillon**, Local Growers, Rockford, Barossa Valley (page 34)
- **Semillon**, The Willows Vineyard, Barossa Valley (page 41)
- **Viognier-Pinot Gris**, Heartland, Langhorne Creek (page 36, 142)

SWEET
- **Botrytis Semillon**, Hermits Hill, Riverina, New South Wales (page 115)
- **Botrytis Semillon**, Noble One, De Bortoli, New South Wales (page 115, 142)
- **Orange Muscat & Flora**, Brown Brothers, Milawa, Victoria (page 117)
- **Rutherglen Grand Muscat**, Chambers Rosewood Vineyards, Victoria (page 145)

SPARKLING
- **Jansz** (page 143)

⑪ 2004 The Fergus, Tim Adams,
🍷 **Clare Valley, South Australia, £9.99, Tesco**
In some vintages The Fergus is wilder than this, but it's always a wonderfully gushing, juicy, party animal of a wine – and it's the Grenache grape that does it – 15% alcohol, pure happy juice, a joyous syrup of mint leaves and cherry, a touch of strawberry, even a touch of chocolate, and a good deal more than a touch of eucalyptus. Are you brave enough to party with this baby?

⑫ 2002 Semillon, Local Growers, Rockford,
♀ **Barossa Valley, South Australia, £10.99, Australian Wine Club**
This is a lovely restrained Aussie style, just starting to show maturity at 4½ years old, but promising at least another 10 years of development if you're interested in the fascinating paradoxical mix of richness and haughty austerity that mature Semillon brings. At the moment the wine is a mighty mix of lemon and honey syrup, leather, petrol and hot rocks. There's cashew nut and cream as well, but they can't avoid the drip, drip, drip of petrol.

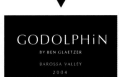

⑬ 2004 Shiraz-Cabernet Sauvignon, Godolphin,
🍷 **Glaetzer Wines, Barossa Valley, South Australia, £22.95, Great Western Wine**
Now hang on, fellas, who's gonna drink this? And how? It's 15.5% alcohol. Couldn't you have made it at 14% or so? I know it wouldn't have had quite the dramatic intensity, but at 15.5% dramatic becomes soporific very quickly. But, dammit, it is good. It's heaped with burly tannin, the resinous rasp of herbs and black chocolate, the gagging of rock dust, but somehow through all this emerges sweet black plum and blackberry fruit mellowed by fudge and sprinkled with mint. I don't know how they keep it so fresh.

⑭ 2005 Chardonnay, McLean's Farm,
♀ **Barossa Valley, South Australia, £8.99, Australian Wine Club**
This is interesting – a Chardonnay grown on the Kalimna vineyard, which is one of the Barossa Valley's great Shiraz vineyards. What's Chardonnay doing there? Oh, don't ask. Luckily Bob McLean saw the fantastic quality of this unlikely Chardie vineyard and bought the fruit. And he's made a wine that's deep, powerful, but balanced and fresh, mixing melon and pear and white

peach in a lush, beguiling brew sharpened just a little by lemon. This is how Aussie Chardie used to be, and well done Bob McLean for resurrecting it.

⓯ 2002 Madiran, Cuvée Charles de Batz, ♀ Domaine Berthoumieu, South-West France, £9.85, Les Caves de Pyrene

Here's a trailblazer in an almost lost appellation of the profound south-west of France – Madiran. These are historically just about the toughest wines in France, and correspondingly good for your heart, I'm told. This is dense and quite tannic, but it isn't chewy and tough – it's damson skins and juice and a hint of blossom. That said, the real character of the wine isn't juice, or scent. There is a hardness there, like hazelnut husks, there's some bitter black chocolate, a cold streak of graphite and a meaty density like the dried-out bit on the end of a ham.

⓰ 2004 Riesling, Cono Sur, ♀ Bío Bío Valley, Chile, £7.99, Majestic

There's a growing move towards single vineyard wines in Chile, and a growing confidence in the quality of the far south. This comes from the Quitralmán vineyard in cool, southerly Bío Bío, and it's a delight – slatey, minerally, with a gentle orange zest and mild lemon juice acidity. There's a touch of flowers, but the earthy minerality keeps coming back, reminding me of Rieslings from the red clays of Nackenheim in Germany. Then I read the back label. The vines grow on red clay beneath the Autuco volcano. Riesling is nothing if not transparent of its place.

⓱ 2004 Syrah EQ, Matetic, ♀ San Antonio, Chile, £16.99, Oddbins

San Antonio is for the most part an amazingly cool part of coastal Chile, brilliantly suited to really snappy Sauvignons, aromatic Rieslings and Gewürztraminers and succulent Pinot Noirs. But there is one enclave, one amphitheatre of vines further inland where it is much warmer, where Matetic have planted Syrah – and the result is fantastic red wine that would feel at home in the top vineyards of the northern Rhône in France. It's got a daunting but thrilling aroma of licorice and tar, smoke and baked blackberries, black cherries too – all wrapped in a beautifully balanced package that is re-writing the possibilities of Syrah in Chile.

Serenin.
2005
SAUVIGNON BLANC
MARLBOROUGH
NEW ZEALAND

⑱ 2005 Sauvignon Blanc, Seresin,
♀ Marlborough, New Zealand, £11.67, Armit
Seresin is a top Kiwi outfit owned by a Hollywood film guy; it's probably popular with the cool dude set and that might explain what is, frankly, rather a high price. But this is the best Sauvignon they've made for some time. It had become too syrupy and stodgy, perhaps to please the American market, but this is much more like it: loads of gooseberry fruit and capsicum and nettle snap, just a little syrupy richness and a good streak of Wairau riverbed stones.

⑲ 2003 Syrah, Haras Character,
♟ Viña Haras de Pirque, Maipo Valley, Chile, £12.95, Friarwood
These Haras de Pirque guys make powerful reds, and this wine demonstrates that Syrah, or Shiraz, is going to be a seriously important player in Chile's wine future. This is majestic but not beautiful, smelling of a powerful mix of new tyre rubber, chocolate and prunes. It's a real Formula One smell. It's fascinating, because there's a great seam of black fruit and black chocolate at the core of the wine and some licorice toffee bitter sweetness to soothe the tannin. Put a flank of fighting bull on the barbie and this could be perfect.

⑳ 2005 Viognier-Pinot Gris, Heartland,
♀ Langhorne Creek, South Australia, £8.95, Great Western Wine
Langhorne Creek fruit is so soft and lush, and Heartland make such good use of it. Viognier and Pinot Gris, two schmoozer grapes, could really be too much of a good thing, but here they're a velvety delight: soft pear flesh, the delightful rasp of apricot skin, mingled with ripe grapefruit acidity and apple flesh so fluffy it would melt on your tongue. Sheer delight.

㉑ 2003 Catharina, Steenberg,
♟ Constantia, South Africa, £12.98, Armit
Steenberg is one of my favourite Cape producers and one of the only ones in the Constantia region to excel equally with red and white wines. This one is a Cape take on a Bordeaux style and it works very well, with a mouthwatering mix of ripe blackcurrant fruit and tangy blackcurrant leaf, smoky coffee beans and a drop of traditional eucalyptus oil. These aren't all just leaping out of the

Explore a New World
Chile - A great place to make wine

The long, thin country running down the west coast of South
America - blessed with perfect conditions for winemaking.

Wine Regions

- Elqui Valley
- Limarí Valley
- Aconcagua Valley
- Casablanca Valley
- San Antonio Valley
- Maipo Valley
- Cachapoal Valley ⎫
- Colchagua Valley ⎭ Rapel Valley
- Curicó Valley
- Maule Valley
- Itata Valley
- Bío Bío Valley
- Malleco Valley

WINES OF CHILE

If you want further information about Chile's wines, please contact Wines of Chile UK
info@winesofchile.org.uk Tel: 01344 872229 www.winesofchile.org

Chile
All Ways Surprising

glass – the wine has got a fair degree of good manners – but they become wonderfully sweet as they part the curtains of tannin and leave your palate ravenous for fresh-grilled flesh.

㉒ 2003 The Society's Exhibition Gigondas, ♥ Rhône Valley, France, £10.95, The Wine Society

This is made by the excellent Saint-Cosme outfit and is exactly what a Gigondas should be – big, ripe, brawny, powerful but sweet at the core. When Gigondas gets it right, there is heady, almost rich, dark red fruit swirling about, blood-dark loganberry, dark strawberry and crimson cherry, lightly stewed and mashed into a summer fruit coulis, and tempered by tannin and the broody aroma of baked vineyard stones.

㉓ 2001 Santenay 1er Cru, 'Beaurepaire', J-M Vincent, ♀ Burgundy, France, £15.99, Raeburn Fine Wines

It's not easy to find good *red* Santenay, and it's not at all easy to find good white. But this is very tasty stuff, punching above its weight and tasting more like its considerably more expensive neighbour Chassagne-Montrachet. It has an enticing green-gold colour and smells savoury and reserved, of leathery oak and green-stemmed fruit. The palate's more forthcoming: ripe, round, with dry glycerine and soft white peach flesh, unsalted cashew nut richness and the cold drag of stones. No fruit richness at all. Very nice, restrained, serious Burgundy.

㉔ 1999 Rioja Reserva, Viña Ardanza, La ♥ Rioja Alta, Spain, £16.95, Laymont & Shaw

Classic old-style Rioja – and thank goodness for that. Traditional Rioja has a unique ability to blend savoury flavours with cream and strawberries. The savoury flavours can be meaty, or nutty, and Ardanza manages both, matching squashy strawberries with an attractive meat-pie meatiness, bone-dry vanilla and hazelnut cream and a dry, rich finish like melted butter.

㉕ 2003 Priorat, Creu Celta, Viñedos
♥ McAlindon e Hijos, Cataluña, Spain,
£14.99, Direct Wine Shipments
I know these McAlindon lads in Belfast. I've got pretty wobbly-kneed with them, so I know the kind of wines they like, and the kind of quantities they like them in. But I didn't expect them to go off and start making their own! But of course, what a suitable choice. Priorat. Great big beefy powerhouse reds to warm an Ulsterman's heart in the depths of the Belfast winter. And they've done well. This isn't just an over-strength sun-spoiled mess of dates and raisins – this manages to keep a fresh plum depth, and when you mix that with figs and dates and prunes, some fairly mighty tannins and a rather lifted acidity, it's as though all the red wine flavours have been baked into a sticky Saharan stew. And it's smashing. Well done, lads. *Slainte.*

㉖ 2003 Chassagne-Montrachet, Vieilles Vignes, F & L Pillot,
♥ Burgundy, France, £14.95, Lea and Sandeman
2003 was a very challenging year for Burgundy. Most of the whites got a bit too hot and flustered and are now losing their transitory, podgy charm. For reds, though, it was a vintage of great opportunity if you knew what you were doing. The vineyards did get impossibly hot and there are quite a lot of hard-baked monsters as a result – and a few beauties. Note 'Vieilles Vignes' on the label. Old vines, with deep roots, able to withstand drought and produce a red that *is* tannic and will improve for 10 years, but has lovely red cherry and plum fruit, strawberry scent and a sensitive dry oak richness. In 10 years you'll get supreme flavour at half the price of a Pommard or Volnay.

㉗ 2004 Shiraz, Hazyblur, Baroota,
♥ South Australia, £15.99, Oz Wines
Fascinating stuff. This one comes from Baroota – hardly a household name – and has a tannic bite that initially seems a bit edgy, but which becomes welcome as it turns into a dry, herb-scented rasp that acts as a really good seasoning to the deep, soft, black and red cherry and plum fruit. Give it 2–5 years and it'll be even better.

28 2004 Salento Rosso, Armentino, Schola Sarmenti,
Puglia, Italy, £11.50, The Winery

This comes from way down in the far south of Italy, and is a sister wine to Salice Salentino and Copertino, both of which have done the region no end of good with their rich, almost overripe styles of red. This is the same idea taken up a step, with a rich flavour of dried fruits – dried fig, sultana and prune and loads of dates – but the Salento magic is that there's a pool of sweet fresh perfumed black plum there too – dense, overripe, mixed with fresh and bright-eyed orchard fruit.

29 2005 Semillon, Ashbrook,
Margaret River, Western Australia, £10.75, Vin du Van

This has that wild sweaty smell that full-bodied New Zealand Sauvignons sometimes boast. It can be slightly unnerving, but locals say it disappears in time and is replaced by ripe tropical fruit. In New Zealand that is. This wine is from Western Australia so may not behave in the same way, and anyway it's a different grape, the Semillon. But they've evidently gone for a Sauvignon style: sharp, snappy, full of green fruit – fresh fig, kiwi fruit, coffee bean, capsicum and that strange but attractive green Meltis Fruit – that's showing my age! There's some custard apple richness that will deepen with age and get coated in leather, so it's a green delight now and will mature over the next 5 years.

30 2003 Zinfandel, Lowe, Mudgee,
New South Wales, Australia, £12.95, Vin du Van

Zinfandel is supposed to be California's calling card, but, bit by bit, California is having its supremacy usurped. This is the third or fourth Aussie Zin I've had this year, and they've all been very good. This one has a rich, classic Zinfandel flavour of fig and date and sultana, and some super-ripe blackberry, all awash in a soup of squashy brown fruit and demerara sugar syrup sprinkled with tobacco. This is exactly what good Zinfandel should taste like.

31 2002 Bourgogne Blanc, Domaine Rémi Jobard,
Burgundy, France, £10.95, Lea and Sandeman

Jobard is a top Meursault producer and this wine is a blend of Meursault barrels that didn't quite suit the Meursault labels, wine from bits of land just outside the Meursault boundaries – that kind of thing. But you get Meursault expertise, Meursault personality, Meursault in all but name – and price. This is half the price of a similar wine with 'Meursault' writ large on the label. It's dry, but with a lovely mellow quality: that slightly sweaty oatmeal which doesn't sound nice but is at the core of so many good Meursaults, its fruit is ripe eating apples and nuts coated with beeswax and the oak has the irresistible sweetness of buttered brazils.

32 2004 Collio, Zuani,
♀ Friuli-Venezia Giulia, Italy, £12.95, Lea and Sandeman

This doesn't taste much like most of the Collios I've tasted, but it does have the explosive arresting quality I've heard about but rarely experienced. It is *not* a mainstream north-east Italian white – it's powerful, unpredictable, shocking. I don't know how much lava they have in their vineyards but this wine tastes as though a lava flow ran right through the winery, boiling everything in its wake, frying the stones, desiccating the apricots and searing the meat. And with all this, the wine has a really attractive texture and somehow the mineral/lava character seems perfectly judged.

33 2002 Semillon, The Willows Vineyard,
♀ Barossa Valley, South Australia, £8.99, Australian Wine Club

Wild wine. This is *not* typical Aussie Semillon. Given that The Willows are experts at stonking great hedonistic reds, I suppose I should expect them to go slightly mad on the whites. Well, here goes. You do get the feeling they've squeezed all the available character out of these grape skins – the lime zest really rips into your tonsils, the acrid fumes of Vicks Vapour rub prickle in your nostrils, while the lick of honey, the quince syrup and the scented leather try to calm your hyperactive palate.

34 2005 Pinot Gris, Gladstone, Wairarapa,
♀ New Zealand, £11.95, Lea and Sandeman

Pinot Gris is big in New Zealand right now, but I'm not convinced they all know quite what to do with it. Well, Gladstone's version would be a good place to start. This is a lovely style – soft pear, banana and white peach fruit, a hint of honey and sultana and a whiff of tobacco. This is like a cleaner, fresher version of classic Alsace Pinot Gris – exactly the kind of Pinot Gris the world needs more of. What we don't need is oceansful of tasteless, flat Pinot Grigio from Italy, New Zealand or anywhere else.

35 2004 Chenin Blanc, Te Arai Vineyard, Millton Vineyards,
Gisborne, New Zealand, £11.99, Vintage Roots

New Zealand has numerous areas ideally suited to drawing out the best from different white grape varieties. Chenin is a tricky variety, rarely seen at its best in its homeland of France's Loire Valley, or its adopted exile of South Africa. But on New Zealand's East Coast at Gisborne, they get it right. This is full, fat, rich, with beeswax, lanolin and glycerine all coating your tongue, quince syrup and honey freshened by apple juice and a shower of pebbles, then soothed by buttercream and buttered brazils.

36 2001 Chianti Classico Riserva, Riecine,
Tuscany, Italy, £19.90, Tanners

This is a small but utterly quality-focused Chianti property started by an Englishman and continued by Sean O'Callaghan (he doesn't sound Italian either). He makes purists' Chianti – deep, dry, challenging, thought-provoking, but not dense, clumsy and stolid as many currently popular Chiantis are. This has dry but ripe red cherry fruit, a savoury sweetness of sun-dried tomato, herbs and pine needles intertwined and a fine grainy tannin that delightfully and subtly roughens up your tongue.

37 2004 Sauvignon Blanc Laurel Vineyard, Casa Marín,
San Antonio, Chile, £13.95, Lay & Wheeler

San Antonio is one of Chile's coolest regions – in temperature and style – with vineyards in sight of the Pacific Ocean. Casa Marín was founded in 2000 and the owner is ambitious and quality-obsessed. She let this Sauvignon fruit hang on the vine until April to intensify flavour, yet the cool conditions meant it never overripened. The result is a wine with an amazing aromatic flavour of jalapeño peppers, an acidity sharp yet soft, like the zest of boiled lemons, and a richness as fresh and mouthwatering as apple syrup.

38 2003 Nero d'Avola-Cabernet Sauvignon, Feudo di Santa Tresa 'Nivuro', Sicily, Italy, £8.99, Oddbins

Nero d'Avola is a fantastic Sicilian grape full of rich, dark fruit and ecclesiastical scent. It's also a good blender and gives the Cabernet a personality it might otherwise lack in this deep plummy red wine, its fruit wrapped in fruit cake, coconut and vanilla, and lingering at the rim of the glass the smell of cedarwood and scented candles.

39 2003 Cento, IGT Salento, Castel di Salve, Puglia, Italy, £15, Bat & Bottle

From the heel of Italy, this red has an air of antiquity, touched by scents of the bazaar and a thousand years of trading across the Mediterranean sea. It's a rich wine, but it's as though all the flavours are desiccated fruit – sultanas, prunes, apricots – it's like an essence squeezed out from whatever liquid remained from a pile of exotic dried fruit. Remarkably there's still room for some fresh fruit to emerge – dark sloes and black plum, softened by rice pudding, cream and a pinch of salt. Part modern, but a lot more ancient, that's Salento.

40 2004 Carignan, Vin de Pays Catalan, Ferrer-Ribière, Languedoc-Roussillon, France, £8.95, Yapp Brothers

I couldn't resist this. Carignan as a grape variety is much reviled by the pundits, and poor Carignan has probably been the chief component of a lot of the thinner, meaner cheap campsite reds we've drunk in southern France. But old vine Carignan is a totally different matter. These Carignan vines are 127 years old and counting, in the fabulous Pyrenean foothills that clamber up towards the Spanish border near Collioure. And this is feisty stuff. It doesn't have a modern pinging focus of fruit, but instead it has a grainy power, a dark, indistinct but satisfying fruit, half blackberries, half tar, with the smoky smell of grilled wild boar and a sharp, unrepentant acidity.

From £7 to £10

I often think that there should never be any need to pay more than a tenner for a good bottle of wine. With the exception of rare luscious sweet wines, there's only so much that you can do to a wine and, adding the costs up, you should be able to make a decent profit at ten quid. Obviously some Bordeaux château owners and Napa Valley Cabernet Sauvignon producers would disagree with me, but that's because they've persuaded the world that their wines are worth more than they really are, and are still finding rich people prepared to pay. Some Burgundy producers might, more reasonably, say that they make so little of particular wines they feel justified in charging for the rarity value. And they're probably right. That doesn't upset me. If I get sufficiently enthused, I don't begrudge them the money. But people who make tens of thousands of cases of wine and still charge the earth, I have little time for. You won't find any of these in my selection here – just loads of character, lots of flavour, and a fair price.

❶ 2005 Sauvignon Blanc, Ventolera, Viña Litoral,
♀ Leyda Valley, Chile, £8.50, The Wine Society
If you ever thought the Wine Society might be a bit stuffy, think again. They are constantly probing the four corners of the earth for new taste experiences, whilst also providing a Rolls Royce service for those who prefer something traditional. This wine is one of their taste-probing jobs – Sauvignon from one of the newest top-quality vineyard areas in the world, Leyda Valley in Chile. These are really cool-climate vines, right next to the Pacific with its icy Humboldt current, and you can taste the ice in the pure intensity of the fruit here. It's perfect for Sauvignon Blanc – it may yet prove to be one of the world's greatest Sauvignon sites – and the intense flavours are quite different from those of New Zealand. This smells forcefully of lime zest and of orange zest too. It offers a riot of green flavours – nettles and capsicum, green apples, kiwi fruit and passion fruit – usually you only get one or two of these, but here you get the whole shopping basket. This

Please bear in mind that wine is not made in infinite quantities – some of these may well sell out, but the following year's vintage should then become available.

could imply that the wine is sharp, but isn't. It has a succulent texture that might be too much were it not for an insistent mineral dryness rubbing on your tongue like pumice stone.

② 2004 Pinot Noir, Momo,
♀ (Seresin Estate), Marlborough, New Zealand, £9.95, Armit

Seresin's Pinot Noirs have been lauded to the skies for several years now, but I've often found them a little too rich. This one seems to get the balance just right. The texture is rich, but it never cloys because the juice is so bright and focused: strawberries and red plums in a delicate syrup, toughened up by a little tannin and stony undertow, and seasoned with a whiff of smoky oak, a twist of pepper and a rather sappy green streak as though they'd left some of the vine stems in the vat when they were fermenting the wine. Perhaps they did. *Also at Harvey Nichols, Noel Young*

③ 2004 Shiraz, Heartland, Langhorne Creek-Limestone Coast,
♀ South Australia, £7.95, Great Western Wine

They've changed the blend since I last tasted this. When I queried this with Ben Glaetzer, the winemaker, he said they'd thrown in rather more soft, fleshy Langhorne Creek fruit this year because the Limestone Coast Shiraz was simply too extreme. I told him that it was the 'extremeness' that turned me on about Heartland reds. He gave me a slightly worried look, but I think he understood. Look out for the 2005, he said. Extreme is back. But until then this 2004 is still delicious stuff, even if it is a touch more mainstream. Pretty gorgeous mainstream – rich black treacle, rich black plums, lovely mint toffee sweet perfume and a quiver of eucalyptus. I think I could be persuaded. *Also at deFINE, Nidderdale, Oz Wines, Playford Ros, Stone, Vine & Sun, Villeneuve*

④ 2004 Carmenère-Shiraz, Doña Dominga Reserva
♀ Colchagua Valley, Chile, £7.99, Waitrose

This is a beauty. They've really thought carefully about this wine, because with two very proud, assertive grape varieties like Carmenère and Shiraz, this could easily have turned into a fist-fight. But it didn't. It's more like a reunion of old buddies, which may not be so removed from the truth: Shiraz and Carmenère used to be planted next to each other in a few Bordeaux vineyards in the 19th century. It's only in Chile that happens now. And the result is this ripe, lush embrace of black plum and blackcurrant fruit which is kept from getting sentimental by a ripe apple acidity, soft creamy wood, and some grainy tannins that help rather than hinder the pleasure.

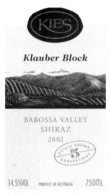

❺ 2002 Shiraz, Klauber Block, Kies Estate
❢ Barossa Valley, South Australia, £9.99, Nidderdale Fine Wines

I've tasted this wine several times in the past year or so and it's evolving and maturing a bit like a punch-drunk prizefighter. Unpredictable but always likely to pull something brilliant out of the bag. And they do share one characteristic: they're both thick. They're dense, and that probably suits the wine more than the prizefighter. The denseness here relates to texture and this texture is made up of layer upon layer of licorice and bitter black treacle intertwined with melted caramel and scented milk chocolate then overlaid with the rough male smell of hard-ridden leather and the altogether more sophisticated scent of sandalwood.

❻ 2004 Bourgogne, Les Raverettes, P & M Guillemot-Michel,
♀ Burgundy, France, £9.95, The Wine Society

I can't tell yet whether biodynamic farming works or not, but when you can turn your biodynamic grapes from a somewhat nondescript Mâcon village like Clessé into wine like this, I do begin to think there must be something in it. Above all, what texture. The savoury, oatmeal, creamy white Burgundy texture is the best white wine texture in the world when they get it right – and they do here. The wine ripples with honey, toffee – and acidity. That acidity is crucial, because it allows the creamy oatmeal, the hazelnut syrup and the lick of honey full expression without ever losing balance. And that texture. Is *that* what biodynamics brings?

❼ 2005 Greco di Tufo, Vesevo
♀ Campania, Italy, £9.99, Liberty Wines

Fascinating stuff. This is way off mainstream and all the better for it. I suppose that's not surprising when you have Mount Vesuvius as your next-door neighbour and you don't merely contemplate the effect the lava soil is having on your vines but have to fret that at any moment your vines could be six feet under a brand new lava flow – and you with them. And I'm sure you can taste the lava. The wine is so marvellously curious it can't be just the grape variety. It has a weirdly attractive mixture of fresh sweat, apple peel and lemon, then herbs like rosemary and thyme. And it has a tannic nip – in a white wine! Cool! Although it's aggressive it does have a nice ripe feel to it. And there's another fruit. Smoky, sweet, bitter to the tongue. Persimmon. Yes. *Very* interesting.

8 2004 Pinot Noir, Las Brisas Vineyard, Viña Leyda,
Leyda Valley, Chile, £7.95, The Wine Society, £8.99 Sainsbury's

A single-vineyard Pinot Noir from one of the newest fine wine areas of the world is about as cutting edge as you can get. But the flavours are so reassuringly delicious you could fool yourself that they were predictable. Well, they aren't. The only thing that's predictable about Pinot Noir is its unpredictability. Except that every Pinot I've drunk from Leyda has had beautiful ripe red cherry, red plum and strawberry fruit, swathed in syrup. But this one has something extra – a kind of yeasty creamy veil that adds extra lustre – as if the flavours needed it. Leyda seems to accentuate all flavours, red or white, and this is a fine example.

9 2004 Massaya Classic,
Sami & Ramzi Ghosn, Bekaa Valley, Lebanon, £7.70, Tanners

Every two years I go to the Vinexpo World Wine Fair in Bordeaux, and I seek out the Lebanese guys – partly because Serge Hochar of Château Musar is one of the great wine and life philosophers, and partly because I can really sense the improvements that have been made in recent years, while the country enjoyed a period of stability. And the flavours are fascinating – as they should be from a country like Lebanon. This is a wild mix of soft strawberry freshness with date and dried fig richness, some quite serious but not rough tannin and an acidity rather like loft apples, a definite stony rasp and a perfume that hangs in the air halfway between pepper tree and pine resin. It briefly, but pleasantly, reminded me of carbolic soap.

10 2002 Ribera del Duero Reserva, Altos de Tamaron,
Castilla y León, Spain, £9.99, Morrisons

Morrisons' Spanish wines have been impressive this year. This one's a class act from one of Spain's most expensive DOs, Ribera del Duero. 2002 wasn't an easy year, and this is still young, ready to age for two to five years. But it's the real thing, with classic Duero flavours: dark blackcurrant fruit, still dry but getting sweeter when the bottle's been opened a bit; reasonable tannic toughness – but that's no problem if you're drinking this with a steak; and lovely mint and buttercream scent.

Pinot Noir, the classic grape of red Burgundy, thrives in cool
climates in many countries

⑪ 2005 Chiroubles, Georges Duboeuf,
♥ Beaujolais, France, £7.99, Waitrose

The 2005 Beaujolais are the best I can remember. Old timers talk about them being as good as in 1985, when a jug or two caused outbreaks of dancing in the streets, they were so delicious. Whether this will get me into my tutu, I'm not sure, but it's exactly the sort of wine Beaujolais should be – a torrent of bright, fresh, gluggable red fruit, a gale of blossomy perfume, crunchy apple acidity and some real ripe weight. This is a wonderful picnic red: a bottle of this, some saucisson, some sun = O.C. zonked but still smiling.

⑫ 2003 Sylvaner, Charles Schleret
♀ Alsace, France, £7.95, Yapp Brothers

Fascinating dry white made from the very unfashionable Sylvaner grape. It has a golden colour from the boiling 2003 vintage, and a strange but beguiling flavour of round, soft honey and grapes allied with unripe apple peel and green beans. There's some ripe tomato too, and a sprinkling of dust, all swimming in honey syrup. But that's Sylvaner for you – always mixing fruit and veg flavours and, in the hands of an expert like Schleret, getting away with it. *Also at Harvey Nichols*

⑬ 2005 Pinot Gris, Tim Adams,
♀ Clare Valley, South Australia, £9.99, Australian Wine Club

Pinot Gris is being touted as the next big thing in Australia and New Zealand, yet few growers seem to know what to do with it. Tim Adams always seems to know what to do when he tries something new and, typically, he's made an excellent Pinot Gris here, although he's only been at it a couple of years. This isn't quite dry – a lot of the best Alsace Pinot Gris aren't either – but has superb balance. Chill this down and you'll taste a brilliant Bramley apple purée, washed with a lemony zesty syrup and scented with smoky grilled nuts. It's rich, upfront and very good.

For more wine recommendations see Oz Clarke's
Wine Style Guide, pages 136–145

Another corking year.

Waitrose has won many more of the major wine awards than any other supermarket.
The reason isn't hard to find. We have 4 Masters of Wine - more than any other supermarket.
We have a range of no less than 650 wines. And we have wine specialists on hand in
branches to guide our customers. The fact is, at Waitrose we take our wine very seriously.
And you can enjoy the fruits of our labour by visiting any branch or waitrose.com/wines

French reds

- **Ch. de l'Abbaye de Sainte-Ferme,** Bordeaux (page 122)
- **Ch. Barreyres,** Haut-Médoc (page 122)
- **Ch. Bauduc,** Bordeaux (page 122)
- **Beaujolais,** Dom. Chatelus de la Roche (page 81, 136)
- **Ch. Bel Air,** Haut-Médoc (page 123)
- **le Blason d'Issan,** Margaux (page 123)
- **Cahors, Le Cèdre,** Ch. du Cèdre (page 28)
- **Cahors, Le Prestige,** Ch. du Cèdre (page 33)
- **Carignan,** Vin de Pays Catalan, Ferrer-Ribière (page 43)
- **Chassagne-Montrachet,** Vieilles Vignes, F & L Pillot (page 39)
- **Châteauneuf-du-Pape,** Le Vieux Donjon (page 17)
- **Chiroubles,** Georges Duboeuf (page 50, 136)
- **Ch. Clos Renon,** Bordeaux (page 123)
- **Corbières,** Ch. Pech-Latt (page 65, 138)
- **Cadet de Gascogne,** Côtes de Gascogne, Vasconia (page 88)
- **Côtes de Castillon,** Seigneurs d'Aiguilhe (page 138)
- **Côtes du Rhône-Villages** (page 98)
- **Côtes du Rhône Villages,** Plan de Dieu, Dom. de la Meynarde (page 91)
- **Côtes du Roussillon-Villages,** Le Roc des Anges, Dom. Segna de Cor (page 23)
- **Crozes-Hermitage,** Alain Graillot (page 20)
- **Crozes-Hermitage,** Cuvée Albéric Bouvet, Dom. Gilles Robin (page 31)
- **Cuvée Chasseur,** Vin de Pays de l'Hérault (page 103)
- **Cuvée de Richard,** Vin de Pays de l'Aude (page 101)

- **Fleurie,** Christian Gaidon (page 54)
- **Le Haut-Médoc de Giscours** (page 123)
- **Ch. Grand Village,** Bordeaux (page 124)
- **Grenache,** Fruits of France, Vin de Pays d'Oc (page 100)
- **Ch. La Gurgue,** Margaux (page 124)
- **Lirac, La Reine des Bois,** Dom. de la Mordorée (page 20)
- **Madiran, Cuvée Charles de Batz,** Dom. Berthoumieu (page 35)
- **Old Vines Grenache Noir,** Vin de Pays des Côtes Catalanes (page 90)
- **Ch. Pey la Tour,** Bordeaux (page 124)
- **Ch. Peyrabon,** Haut-Médoc (page 124)
- **Ch. Pierrail,** Bordeaux (page 124)
- **Ch. Potensac,** Médoc (page 126)
- **Ch. Robin,** Lussac-St-Emilion (page 126)
- **Ch. Ribeyrolles,** Bordeaux (page 126)
- **Avery's Fine St-Emilion,** (page 126)
- **Saumur-Champigny,** Dom. Filliatreau (page 53, 136)
- **Saumur-Champigny,** Dom. des Roches Neuves (page 32)
- **Ch. Segonzac,** Premières Côtes de Blaye (page 126)
- **Seigneurs d'Aiguilhe,** Côtes de Castillon (page 126)
- **The Society's Exhibition Gigondas** (page 38)
- **Syrah,** Camplazens, Vin de Pays d'Oc (page 70)
- **Ch. Tire Pé,** Bordeaux (page 128)
- **Ch. Villars,** Fronsac (page 128)
- **Ch. Villepreux,** Bordeaux (page 128)
- **Vin de Pays du Comté Tolosan,** Vieille Fontaine (page 103)

⑭ 2001 Rioja Reserva, Coleccion Personal, Marqués de Griñon,
♥ Spain, £8.35, Budgens
Very good traditional-style Rioja – the kind that most of us like because it
offers such a reliably satisfying red wine experience when all around us things
seem to change with every vintage. This is rich, squashy, almost like a
strawberry smoothie, coated with coconut and vanilla and exhibiting that Rioja
genius of mixing freshness with maturity that keeps us coming back for more.

⑮ 2003 Chardonnay, Allandale,
♀ Hunter Valley, NSW, Australia, £9.99, Wimbledon Wine Cellar
Full, rich, classic Hunter style Chardonnay, with a leathery, nutty, smoky toffee
smell and then a big broad texture when you taste it. Lanolin, syrup, a
beeswaxy weight – and that leather and smoky toffee flavour keeps on right to
the end. It's an old style of Chardonnay, but it's very good.

⑯ 2004 Cabernet Sauvignon, Coonawarra,
♥ South Australia, £7.99, Marks & Spencer
This comes from the vineyards of Lindemans in Coonawarra. Nowadays we
often think of Lindemans as a label for cheap Aussie whites, but in fact they
are one of the great old-time vineyard owners in Coonawarra and have some
of the best sites. M&S have chosen well: this is classic Coonawarra – gentle
texture, lean yet ripe blackcurrant fruit lifted slightly by a flicker of leaf and
herbs, scented with mint and wrapped in creamy oak.

⑰ 2004 Cabernet Sauvignon, Kangarilla Road,
♥ McLaren Vale, Australia, £9.99, Majestic
McLaren Vale is a pretty warm part of South Australia, but this is from higher
vineyards that are significantly cooler and the wine is immediately perkier and
better balanced. It's almost slightly stony, in a Bordeaux way, but it has a much
stronger flavour of blackcurrants, mint toffees and trademark Aussie
eucalyptus than you would ever find in Bordeaux.

⑱ 2004 Saumur-Champigny, Domaine Filliatreau,
♥ Loire Valley, France, £8.50, Yapp Brothers
Good red Loires are such a delicious, refreshing style of wine that sometimes
they fit the bill like no other. Yet merchants despair of being able to sell them.
Well, Yapp were the virtual pioneers of these wines in England and Filliatreau

is Saumur's top red performer – so can I persuade you to try this wine? It's got lovely fresh raspberry fruit, grainy tannin and intense minerality, and the aftertaste is as though you've been licking the local chalk cliffs smeared with raspberry coulis – cold, refreshing, moist and very pure.

⑲ 2004 Seven Sleepers/Siebenschlafer, Kurtz Family,
❢ Barossa Valley, South Australia, £8.95. Vin du Van
You can call this Siebenschlafer if you want – I think it sounds a bit more intriguing. It is made from seven different types of old vines in the Barossa Valley – and is a good example of the best type of deep Barossa style. Barossa is best when it's soft and rich but not OTT. This is a gorgeous drink, full of rich plum and cherry fruit, baked apples and cream richness and a little apple blossom scent. *Also at D Byrne, Halifax Wine Co*

⑳ 2001 Rioja Reserva, Bodegas Palacio,
❢ Spain, £9.99, Morrisons
Morrisons are clearly taking their Spanish selection seriously; this is a Reserva from an important producer at a very fair price. It's a fairly dry style and there's a little edgy tannin, but that will allow this wine to age for five to ten years without any trouble because there's a good depth of dark fruit flavour nicely wrapped up in oaky vanilla.

㉑ 2005 Fleurie, Christian Gaidon,
❢ Beaujolais, France, £8.95, The Wine Society
Sheer delight. A gorgeous, bright, busty, ripe juicy red, packed with raspberry and cherry and banana fruit, reeking with the scents of vintage time. Is it complex? No. Will it age? Why worry? Is it delicious and should I pour it wantonly down my throat? Definitely.

㉒ 2004 Cabernet Sauvignon, Pirque Estate,
❢ Maipo Valley, Chile, £6.99, Marks & Spencer
This comes from the top Haras de Pirque estate: another example of M&S going to top producers and making up delicious blends from their barrels. Haras de Pirque make powerful, burly, dark wines drenched with black fruit, tannins and dark promise. They've lightened up a little here: it's still a dense

wine with enough tannin to make your gums shudder, but the massive weight of black plum and black cherry juice and black chocolate richness loaded with spice makes it a triumph. Me? I'd buy it and age it five years.

㉓ 2003 Shiraz Reserve,
Buckingham Estate
Western Australia, £7.99,
Morrisons
Soft Shiraz, but ripe and tasty. You don't mind Shiraz being soft if there's loads of flavour, and there is here – rich chocolate texture, deep plum and prune fruit and a come-hither minty, floral scent. Lovely, easy to drink red with satisfying depth to boot.

㉔ 2004 Riesling, Clifford Bay Estate, Single Vineyard,
Marlborough, New Zealand, £9.95, Friarwood
Clifford Bay is an extremely good estate at the mouth of the Awatere River in Marlborough, New Zealand. It's well known for its Sauvignon, less so for its Riesling, but its wines always have intensity of flavour. I smelt this and wondered if it had too much flavour, but taste it and it's just right – ripe, with a waxy, honeyed weight, but also lots of citrus zest acidity, excellent minerality and refreshing white peach and apple fruit.

㉕ 2005 Chardonnay, Twin Wells,
Hunter Valley, NSW, Australia, £7.99, Marks & Spencer
This type of Hunter Valley Chardonnay was probably more popular five years ago, but this is a very good example, even if the style is less trendy than it used to be. It has a lanolin-smooth weightiness, golden peach fruit that is vague rather than focused, and quite a bit of clove and cinnamon oak spice. It's weighty, but it's dry too, and its braggadocio is greatly reduced from the Hunter's glory era of a decade and more ago.

*The JMB labelled wine
was £9.99.*

26 **2005 Chablis, Sainte Celine (Jean-Marc Brocard),**
♀ **Burgundy, France, £7.99, Sainsbury's Taste the Difference**

Brocard is one of the most passionate producers in Chablis, able to please a
large outfit like Sainsbury's, and unwilling to compromise his commitment to
making crisp, minerally, classic Chablis wines. You can taste the ripeness of
2005 in this wine, but it's the crisp ripeness of good eating apples, balanced
by yeast softness, lemon acidity, a little perfume and an overriding sense of
the sun-warmed summer soils of the vineyard.

27 **2002 Montagny 1er Cru, Caves des Vignerons de Buxy,**
♀ **Burgundy, France, £8.99, Morrisons**

What an interesting wine, mainly because it has a maturity that it's rare to find
in the High Street. 2002 was a lovely year for white Burgundy, and Montagny is
a dry, chalky white Burgundy style that benefits greatly from aging. It stays dry,
almost slightly austere, but the extra age creates a delightful lean yet soft mix
of apples and hazelnut, mineral stoniness and a savoury, glycerine aftertaste.

28 **2005 Grenache, Willunga 100,**
🍷 **McLaren Vale, South Australia, £7.99, Sainsbury's**

The Grenache grape in Australia makes some of the planet's most
dangerously gluggable wine, partly because the wine has loads of flavour but
it never gets dense or challenging. This is a jumble of all things red plus a
handful of herbs – even the acidity is cranberry acid, redcurrant acid and the
fruit is a great blast of red cherry, red plum and strawberry essence soaked in
red syrup.

29 **2004 Riesling, Erdener Treppchen Vineyard,**
♀ **Mosel-Saar-Ruwer, Germany, £9.99, Marks & Spencer**

This is such a lovely style of wine; it used to be regarded as the height of
sophistication a generation ago, yet nowadays hardly any of us touch it. The
Mosel Valley is steep, treacherous and home to Germany's most challenging
but rewarding vineyards, and Ernie Loosen, the maker of this wine, is a quality
leader there, intent on delicacy but never fragility. This is off-dry – many of the
best German wines are – slightly spritzy, a mouthwatering mixture of green
leaf, green apple, orange blossom and liquid honey that lingers on your
tongue long after the wine is gone. Sheer delight. And you could age it ten
years if you wanted to.

French whites

- **Bordeaux**, Château Selection, Ch. Limouzin (page 103)
- **Bourgogne, Les Raverettes**, P & M Guillemot-Michel (page 46)
- **Bourgogne Blanc**, Dom. Rémi Jobard (page 40)
- **Bourgogne, Vieilles Vignes**, Le Chat Blanc, Bruno Fèvre (page 141)
- **Chablis**, Sainte Celine (Jean-Marc Brocard) (pages 56, 140)
- **Chardonnay, 'Le Petit Ange'**, Dom. Begude, Vin de Pays d'Oc (page 81)
- **Chardonnay, H**, Dom. Saint Hilaire, Vin de Pays d'Oc (page 72)
- **Chassagne-Montrachet**, Vieilles Vignes, Vincent Girardin (page 141)
- **Cheverny**, Dom. des Marnières, Delaille (page 58)
- **Colombard**, Vin de Pays des Côtes de Gascogne, Calvet (page 140)
- **Coteaux du Languedoc Picpoul de Pinet**, Dom. de Peyreficade (page 78)
- **Cuvée Pecheur**, Vin de Pays de Comté Tolosan (page 102)
- **Gewurztraminer, Herrenweg**, Zind-Humbrecht (page 142)
- **Gewurztraminer, Cave de Turckheim** (page 68. 142)
- **Graves, Clos Floridène** (page 141)
- **Grenache-Viognier**, Dom. la Croix Belle, Vin de Pays des Côtes de Thongue (page 75)
- **Jasnières, Cuvée Tradition**, Bénédicte de Rycke (page 24)
- **Jurançon Sec**, Vitatge Vielh de Lapeyre (page 27)
- **Montagny 1er Cru**, Caves des Vignerons de Buxy (page 56)
- **Muscadet Sèvre et Maine sur lie** (Jean Douillard) pages 93, 140)
- **Muscadet Sèvre et Maine sur lie Réserve**, Ch. du Cléray (page 140)
- **Les Olivettes, Vin de Pays des Vals d'Agly**, Dom. des Chênes (page 76)
- **Pessac-Léognan**, Ch. Tour Léognan (page 141)
- **Petit Manseng Sec**, Cabidos, Vin de Pays des Pyrénées-Atlantiques, Comte Philippe de Nazelle (page 19)
- **Riesling**, Cave de Turckheim (page 82)
- **Rolle**, Vin de Pays des Coteaux de Murviel, Dom. de Coujan (page 82)
- **Santenay 1er Cru**, 'Beaurepaire', J-M Vincent (page 38)
- **Saumur**, La Paleine, Dom. de la Paleine (page 80)
- **Sauvignon-Semillon**, Delor (page 98)
- **Sylvaner**, Charles Schleret (page 50)
- **Vin de Pays du Gers**, Vieille Fontaine (page 103)
- **Viognier**, Nord Sud, Vin de Pays d'Oc, Laurent Miquel (page 70)
- **Viognier**, Dom. de Coudoulet, Vin de Pays d'Oc (page 142)

SWEET

- **Sauternes**, Ch. Doisy Daëne (page 116)
- **Sauternes**, Ch. Guiraud (page 117)
- **Sauternes**, Ch. Liot (page 116)
- **Sauternes**, Maison Sichel (page 117)
- **Sauternes**, Ch. Suduiraut (page 143)
- **Sainte-Croix-du-Mont**, Ch. La Rame Sublime (page 143)

**30 2005 Chardonnay, Kangarilla Road,
McLaren Vale, Australia, £8.49, Majestic**

McLaren Vale Chardonnays used to be popular with the big brand blenders in Australia because they were so fat and rich and could easily add succulence to some inferior brew. Modern McLaren Vale Chardonnay is altogether more sophisticated, nicely acid, with very attractive dry apple and peach fruit and an oatmeal and hazelnut softness that reminds me – distantly – of a good Burgundy.

**31 2004 The Society's Exhibition Chardonnay,
Casablanca Valley, Chile, £8.95, The Wine Society**

This doesn't in any way resemble a good white Burgundy. In fact this style of wine is becoming a rarity nowadays – rip-roaring, gushing, tropical fruit salad Chardonnay packed with figs and melons and pineapple, glyceriny, syrupy even, yet with a stony streak and somehow all subsiding into a delightful balanced drink. Excellent example of an old-style Chardonnay.

2004
WAIPARA WEST

Two Terrace
Chardonnay
WAIPARA
750ml   WINE OF NEW ZEALAND   14%vol

**32 2004 Chardonnay, Two Terrace, Waipara
West, Waipara, New Zealand, £7.99,
Waterloo Wine Company**

This comes from a superb, out-of-the-way vineyard in South Island, New Zealand. It's rich and round, deep and soft with a lovely sense of beeswax and lanolin, earth and a wild, funky, savage quality I keep saying is pheromonal without ever quite working out why – that's pheromones for you – and a final ancient autumn flavour of quince and medlars. Wines like this make Chardonnay interesting again. *Also at Handford Holland Park*

**33 2004 Cheverny, Domaine des Marnières, Delaille,
Loire Valley, France, £7.49, Flagship Wines**

This is pretty rare stuff from a pretty obscure part of the Loire Valley – and it's good. 85% Sauvignon and 15% Chardonnay creates a tangy, aggressive wine with a little softness from the Chardonnay at its edge, but the wine still delivers apple peel and nettle, coffee bean and citrus zest, and an unusual but appetizing metallic twang. This is far better than most Sancerres – and cheaper.

❸❹ 2004 Calatayud, Papa Luna,
🍷 Aragón, Spain, £8.99, Thresher
Big dense red with loads of chewy
plum skins but fleshy, spicy, juicy
flavours as well. It's as though they've
squeezed red cherries and plums,
stewed them with their skins, then
added a ladleful of spice and a squirt
of chewing tobacco.

❸❺ 2002 Cigales Crianza,
🍷 Museum, Castilla y León,
Spain, £8.49, Flagship Wines
Cigales is a new trendy area of Spain
that is making some pretty
interesting reds. This is rich and stewy
and has even got some date and fig
overripeness, but its also got good acidity and a savoury richness like really ripe
tomatoes, all topped off with vanilla oak.

South Africa

WHITE
- **Chardonnay**, Rustenberg (page 142)
- **Sauvignon Blanc**, Fairtrade (page 93)
- **Sauvignon Blanc**, Oak Valley (page 59)
- **Sauvignon Blanc**, Springfield Estate
  (page 140)

RED
- **Cabernet Sauvignon**, Fairtrade (page
  95)
- **Catharina**, Steenberg (page 36, 138)
- **Cinsault-Shiraz**, Fairtrade (page 101)
- **Syrah**, Porcupine Ridge (page 67)

❸❻ 2004 Pinot Noir, Porta Select Reserve, Viña Porta,
🍷 Bío Bío Valley, Chile, £6.49, Thresher
Bío Bío is a cool, damp area in the south of Chile, quite unlike its other vineyard
areas, but it is proving itself to be excellent for aromatic white varieties like
Riesling and Gewürztraminer, and for fragrant, delicate Pinot Noir reds. This is,
in fact, quite full, with lovely gentle ripe strawberry and red cherry fruit of an
almost jelly baby soft consistency, lightly scented with roses and brightly
streaked with eucalyptus.

❸❼ 2005 Sauvignon Blanc, Oak Valley,
🍸 Elgin, South Africa, £9.95, Great Western Wine
Oak Valley is a strange name for a Sauvignon Blanc that is proudly, aggressively
un-oaked, but there you go. Don't let the name put you off, because Elgin
grows some of South Africa's top Sauvignon and this is a good example,
managing to be both soft yet very direct, full of green sensations and
capsicum, coffee bean, nettle and boiled lemon sharpness – yet it's never raw,
always easy and soft.

Austrian wine

Why don't we drink more Austrian wine? Is it because the names are in German and so we presume they will be tainted with the Liebfraumilch brush? Is it because they're quite expensive? But then, if you'd seen the daunting mountain goat vineyards that a lot of them come from, especially in the Wachau region, I can't believe you'd begrudge them the money. You'd probably offer to pay their accident insurance. Is it because, frankly, we're nervous of the unfamiliar? Is it that? Will you please let me reassure you that the unfamiliarity of Austrian wine merely means you have a treasure chest of wonderful new flavours to discover. Check my selection over. Just buy *one* of them. If you don't like it, you don't have to buy another.

1 2004 Riesling, Strasse Gaisberg, Weingut Eichinger, Kamptal, £10.61, Armit

What a beautiful wine. What a fantastic array of flavours and yet what masterful restraint in putting them all together. This is nothing like a German Riesling, nor an Alsace or an Australian one. It shows how the Riesling grape adapts to each place that it grows and produces thrillingly different flavours. This is honeyed but dry, floral with delightful jasmine scent, almost grapey, too. But the restraint is majestic. Initially the flavour seems full but dry, and then the lovely fruit and perfume slowly build and stay in your mouth as a strong stony undertow tugs at any indulgence and keeps the wine so fresh and dry and appetizing that it barely seems fully ripe. At 12.5% alcohol, perhaps it isn't, and it's all the better for it.

2 2005 Riesling, Gobelsburger, Kamptal, £7.69, Waitrose

An excellent example of why we should be drinking more Austrian wine. It's completely different from other Rieslings around the world and yet its flavour is classic – the shimmering thread of true Riesling personality runs like a rapier through the wine. It manages to be full yet lean, with a fruit made up of apple peel and lemon, a cleansing, scouring dryness of river bottom

WINES FROM
AUSTRIA
A TASTE OF
CULTURE

WINES FROM AUSTRIA

warm days, cool nights - aromatic wines

Good food deserves good wines. www.winesfromaustria.com

pebbles, resinous herbs and the sprinkling of river bank summer dust. All this with lovely acidity, and a floral finish.

③ 2005 Grüner Veltliner, Gobelsburger,
♀ Kamptal, £6.49, Waitrose

Grüner Veltliner for me offers a unique Austrian flavour – full, savoury, ripe, yet memorably peppery and refreshing. This is ripe all right, with a hint of honey and jasmine and sweet apple fruit and a lovely full, weighty autumn orchard sunshine texture, but mixed in there's a scent of leather, the rasp of stones and the crackling crunch of fresh ground pepper.

④ 2004 Grüner Veltliner, Spitzer Point Federspiel, Johann Donabaum,
♀ Wachau, £9, Connolly's

The Wachau makes famously mineral wines from its scarily steep slopes, and here's a top example. It's full and dry but the texture is ripe and you'd almost expect a little honey, but you won't get it. What you *do* get is a wine that is zesty but not aromatic, a strong flavour of lemon and white pepper, and an appetizing acidity which is as cool and dry as rock: you can sort of taste the lemon, yet you can't. There's a hint of spritz and the whole delicious experience is as cool and dry as rock, the flavour washed with cold, clean rocky mineral dust.

⑤ 2005 Grüner Veltliner, Hochterrassen, Weingut Salomon-Undhof,
♀ £6.95, Lea and Sandeman

A gorgeous wine showing all the thrilling 'different-ness' of the Grüner Veltliner grape. This is so bright, so cold, with its sprinkling of white pepper, its lean apple peel and lemon zest fruit, tobacco scent and a strong sense of the gaunt stones of sheer Danube rockface. Yet this isn't an aggressive wine; it manages to be austere yet soft and its aftertaste is refreshingly citrus and thirst-quenching.

⑥ 2003 Grüner-Veltliner, Schneiderberg, Weinrieder,
♀ Weinviertel DAC, £8.25, Waterloo Wine Company

Remember how hot 2003 was? Well this Grüner-Veltliner is both mature – 3 years old – and from a broiling vintage. The colour is full gold and the wine is rich, round, with a fatness of ripe apples and pastry cookies, a scent of white pepper and curry plant and an overriding sensation of warm stones soaking up the heat on the river shore.

7 **2005 Grüner Veltliner (organic), Meinklang, Michlits Werner, Burgenland, £6.95, Vintage Roots**
Slightly fuller and softer than some other Grüner Veltliners, but it's still nice and dry, with lemon acidity, apple fruit and a good mineral rub of dry stones. No pepper, but there's a tasty lick of celery.

8 **2004 Grüner Veltliner, Salomon Groovey, Weingut Salomon-Undhof, £6.49, Oddbins**
Good white pepper, celery and ripe apple flavours with a decent chunk of mineral rocks in this dry, soft Grüner Veltliner that really is trying to be groovy – the label shows a hip fish wearing shades.

And Austria makes red wine, too:

9 **2002 Blaufränkisch, Erwin Tinhof, Burgenland, £7.95, Savage Selection**
We see even fewer Austrian red wines than whites, but they're worth seeking out for a *very* different experience. Typically, Mark Savage has a good example – it's slightly oakier than it need be, but the toasty warmth goes very well with the herby scent and the ripe yet acidic redcurrant fruit.

10 **2004 Blaufränkisch, Feiler-Artinger, Burgenland, £8.99, Waitrose**
This is quite gentle in texture for an Austrian red, and its time in old oak barrels has left a pastry softness that blends nicely with the juicy red and black plum fruit and the fresh nip of peppercorn and green leaf.

From £5 to £7

The price segment above the dreaded £4.99 point is enormously important because it allows the vendor or retailer some freedom, some flexibility, and allows him to talk quality and personality with his customers and with his suppliers. It seems we drinkers are beginning to agree. I've just seen a report that said there's been a 29% increase in wine purchases between £6 and £7. Brilliant. Just so long as this wasn't souped-up New World brands with artificially inflated prices. Last year, we recommended 20 wines in the £5–7 slot. But it's so important that this year I've chosen 50 gorgeous, affordable reds and whites.

1 2004 Rioja Blanco, Barrel-Fermented, Monopole, Cune,
♀ **Spain, £6.49, Waitrose**
A fantastic price for a genuine, old-fashioned class act. When all around new styles and new producers are sprouting like mushrooms – and nowhere is this more true than in Spain – one of the oldest established Rioja companies, Cune (officially they're Compañía Vinícola del Norte de España), realize that there's absolutely nothing wrong and everything right with the way they make their white Rioja, so how about leaving it as it is? Revolutionary stuff. But if you're tired of Chardonnay, and many people are, but still like a rich, oaky wine, well, this is a true original, a deep, dry style, tasting of custard and brazil nut flesh, wax and glycerine, kept fresh with orange juice acidity. Unlike any other white in the world. And yours for £6.49.

2 2004 Corbières, Château Pech-Latt,
❗ **Languedoc-Roussillon, France, £5.99, Waitrose**
The savage hills of the Corbières, down towards the Pyrenees, are some of my favourite places in France, and there's been a wine revolution going on during the last decade or so. Corbières used mostly to be pretty hard work, rather bitter, stringy, ungenerous, speaking not so much of the wild grandeur of the mountains but more of the miserable time most producers were having trying to ripen their grapes and make a half-decent mouthful. But now Corbières is

Vineyards in Corbières, in the foothills of the Pyrenees

DISCOVER THE ART IN WINE

Spier wines offer a gallery of exceptional works of art
- wines with superb varietal character, on a canvas of
distinct individuality and expression.

Our wines are the result of the winemaker's passion
- to bring the ultimate truth in wine, to all. Choose from
our Discover range of wines for all occasions,
to our premium collections with a host of star ratings,
accolades and awards.

Discover the true art in wine with Spier - a combination
of creative expression, knowledge and skill, in a palette
of wisdom, since 1692

DISCOVERING THE ART IN WINE SINCE 1692

INTERNATIONAL WINE & SPIRITS COMPETITION
LONDON 2005

Spier Vintage Selection   Shiraz - Mourvèdre - Viognier 2003

Spier Private Collection   Pinotage 2003

full of confident wine-growers prepared to modernize their approach in the vineyard and the winery, and the result is an increasing number of really gutsy reds reeking of the mountain glen. This vineyard was first planted in 784, and it's organic. The wine is dark and rich, beautifully ripe without being at all overdone, a lovely deep syrup of blackberry and black plum seasoned with allspice and coriander seed and swished with mountain herbs. And it's only £5.99. Sometimes the good guys *do* win.

③ 2002 Cabernet Sauvignon, Coonawarra,
♀ South Australia, £6.99, Sainsbury's Taste the Difference
Taste the difference, the label says. Well, if it's there we will, and with this cracker it's there all right. This is made for Sainsbury's by Katnook Estate, one of the top producers down under, who still try to preserve the special flavours of Coonawarra; some of the other, bigger, producers don't. That means a dark, dry red wine with loads of piercing, ripe blackcurrant fruit, a little pastry softness from oak barrels and a beguiling mint leaf and eucalyptus scent, a sure sign in Australia that the grapes grew in cool conditions. Coonawarra's king of cool, and this wine shows how 'cool' cool can be.

④ 2005 Pinot Noir, Secano Estate, Leyda Valley,
♀ Leyda Valley, Chile, £6.99, Marks & Spencer
Some people say Pinot Noir is impossible to do well at a low price. So how come M&S are so good at it? Their £4.99 Pinot Noir from the Casablanca Valley (see page 94) is very good. This one, at £6.99, is an absolute star. It comes from the Leyda Valley, the closest vineyards in Chile to the sea, and some of the coolest. But the sun shines every day, and the fruit has the brilliant acidity of cool conditions as well as the proud ripeness of sunny skies. This Pinot is fresh, alert, the fruit gentle yet concentrated, all sweet raspberry and cherry syrup, no hard edges – but there's an appetizing flash of metallic minerality running through the wine.

⑤ 2005 Syrah, Porcupine Ridge,
♀ Boekenhoutskloof, Franschhoek, South Africa, £6.99, Waitrose
This is a really encouraging wine from South Africa. It started out life as a few barrels of off-cuts from the extremely classy, if unpronounceable, Boekenhoutskloof operation, but rapidly took on a life of its own and is now a big-volume niche brand. Well, not 'big' like Blossom Hill et al, but they have to

go out and source the grapes because they can't grow them all themselves – yet the quality is unerringly high. This wine is exciting for its own sake and it also shows the fantastic potential at this £6.99 price point for other important producers – but they must be demanding and ambitious, like Porcupine Ridge's Marc Kent. And the wine? It's a great hotchpotch of sweet damson fruit, red cherry syrup, charcoal smoke and a delightful scent of lilies. The balance is spot on. More like this, please.

6 2003 Rioja, Club Privado, Baron de Ley,
Spain, £6.99, Morrisons

If Morrisons are genuine about keeping up their wine range and their image along with it, then this is the kind of wine that'll help them. It's a serious Rioja from a serious producer and it isn't as pricy as many of the other smart names. And it manages to be very modern but not lose track of why we all like Rioja so much. Softness, succulence, a little savoury cream to go with the strawberry and cherry red fruit, brioche softness, and in this case a little blossom perfume too.

7 2005 Gewurztraminer, Alsace,
Cave de Turckheim, France, £6.99, Marks & Spencer

Pretty much all of the supermarkets have decent spicy Gewurztraminers and most of them come from the same producer, the large co-operative at Turckheim, but M&S seem to have secured the best blend. Which is exactly what you'd expect and demand of M&S. This is absolutely delightful stuff, with a scent like Nivea face crème, Fry's Turkish Delight, rose petals and lychee, and a perfumed softness that is chubby and irresistibly squeezable.

8 2004 Touriga Nacional,
(Jose Neiva), Estremadura, Portugal, £5.99, Tesco Finest

This is perhaps my favourite of all the Tesco Finest range, because it has so much boisterous ripe personality. It just sings out its Touriga Nacional origins and its proud Portuguese roots. Touriga is a fantastic grape: a lot of top ports use it for its colour and dense fruit and, wow, you can see why. This has an almost syrupy blackberry richness, but it never cloys because there's a barrage of beautiful bitter-sweetness, licorice and black treacle, that makes this fascinating, satisfying, original stuff.

Please bear in mind that wine is not made in infinite quantities – some of these may well sell out, but the following year's vintage should then become available.

Tesco.com Wines by the Case.

We've an exclusive online selection.

Whether you fancy a vintage vin rouge or a fruity vin blanc.

We'll deliver.

In our big van bleu.

To order go online to
www.tesco.com/wine
or call 08456 775577

www.tesco.com | *Every little helps*

9 2005 Viognier, Nord Sud, Vin de Pays d'Oc, Laurent Miquel, Languedoc-Roussillon, France, £6.99, Majestic

Viognier is a wonderful grape, but it's capricious, it's difficult to control, because it wants to give you rather more of its voluptuous charms than you can really cope with. Brash, big-lipped, flirtatious, Viognier needs to be tamed. Well, these guys have done a lovely job of it. No more overbearing heady scents and thick jowly fruit, but instead a gentle fresh flavour that slowly builds in your mouth, like apricot skins, the kind you get in good apricot jam, sweetened with a little pear juice and scented with honeysuckle. Chewy, rich, fragrant, and not at all suffocating.

10 2005 Carmenère Reserva, Mont Gras, Colchagua Valley, Chile, £6.99, Waitrose

2005 was a thrilling vintage in Chile, producing wine of pronounced fruit and real pinging focus. So if you don't know what Carmenère – Chile's great original variety – tastes like, this would be a good place to start. It has impressively rich blackberry and black plum fruit, a green, leafy freshness and a winter stew-like savouriness of coal dust, ground pepper and long-casseroled vegetables. And that's exactly what it should taste like.

11 2005 Syrah, Camplazens, Vin de Pays d'Oc, Languedoc-Roussillon, France, £6.49, Majestic

Vin de Pays d'Oc Syrah could mean anything, quite frankly. Luckily the British couple who own this vineyard have chosen a top patch of land in an area called La Clape near Narbonne and the Syrah they grow there is textbook stuff that could easily hail from the Rhône Valley at more than twice the price. Its perfume is an unlikely but beautiful mix of violets and peppercorns and the taste manages to mix that pepper with licorice, full creamy damsons and plums and the slight sizzle of hot stones.

12 2005 Cabernet Sauvignon-Carmenère, Porta Reserve, Viña Porta, Maipo Valley, Chile, £5.99 (£3.99 3 for 2), Thresher

This is good value at £5.99. But Thresher shops operate a three for the price of two policy, so it's brilliant value at £3.99 when you buy three. This wine demonstrates the point that a lot of wine experts make when they say a blend is often better than the varieties kept separate. I can see that here. There's excellent rich blackcurrant – that's the Cabernet – and black plum skin fruit –

that's the Carmenère. It's chewy – Cabernet – yet there's also a kind of rasping richness like the skin and flesh of a really ripe peach to go with the dark, dense fruit. If I had to guess I'd say that was Viognier, but I'll presume it's yet another guise Carmenère takes on now and then.

QUINTA
DE AZEVEDO
Vinho Verde
DENOMINAÇÃO DE
ORIGEM CONTROLADA
Engarrafado por Sogrape
Vinhos, S.A. Vila Nova de
Gaia- Portugal. Product
of Portugal. VINHO BRANCO

2005

10.5% vol   750 ml ℮

⓭ 2005 ♀ Vinho Verde, Quinta de Azevedo, Portugal, £5.25, The Wine Society

At the price, we'd have let this into the 'around a fiver' section, but we thought it was so good it could hold its own among more expensive wines. If you've not tried Vinho Verde – proper, bone-dry Vinho Verde from a good single estate – you're missing a treat. I drank a bottle of this on the terrace of the Quinta with the owner. It was a baking afternoon, the Vinho Verde was ice-cold and crackling in the glasses. It was damn near perfect. Back in Blighty, with winter setting in, it may not be quite so perfect, but it's still brilliant wine – a very mild fizziness, delightful Bramley apple and white peach fruit, quite sharp lemon acidity and a memory of crumbly summer earth. And it's 10.5% alcohol. *Also at Booths, Majestic, Robersons, Stevens Garnier, Wright Wine*

Portugal

WHITE
- **Alentejo**, Marquês de Borba, J Portugal Ramos (page 72)
- **Vinho Verde**, Quinta de Azevedo (page 71)
- **Vinho Verde**, Quinta de Simaens (page 78, 140)

RED
- **Douro**, Sainsbury's (Quinta do Crasto) (page 74)
- **Touriga Nacional**, Estremadura (Jose Neiva) (page 68)
- **Trincadeira**, J Portugal Ramos (page 77)

PORT
- **The Society's Late Bottled Vintage Port** (page 120)
- **10 Year old Aged Tawny Port**, Marks & Spencer (page 121)
- **Crusted Port**, Dow's (page 121)
- **Finest Reserve Port**, Marks & Spencer (page 121)
- **Vintage Port**, Graham's (page 145)

For more wine recommendations see Oz Clarke's Wine Style Guide, pages 136–145

⑭ 2003 Chardonnay, H, Domaine Saint Hilaire, Vin de Pays d'Oc, ♀ Languedoc-Roussillon, France, £6.25, Christopher Piper Wines

Made by a British operation – the Brits seem to be making quite a difference down in the south of France – and showing just how gorgeous carefully crafted Chardonnay can be. It's quite rich, but it hasn't lost any freshness, and the oak is subtly woven into the wine. The fruit is like a very ripe apple drizzled with honey, the oak spice is like a single clove dipped briefly in pineapple and cling peach syrup. It's lush, yet it's dry. Californian and Australian winemakers please take note.

⑮ 2005 Chardonnay, Windy Peak, De Bortoli, ♀ Victoria, Australia, £6.99, Sainsbury's

This wine is based on fruit from Victoria's cool Yarra Valley; in French terms that's still not exactly cool, but this gives you the big Aussie flavour without the sugar and the flabby overripeness. It's got very attractive nectarine, pear flesh and syrup ripeness, the oak adds a little spicy vanilla, but the acidity holds it all in check, so you get that extra Aussie fruit but you also benefit from a positively European freshness and acid balance.

Marquês de Borba

I PORTUGAL RAMOS

⑯ 2005 Alentejo, Marquês de Borba, J Portugal ♀ Ramos, Portugal, £7.35, Tanners

J Portugal Ramos – good name, you don't have to ask where *he*'s from – is one of Portugal's leading consultants and, increasingly, he's making his own wine. This is a smasher. From a really hot part of the country, he's managed to create a firm, soft, but acid-fresh style smelling of orange blossom and tasting of nectarines and ripe Cox's apples tempered and toughened by orange citrus acidity and the rough kiss of stones.

⑰ 2005 Sauvignon Blanc, Budai, Nyakas, ♀ Buda, Hungary, £5.77, Wines of Westhorpe

This is smashing. I'd like bottles of this to be sent to the syndicates who control places like Sancerre and white Bordeaux, asking 'why can't you do this?' But why bother? Better to encourage the Hungarians in a style that they understand and do really well. There are cheaper Hungarian Sauvignons, and they're snappy and good, but this one is a notch up. Bright, aggressive, packed with zingy grapefruit, nettle, capsicum and kiwi fruit greenness, elderflower scent and a hint of crunchy green grape – full, balanced, aggressive, excellent.

⓲ 2004 Tryst, Cabernet-Tempranillo-Zinfandel,
🍷 Nepenthe, South Australia, £6.99, Waitrose
A beaut from the Nepenthe mavericks in the Adelaide Hills. This mixes the intercontinental combo of Cabernet, Tempranillo and Zinfandel and it works so well I'd love to suggest to France, Spain and California (the homes of the three varieties) that they give it a go. But they wouldn't be growing these three varieties together in the same region, let alone the same vineyard. In fact, France simply couldn't do it: she doesn't allow these three to be planted together. This is something really special. It's got a seductively easy-drinking character and you could even chill it down for an hour if you wanted to, but not too much because you don't want to flatten the brilliant flavour of eucalyptus and ripe black plums and stem ginger – yup, the stuff in the jar – dashed with some lime acidity and blackcurrant leaf. *Also at Ballantynes, Oddbins*

⓳ 2005 Petit Verdot-Shiraz, Inkwell, Salena Estate
🍷 South Australia, £5.99, Laithwaites
Petit Verdot is such a good stern, dark grape, oozing with black fruit and sometimes with a delightful violet perfume, rather like a rugby forward wearing girl's cologne – just for the fun of it, or the laughs, mind you. I'd leave it unblended, but if you want to soften it and sweeten it, well, juicy sweet-hearted Shiraz is the partner to choose, and it works very well here. The fruit is dark cherry and blackberry syrup and the Petit Verdot has added a tasty black chocolate bitter bite, but there's also a softness like buttercream and daisy cakes – and there's a whiff of floral cologne too.

⓴ 2004 Cabernet-Shiraz, Margaret River,
🍷 (Evans & Tate), Western Australia, £6.99, Marks & Spencer
I met the bloke who made this last year. He asked why didn't I like his wines more. I said I did, so long as they were blended by M&S – just get all his stuff up to M&S level and I'll *love* his wines. It's true. M&S do a really good job on this powerful red and sell it at a very fair price, because Margaret River is one of Australia's most expensive areas. This is a dry, earthy red, but the earth is so washed with blackberry and black plum fruit, scented with herbs and massaged with vanilla oak, that you realize this is like a super-ripe, but not ridiculously overripe, Bordeaux – and that's exactly what Margaret River aims to do.

㉑ 2004 Douro,
🍷 Portugal, £6.99, Sainsbury's Taste the Difference

The Douro river in Portugal is where they make all the great sweet ports; increasingly they're making excellent unfortified red wines as well. Sainsbury's blend this at Quinta do Crasto, one of the most beautiful properties you'll ever visit, whose winemakers unusually are more obsessed with their table wine than with their port. Well, this is a cracker – tannic and bitter streaked, but I don't mind, it gets the tastebuds drooling – and it has such a delightful lily scent matched by damson and blueberry fruit that the whole effect is both muscular and scented, and that's quite a combination to pull off.

㉒ 2004 Kékfrankos, Tamas Gere & Zsolt,
🍷 Villany, Hungary, £5.93, Wines of Westhorpe

If you want to shock – well, amaze – your friends with your originality, look no further than this weird but wonderful delight from Hungary. It's a whopping great Transylvanian stew of ripe red plums and damsons, grilled red capsicum peppers, lovage, peppercorns and savory. Bright, beautifully balanced and genuinely different. Just what your Sunday lunch table needs.

㉓ 2002 Carmenère Reserve, Peteroa,
🍷 Central Valley, Chile, £5.77, Wines of Westhorpe

Westhorpe are experts in Hungarian wine, but they were also one of the first companies to take Chile seriously. They've listed Peteroa for decades, and now it's better than ever. This really shows you what steamy, dark-blooded tearaway Carmenère is like, stinking beautifully of tarmac and licorice and coal black fruit, tasting smoky and dense, its seams bursting with plum and blackcurrant richness, soy sauce savouriness and the grainy tough edge of coal dust.

㉔ 2005 Chenin Blanc, Peter Lehmann,
🍸 Barossa Valley, South Australia, £5.99, Waitrose

This remains one of the great bargains in Aussie whites, and you won't find many better dry Chenins than this in the grape's heartlands of South Africa and the Loire Valley. It's bone dry, sharply acidic, but not for long, as a waxed leather softness takes control and orange blossom scent seems to rise from the glass. This is a lovely thirst-quencher now. In 5–10 years it will be transformed into a marvellous mouthful of honey, nuts, orange marmalade and quince. *Also at Budgens*

㉕ 2004 Falanghina del Molise, ♀ Ramì, Di Majo Norante, Italy, £7.05, Lea and Sandeman

Lea and Sandeman never cease to amaze and delight you with genuinely different flavours. Don't go to them for reassurance. Go to them when you're fired up by excitement at what frontiers of wine experience you haven't yet touched. This is a most unusually styled, perfumed yet leathery white, almost yeasty fat in its pear and banana fruit, but crackling with apple peel and steel blade acidity. And I think it'll taste of milk chocolate if you keep it for a couple of years.

New Zealand

WHITE

- **Chardonnay**, Two Terrace, Waipara West, Waipara (page 58)
- **Chenin Blanc**, Te Arai Vineyard, Millton Vineyards, Gisborne (page 42)
- **Pinot Gris**, Gladstone, Wairarapa (page 41)
- **Riesling**, Clifford Bay Estate, Marlborough (page 55)
- **Riesling**, Private Bin, Villa Maria, Marlborough (page 76)
- **Sauvignon Blanc**, Jackson Estate, Marlborough (page 140)
- **Sauvignon Blanc**, Seresin, Marlborough (page 36)

RED

- **Pinot Noir**, Momo, Marlborough (page 45)
- **Pinot Noir**, Rippon, Central Otago (page 27, 137)

SPARKLING

- **Pelorus**, Cloudy Bay (page 106, 144)

㉖ 2005 Grenache-Viognier, ♀ Domaine la Croix Belle, Vin de Pays des Côtes de Thongue, Languedoc-Roussillon, France, £6.95, Lea and Sandeman

This property is in the foothills north of Béziers and is another example of how many good single-domaine wines there are in France's far south, once you get away from the dead-end co-operatives and wine factories of the big brands. This delightful white is soft, scented, round and creamy, with a perfume like peach blossom and talcum powder, a flavour of apricots and banana, ginger and cinnamon.

㉗ 2004 Riesling, Private Bin, Villa Maria,
♀ Marlborough, New Zealand, £6.99, Budgens

New Zealand Riesling is a little softer and more scented than Aussie versions, but it's still pretty dry and appetizing. This one is not totally dry but that doesn't matter, because it's got a lime leaf oiliness as though you'd scraped the skin of the fruit, tangy acidity and delightful fruit, a cross between apple purée, lemon curd and lemon meringue pie. My mum would love this.

㉘ 1998 Navarra Gran Reserva, Cabernet Sauvignon-Merlot, Aldabea,
♦ Spain, £6.95, Avery's

Navarra got into Cabernet and Merlot before the rest of Spain in an attempt to differentiate itself from its rather overbearing neighbour Rioja, and for a long time held a virtual monopoly on Cabernet in Spain (Torres in Penedès excepted). Well, Navarra Cabernets don't taste like typical Cabs, but they're very interesting, and this one mixes an attractive leafy blackcurrant fruit with mint spice, but also a soothing savoury quality like a cream soup made out of sun-dried tomatoes.

㉙ 2004 Les Olivettes, Vin de Pays des Vals d'Agly, Domaine des Chênes,
♀ France, £6.95, Lea and Sandeman

Lovely domaine right on the edge of the Corbières mountains but just benefiting from the extra warmth of Roussillon, and run by a member of the staff from Montpellier wine school – a top wine school, by the way. His expertise shows in this full, dry, but musky wine, with a talcum and floral scent, and an apricot ripeness so musky it's as though the apricot is still hanging on the bough on a warm summer's evening in the orchard.

㉚ 2004 Cabernet Sauvignon, Miru, Beelgara Estate,
♦ Coonawarra, South Australia, £6.25, Avery's

Beelgara are an ambitious mob who I first visited a couple of years ago, and I tasted this from the barrel. It's turned out well, although it's not particularly typical of the Coonawarra style. It's got good, rich yet dry blackcurrant fruit, a whiff of smoke and pepper and a gooiness like those chocolate cream bars I used to love when I was a kid.

㉛ 2005 Sauvignon Blanc-Semillon,
♀ Western Australia, £6.99, Sainsbury's Taste the Difference

Sainsbury's has sourced this tangy little number from Capel Vale, a producer in the decidedly cool Western Australian boondocks of Pemberton, sort of in the middle of nowhere in the far south-west. Pemberton is increasingly popular with winemakers from more populous regions because of the intensity of its icy fruit. And here's why it's popular – a leafy, earthy smell translates into a dry white packed with green pepper and green apple, nettle and coffee bean flavour; it does still have a little earthy undertow but that adds to the experience rather than diminishing it.

32 2004 Trincadeira, J Portugal Ramos, Portugal, £6.99, Waitrose

Here's a really interesting flavour from one of Portugal's fascinating indigenous grape varieties. Oak aging has given this a savoury smell like cashew nuts being roasted and scattered with spice, while the Trincadeira fruit is very juicy, ripe plums and blackberries, balanced, classy and utterly gluggable.

33 2005 Sauvignon Blanc, Veramonte, Casablanca Valley, Chile, £7.03, Somerfield

Veramonte is part of Constellation – the biggest wine company in the world, which seems to get bigger every time I open the papers – but so far it has held on valiantly to its own individuality as a crucial player at the upper end of Chile's trendy Casablanca Valley. These Sauvignon grapes are grown down by the banks of the river, where cool breezes blow even when the rest of the valley is starting to heat up, and the result is a real full-on lemon and grapefruit blast. It's not perfumed or complex but it is unremittingly aggressive and unreconstructed.

34 2004 Almansa, Marques de Rojas, Bodegas Piqueras Spain, £5.95, Avery's

Big, powerful red grown inland from Valencia. It comes from the Garnacha Tintorera, but ampelographers (grape experts) love to confuse everyone, including themselves, and this isn't Garnacha at all, it's the beefy, brawny, black-as-pitch Alicante Bouschet. Whatever it is, it's top grog – burly, ripe, piled up with plum skin and banana and rock dust. But a word of warning: Alicante's juice is dark purple. So's this wine. Don't spill it on your blouse.

35 **2005 Vinho Verde, Quinta de Simaens,**
Portugal, Waitrose, £5.49

Lovely, almost austere, almost ascerbic but ultimately wonderfully refreshing dry white. Vinho Verde has a poor reputation in the UK because of the big brand sulphurous, sweetish rubbish that's been foisted on us over the years, but real Vinho Verde like this, full of acidity, bone dry, yet packed with apple and lemon fruit, pear blossom scent and a stony rasp is a great alternative to Sauvignon Blanc – and cheaper too.

36 **2005 Chardonnay, McLaren Vale**
South Australia, £6.98, ASDA Extra Special

I know that Aussie Chardie has gone a bit out of fashion, but really, when it's good, it merits a second look. This is a full, gentle mix of nut and cream and porridge oatmeal, and that's what good Burgundy tastes of. It then gets a bit richer, pineapple and melon and a hint of smoke, but this is classy white – don't let your prejudices get the better of you.

37 **2004 Coteaux du Languedoc, Picpoul de Pinet, Domaine de**
Peyreficade, Languedoc, France, £6.60, Yapp Brothers

I still haven't worked out how they make such a bright, fresh white as this on the broiling flatlands of France's Mediterranean coast. But Pinet is right next to the biggest oyster beds in the south, and I can only presume that the demand for a lean, dry, lemony white to go with a plateful of number 3s proved that necessity is the mother of invention. Planting Picpoul was a good idea, because this grape is famously acidic and even in the fierce Mediterranean sun it manages to create a delightfully, unexpectedly fresh white, with apple blossom scent, baked apple and lemon rind fruit and a good, creamy, yeasty, soft texture.

38 **2004 The Society's Chilean Cabernet Sauvignon,**
Maipo Valley, Chile, £5.50, The Wine Society

The Wine Society are a top operation, always able to persuade producers to give them really good cuvées, and then they always sell them at a fair price. This impressive Cabernet comes from Chilean giant Concha y Toro and is a classic Cabernet at a very appealing price. It's deep, dark, packed with ripe blackcurrant fruit, scented with eucalyptus and softened by oak.

Best wine under the sun.

In 1853, Thomas Hardy started crafting wines that would soon be prized in markets all around the world. Five generations later, the Hardys winemakers are still making the best of the rich soil and abundant sunshine of Australia's best regions to produce the current family of wines. A range that, without a shadow of a doubt, best expresses our founder's principles of quality, flavour and consistency.

㊵ 2003 Saumur, La Paleine, Domaine de la Paleine,
♀ **Loire Valley, France, £6.30, Tanners**

Wow. I didn't expect this. I know 2003 was hot, but this whopper piles in at 15% alcohol and is still dry – I think. Yes, it's fat. It's overripe. But it is dry. It tastes almost syrupy, the fruit is as old and autumnal as medlars and quince, its texture is like a super-ripe apple coated in thick wax, but, somehow, it is dry. Be brave, try it. *Also at Ballantynes*

㊶ 2004 Cabernet Sauvignon
♀ **Reserve, Casa Leona, Rapel Valley, Chile, £6.99, Marks & Spencer**

M&S started working with Casa Leona years ago. They've now become a large and pretty cool producer, but it's good to see M&S still sourcing wine here –

Italy

WHITE

- **Collio**, Zuani, Friuli-Venezia Giulia (page 41)
- **Falanghina**, Rami, Di Majo Norante, Molise (page 75)
- **Greco di Tufo**, Vesevo, Campania (page 46)
- **Grillo**, Serenata, Sicily (page 101)
- **Pinot Grigio**, La Prendina Estate, Veneto (page 140)
- **Pinot Grigio**, Colli Orientale de Friuli, Friuli-Venezia Giulia (page 140)
- **Verdiso**, Vincenzo Toffoli, Veneto (page 81)

RED

- **Amarone**, Taste the Difference, Valpantena, Veneto (page 139)
- **Cento**, IGT Salento, Castel di Salve, Puglia (page 43)
- **Chianti Classico**, Villa Cafaggio, Tuscany (page 139)
- **Chianti Classico Riserva**, Riecine, Tuscany (page 42)
- **Lacrima di Morro d' Alba**, Rubico, Marotti Campi, Marche (page 137)
- **Langhe Rosso Serrapiù**, Gianni Voerzio, Piedmont (page 139)
- **Nero d'Avola-Cabernet Sauvignon**, Feudo di Santa Tresa 'Nivuro', Sicily (page 43)
- **Teroldego Rotaliano**, Vigneto Lealbere, Roberto Zeni, Trento (page 139)
- **Primitivo-Aglianico**, Dorio, Puglia (page 138)
- **Primitivo-Merlot**, Da Luca, IGT Tarantino, Puglia (page 90)
- **Puglia Rosso** (Casa Girelli), Puglia (page 91)
- **Salento Rosso**, Armentino, Schola Sarmenti, Puglia (page 40)

SWEET

- **Moscato d'Asti**, Nivole, Michele Chiarlo, Piedmont (page 117)
- **Torcolato**, Maculan, Breganze, Veneto (pages 115, 143)
- **Vin Santo**, Il Colombaio di Cencio, Sassodoro, Tuscany (page 114)

and influencing the blends. This is full, ripe stuff, with some bright leaf and eucalyptus scent and big, rich, chocolate, blackberry and black cherry fruit, and some rather exciting savoury soy sauce which makes me think they've popped a bit of Carmenère in there. I wouldn't blame them if they had.

41 2004 Pinot Noir, Yering Frog, Yering Station, Yarra Valley, Victoria, Australia, £6.99, Majestic

Pinot Noir is a grape that demands cool conditions to give of its delicate best, and the Yarra Valley, a hop and a skip out of Melbourne, is historically one of Australia's coolest vineyard regions. Well, that cool climate shows in this very gentle wine, with gentle red plum and strawberry fruit, mild eucalyptus scent and an accommodating streak of acidity that wouldn't want to upset the calm, rather Burgundian style of the wine.

42 2004 Verdiso, Vincenzo Toffoli, Veneto, Italy, £5.95, Savage Selection

I didn't know these Toffoli guys until Mark Savage sidled up rather forcefully and removed any prevarication from the equation. I thought I was busy with something else, but no, suddenly I wasn't, I was tasting this fascinating white. A lot of Italian whites are very neutral and I'm sure the grapes used for this are pretty neutral, but Sr. Toffoli has created a full, deep, dry white with a core of stewed apple and honey splashed with lemon, and a growling undertone of earth dust and nut husk.

43 2005 Beaujolais, Domaine Chatelus de la Roche, Burgundy, France, £7.10, Roger Harris

Ah, Beaujolais as it was born to be. It's not sophisticated, thank goodness. There's nothing sharp and thin about this. Nothing stewy and sullen. Just the sheer delight of gorgeous juicy drink-me-quick red fruit, a rush of peach and red plum and strawberry with a mouthwatering apple peel rasp and a feeling that the wine ran over a bed of dry stones on its way to the bottle.

44 2004 Chardonnay, 'Le Petit Ange', Domaine Begude, Vin de Pays d'Oc, Languedoc-Roussillon, France, £5.99, Majestic

James Kinglake, a refugee from the City rat-race down in the hills of south-west France near Carcassonne, is making some top Chardonnay. This one is pulsing with ripe melon, peach and banana split fruit, freshened by lemony acidity, and its feet are kept firmly on the ground by a cool, dry stream of pebbly calm.

45 2004 Rolle, Vin de Pays des Coteaux de Murviel, Domaine de Coujan
♀ Languedoc-Roussillon, France, £5.99, Maison du Vin

The white wine we see coming out of France's far south is generally pretty flat and quite a lot of it is Chardonnay growing in conditions really too hot and tasting of nothing very much. But this one uses a proper southern grape variety, the Rolle, and grows it up in the foothills north of Béziers, with the result that this is very attractive – and different. It's delightfully dry yet soft, with apple and a little peach ripeness sharpened by lemon, softened by beeswax and perfumed very slightly with leather and Fuggles hops!

46 2005 Riesling, Cave de Turckheim,
♀ Alsace, France, £5.99, Marks & Spencer

Most of the dry Riesling we drink nowadays comes from the New World, usually Australia. But Alsace in northeast France is the original dry Riesling producer and has been making this style for donkey's years. This is an excellent example of this bright, pure, incisive style. It's dry with a good stony mineral texture just fattened up a bit with leesy cream; the fruit is fresh green apples streaked with lemon zest.

47 2003 Malbec, Festivo, Bodega Monteviejo,
♥ Valle de Uco, Mendoza, Argentina, £6.50, Friarwood

An increasing number of people from Bordeaux are getting involved in Argentina, excited by the prospects of working with personality-packed fruit. This time it's a guy from Pomerol, where they make big juicy Merlot-based reds, leaping at the chance to make big juicy Malbec wines right under the brow of the Andes. And this is good Malbec. It has just the right level of ripeness – in other words there's a touch of European restraint. It isn't pretty or lush, and I suppose I'd like a touch more violet perfume if it was on offer, but the texture is soft and mellow, there's a whiff of smoke in the air to go along with the smell of good, clean leather and the flavour of damson jam, stones and all.

48 2005 Sauvignon Blanc, Old Vines, Doña Dominga,
♀ Silva Family Wines, Colchagua Valley, Chile, £6.99 (£4.66 3 for 2),
Thresher

Not a typical tangy Sauvignon Blanc. It's much fuller and broader, in fact it's more like a Sauvignon-Semillon blend, but since those are the two grapes that make up classic white Bordeaux, I'm not too worried. There is lots of green fruit here, but it's ripe and gentle, more like kiwi than lime, and there's a soft pear and apple core fattened out with glycerine and beeswax.

49 2001 Syrah, Peteroa Oak Aged Collection,
♀ Central Valley, Chile, £6.10, Wines of Westhorpe

This isn't a typically plump, juicy Syrah, it's altogether more stern, a bit disciplined and corseted. But it is good and at over 5 years old still has some maturing to do. At the moment the dark plum fruit is coated with black treacle and slightly acrid smoke and there's quite a cold mineral streak running through the wine. Not typical, but I like it, perhaps for that very reason.

50 2003 Petit Verdot, Vat 4, De Bortoli,
♀ South-Eastern Australia, £5.99, Oddbins

Petit Verdot is one of those smashing grapes that kept on being pushed into a corner by mainstream winemakers, as though they were hoping it would just sit there, wan-faced, until everybody had forgotten about it. But one or two of Bordeaux's most innovative, quality-conscious producers – Paul Pontallier at the legendary Château Margaux being the leader – were convinced that this dark, brooding, late-ripening, marginal variety contained a depth of black fruit and violet perfume if only someone could find the key to unlock it. Petit Verdot is now regularly adding scent and excitement to top Bordeaux, and it has discovered another homeland way up in the Australian outback on the banks of the Murrumbidgee River. Here the grapes ripen more quickly, so the wine is richer, seemingly sweeter, certainly less brooding, hardly needing a key to unlock its flavour of deep sweet damson and black cherries, with a scent of peppermint and smoky treacle that is dense but utterly approachable. *Also at Wright Wine Co*

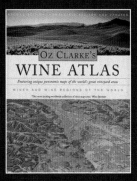
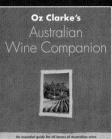

Oz Clarke
& Margaret Rand
Grapes and Wines
The definitive guide to the
world's great grapes and the
wines they make.
£18.99 p/b

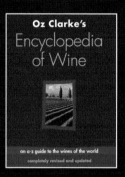

Oz Clarke's
Encyclopedia of Wine
Contains a truly vast amount of
wine information, as well as being
an enjoyable and informative read.
£18.99 p/b

Oz Clarke's
Introducing Wine
The ultimate no-nonsense guide
to wine. No previous knowledge
assumed.
£9.99 p/b

Oz Clarke's
Pocket Wine Book 2007
More information, more
recommendations, more facts, figures,
passion and opinion than any other
comparable guide to wine.
£9.99 h/b

Around a fiver

This is always the battleground in the High Street – everyone wants to hit the £4.99 price point without a) whittling away their profit, or b) diluting the quality. Well, it isn't easy and a lot of £4.99 wines don't stack up, so I've been flexible: wines that are a bit over a fiver but tasted good get into this selection. The supermarkets typically dominate this section but independent Wines of Westhorpe does pretty well with two delicious Hungarian whites.

❶ 2005 SO Organic Merlot,
❢ Maipo Valley, Chile, £4.99, Sainsbury's
Top stuff. 2005 was a beautiful vintage in Chile – they're all pretty good over there – and the fruit in this wine is vibrant and bursting with personality. The blend clearly includes some of the lovely Carmenère grape, and the result is a rip-roaring flavour of black chocolate and herbs and sweet, rich blackcurrant juice. Well done Sainsbury's.

❷ 2005 Chardonnay, Budai, Nyakas,
♀ Hungary, £4.92, Wines of Westhorpe
Marvellously pure Chardonnay. This is what Hungary is becoming so good at: giving the best, simple, pure expression of the grape variety without going OTT. This is Chardonnay without the make-up. It's very fresh, it has a mouthwatering lemony acidity made more aromatic by grapefruit zest, and then loads of apple fruit, lots of pebbly minerals and a touch of honeyed richness.

❸ 2005 Cono Sur, Gewürztraminer,
♀ Bío Bío, Chile, £5.49 Waitrose, £4.99 Sainsbury's
I'm beginning to think that Chile could become my first choice for spicy whites – and at the price, no one can touch them. This has just the right weight and fullness – enough to make you stop and think about the wine for a second, but not so much that you want to dilute it with Perrier water. It's even got some

Vineyards near the village of Markaz, in the Matraalja region of Hungary, northeast of Budapest

acidity – which a lot of Gewürztraminers don't – and it's dry, so that the wonderful eyelid-heavy scent of rose petals, lychees and grapefruit flowers is exhilarating rather than exhausting.

Cadet de Gascogne

Tannat - Cabernet

❹ 2004 Cadet de Gascogne, Vin de Pays des Côtes de Gascogne, Vasconia, South-West France, £4.95, Les Caves de Pyrene
It's not easy to make ripe reds down in Gascony – most of the local wine is pleasantly acidic white to drink, or unpleasantly acidic white to turn into Armagnac brandy. And then they come up with a cracker like this, which has so much plump black fruit, earthy stony drive and blackcurrant leaf acidity that you'd think it was a red Bordeaux at twice the price. *Also at Green & Blue, Wimbledon Wine Cellars*

❺ 2005 Irsai Olivér, Budai, Nyakas, Hungary, £4.82, Wines of Westhorpe
We don't see much Irsai Olivér in this country and when we do it's mainly at a rock-bottom price and tasting vaguely of lime-scented loo cleaner (not a bad flavour, but you have to be in the mood). But this one is lovely, mildly aromatic, gently floral and with a little of the crunchy freshness of green Muscatel grapes. It's got lemony acidity like lemon curd, and a gentle custard cream dry softness. Utterly pleasurable yet restrained.

❻ 2003 Rioja, Vega Ariana, Spain, £5.49, Waitrose
There's some good Rioja around at the moment and this is the best of the bargain reds. It isn't that deep, but has a lovely, mild, mellow flavour of oak barrel creaminess, strawberries, some stylishly squashy apple acidity, and an undertow of stones. Mellow red with spicy flavours. Did I write that? Must be from the label.

❼ 2004 Cabernet Sauvignon, Casillero del Diablo, Concha y Toro, Central Valley, Chile, c.£5.49, widely available
This is made by the biggest wine company in Chile. It shows that big *can* be beautiful and I just wish that the vast conglomerates in places like Australia and California would take note and realize that in the long term, quality

Chile

WHITE

- **Chardonnay**, The Society's Exhibition, Casablanca Valley (page 58)
- **Chardonnay Capitana**, Viña La Rosa, Cachapoal Valley (page 142)
- **Chardonnay-Semillon**, Doña Dominga, Viña Casa Silva (page 94)
- **Gewürztraminer**, Winemaker's Lot, Concha y Toro (page 142)
- **Gewürztraminer**, Cono Sur, Bío Bío (page 87)
- **Riesling**, Cono Sur, Bío Bío (pages 35, 140)
- **Sauvignon Blanc**, Old Vines, Doña Dominga, Colchagua Valley (page 82)
- **Sauvignon Blanc Laurel Vineyard**, Casa Marín, San Antonio (page 42)
- **Sauvignon Blanc**, Misiones de Rengo (page 94)
- **Sauvignon Blanc Reserve**, Montes, Curico Valley (page 94)
- **Sauvignon Blanc**, Ventolera, Viña Litoral, Leyda Valley (page 44)
- **Sauvignon Blanc**, Veramonte, Casablanca Valley (page 77)

ROSÉ

- **Cabernet Sauvignon**, Santa Rita, Maipo Valley (page 96)
- **Merlot**, La Palma (page 139)

RED

- **Cabernet Sauvignon Reserve**, Casa Leona, Rapel Valley (page 80)
- **Cabernet Sauvignon**, Casillero del Diablo, Concha y Toro, Central Valley (page 88)
- **Cabernet Sauvignon**, Peñalolen, Maipo Valley (pages 30, 137)
- **Cabernet Sauvignon**, Pirque Estate, Maipo Valley (page 54)
- **Cabernet Sauvignon**, The Society's Chilean, Maipo Valley (page 78)
- **Cabernet Sauvignon-Carmenère**, Porta Reserve, Maipo Valley (page 70)
- **Carmenère Reserva**, Mont Gras, Colchagua Valley (page 70)
- **Carmenère Reserve**, Peteroa, Central Valley (page 74)
- **Carmenère-Shiraz**, Doña Dominga Reserva (page 45)
- **Merlot**, SO Organic (Sainsbury's) (page 87)
- **Merlot**, Sunrise, Concha y Toro, Central Valley (page 136)
- **Pinot Noir**, Casablanca Valley (Morandé) (page 94)
- **Pinot Noir**, Cono Sur, Rapel Valley (page 90)
- **Pinot Noir**, Las Brisas Vineyard, Viña Leyda, Leyda Valley (pages 48, 137)
- **Pinot Noir**, Porta Select Reserve, Viña Porta, Bío Bío Valley (pages 59, 137)
- **Pinot Noir**, Secano Estate, Leyda Valley (page 67)
- **Syrah**, Haras Character, Viña Haras de Pirque, Maipo Valley (page 36)
- **Syrah**, Peteroa Oak Aged Collection, Vinicola Montealagre, Central Valley (page 83)
- **Syrah EQ**, Matetic, San Antonio (page 35)

pays. It *is* possible to make good wine in large quantities for a fiver – why don't they? They can't serve up coloured sugar water all the time. If they tasted this, they'd probably keel over it's got so much oomph – dark rich plum and blackcurrant fruit, rocky tannins, dense black chocolate and coal dust depth and syrupy nut sweetness from the oak. Powerful. Serious.

8 **2004 Old Vines Grenache Noir,**
🍷 **Vin de Pays des Côtes Catalanes, Languedoc-Roussillon, France, £5.49, Marks & Spencer**
This has got a silly, heavy bottle that might lead some people to think, wow, this *must* be superior, but usually it makes *me* think the wine will be heavy, over-oaked and too expensive. But this is none of those things. The wine *is* powerful. It's 14.5% alcohol, and you can certainly taste it. Thank goodness they haven't added to the power with new oak aging. This is a rich juicy mix of sweet raspberry syrup and raisiny overripeness, swished with a slap of herbs and a fairly tough tannic twang. If the meat course beckons, this is a star. On its own, I'd be wary.

9 **2005 Pinot Noir, Cono Sur,**
🍷 **Rapel Valley, Chile, c.£5.49, widely available**
Cono Sur have been the affordable Pinot experts in Chile for quite a while, and the price has hardly moved, but the quality has got better. Gentle, soft, mild, syrupy sweetness matched with strawberry juice, a little savoury cream and a dry undertow like pebbles in a stream. I've said it before and I'll say it again, Chile is the star when it comes to giving us really good flavours at a fair price.

10 **2004 Primitivo-Merlot, Da Luca,**
🍷 **IGT Tarantino, Puglia, Italy, £4.99, Budgens**
I wouldn't really think of blending the ancient southern Italian Primitivo with the French parvenu Merlot, but this works rather well. To be honest, the Merlot doesn't contribute that much, but the Primitivo is in fine fettle: dark rich dates and figs flavour scented with the casbah, and toughened by tree bark and black chocolate. Loads of flavour for the money.

⓫ 2004 Côtes du Rhône Villages, Plan de Dieu,
🍷 Domaine de la Meynarde, Rhône Valley,
France, £5.49, Marks & Spencer

I remember visiting Plan de Dieu when I was a
student – basically it was a man-made gravel bed
created out of copses and hillocks by a guy who'd
done a deal in earthworking gear with the
Americans after World War II. It took a while to bed in, but he created a pretty
good vineyard and this is a very pleasant mix of quite rich syrupy red berry
fruit, a little tannin and quite a lot of peppertree and lovage scent.

⓬ 2005 Puglia Rosso
🍷 (Casa Girelli), Puglia, Italy, £5.49, Marks & Spencer

There's some really good stuff in southern Italy
nowadays and this is a fine example – bright red
fruit, lots of raspberry syrup ripeness, a lush soft
feel, but refreshing acidity too. It's made by
Veneto stars Girelli, and their northern know-how
clearly pays dividends down south.

⓭ 2004 Garnacha-Tempranillo, La Riada,
🍷 (Bodegas Aragonesas), Campo de Borja, Spain, £4.99,
Threshers, Wine Rack

Threshers have really latched on to the idea that the great
empty plains south of Rioja are a brilliant place to look for really
juicy party reds. Old vines and modern winemaking have created
this smashing cauldron of flavours – a great stew of
strawberries and loganberries, dates and dried figs, seasoned
with pepper and lovage and scorched by hot rocks hurled into
the vat.

⓮ 2005 Rioja, Viura, Sonsierra,
♀ Bodegas Sonsierra, Spain, £5.25, Laymont & Shaw

White Rioja is one of the great undiscovered jewels for people
who like a really dry white style just tempered by yeasty cream
and oak, but still austere. This is positively gentle for a white
Rioja, but the flavour is classic – mild lemon acidity, yeast

Spain

WHITE

- **Priorat**, Blanc de Botes, Clos Berenguer (page 22)
- **Rioja**, Viura, Sonsierra, Bodegas Sonsierra (page 91)
- **Rioja Blanco**, Barrel-Fermented, Monopole, Cune (page 65, 141)
- **Viña Sol** (page 140)

ROSE

- **Navarra rosé**, Agramont (page 96)
- **Tempranillo rosé**, El Prado, La Mancha (page 97)
- **Utiel-Requena**, Bobal Rosado, Viña Decana (page 97)

RED

- **Alicante**, Laderas de El Sequé, Laderas de Pinosa (page 94)
- **Almansa**, Marques de Rojas, Bodegas Piqueras (page 77)
- **Calatayud**, Papa Luna (page 59)
- **Cigales**, Museum (page 59)
- **Garnacha-Tempranillo**, Gran López, Campo de Borja (page 98)
- **Garnacha-Tempranillo**, La Riada, Bodegas Aragonesas, Campo de Borja (page 91, 136)
- **Jumilla Monastrell**, Casa de la Ermita (page 139)
- **Navarra Gran Reserva**, Cabernet Sauvignon-Merlot, Aldabea (page 76)
- **Priorat**, Creu Celta, Viñedos McAlindon e Hijos (page 39)
- **Priorat**, Vi de Guarda, Clos Berenguer (page 24)
- **Ribera del Duero Reserva**, Altos de Tamaron (page 48)

- **Rioja**, Club Privado, Baron de Ley (page 68)
- **Rioja**, Vega Ariana (page 88)
- **Rioja Reserva**, Bodegas Palacio (page 54)
- **Rioja Reserva**, Coleccion Personal, Marqués de Griñon (page 53)
- **Rioja Reserva**, Viña Ardanza, La Rioja Alta (page 38, 137)

SPARKLING

- **Cava Brut Blanc de Blancs** (page 111)
- **Cava Brut Rosé** (page 109)
- **Cava Brut Vintage** (page 109)
- **Cava Reserva, Rosado** (page 110)

SHERRY

- **Amontillado del Duque**, González Byass (page 145)
- **Fino Inocente**, Valdespino (page 145)
- **Manzanilla**, Extra Dry Sherry (Williams & Humbert) (page 120)
- **Manzanilla la Gitana**, Hidalgo (page 118)
- **Manzanilla Pastrana**, Hidalgo (page 118)
- **Manzanilla San León**, Herederos de Argüeso (page 145)
- **Oloroso Solera 1842**, Valdespino (page 145)
- **Oloroso Viejo Matusalem**, González Byass (page 145)
- **Palo Cortado**, Waitrose Solera Jerezana, (Diego Romero) (page 120)
- **Pedro Ximénez**, Fernando de Castilla Antique (page 114, 145)

creaminess and a touch of custard lightly streaked with citrus zest. *Also at Villeneuve Wines*

⑮ 2004 Grenache, Lime Tree, Murray-Darling,
❢ South-Eastern Australia, £4.49, Co-op
If you want beautiful great gobfuls of juicy red fruit soaked in alcohol, Australian Grenache is the place to start. It comes in more powerful versions than this, but look at the price. And this has got great chunks of squashy strawberry fruit and a touch of herbs too.

⑯ 2005 Sauvignon Blanc, Fairtrade,
♀ Western Cape, South Africa, £4.99, Co-op
The large Du Toitskloof co-operative is probably the most encouraging Fairtrade venture in South Africa and earlier this year the Co-op went down and handed over a Fairtrade premium cheque of £64,000, with more to come. They deserve it. The wine is very easygoing, attractively appley, with some melon scent and lemon zest and sherbet. And even a whiff of minerals.

⑰ 2003 Shiraz, Pinnacle, Palandri,
❢ Western Australia, £4.99–£5.99, Waitrose, Somerfield
The price went up just as we went to press – but it'll be discounted back down to £4.99 periodically. Even at £5.99 this is very good value from Western Australia – usually among the more expensive of Australia's wine-producing regions. A big wine, serious, but not subtle, deep, solid, with chunks of chocolate and nut and savoury black plum.

⑱ 2005 Muscadet Sèvre et Maine sur lie (Domaine Jean
♀ Douillard), Loire Valley, France, £4.99, Sainsbury's Taste the Difference
If we're ever going to start drinking Muscadet again, it'll be with wines like this that don't try to put on airs and graces and pretend they can offer big ripe flavours but which accept that Muscadet – good Muscadet – has a fairly neutral flavour but, if

the acidity and texture are right, can be a delightful drink. This is just full enough, with a mild loft apple and apple peel flavour, lemon zest scent and a stony mineral finish – and that delightful suggestion of yeasty cream that good Muscadets possess. Everything in pastel shades, but good.

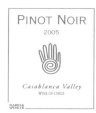

⑲ 2005 Pinot Noir, Casablanca Valley,
🍷 (Morandé) Chile, £4.99, Marks & Spencer
This is M&S's basic Chilean Pinot Noir but it's punching above its weight and is top stuff for £4.99. Slightly stewy in style, but stewed plums and stewed strawberries are a pretty nice flavour, especially when you add in a handful of dried herbs and a little nip of tannin.

⑳ 2005 Sauvignon Blanc, Misiones de Rengo,
🍷 Maule Valley, Chile, £4.99, Morrisons
12.5% alcohol is nice and low for the New World and it means they picked this wine fresh and early to maximize its tangy flavour. And it's worked. This has a good grapefruit bite, strong green apple peel fruit and an extra flavour rather like a promising but unripe peach.

㉑ 2004 Alicante, Laderas de El Sequé,
🍷 Laderas de Pinosa (Artadi), Spain, £5.49, Connolly's
When you see Alicante on a bottle of Spanish wine you should prepare yourself for a ripsnorter. Yet this is surprisingly fresh, and although there is a slight sense of the baking sun's heat, it's the good gutsy black fruit still holding onto a modicum of its freshness that wins out in the end.

㉒ 2005 Chardonnay-Semillon, Doña Dominga,
🍷 Viña Casa Silva, Colchagua Valley, Chile, £4.99, Oddbins
They mix these two grapes together very successfully in Australia, but it isn't often done elsewhere. Yet the Semillon does a pretty good job of calming down the Chardonnay, adding a little acidity and a bit of dry leathery savouriness. The effect here is a soft round white with pleasantly weighty bananas and pear juice fruit and a touch of toasty oak. Different to the Aussie stuff, but good.

㉓ 2004 Grenache, Peter Lehmann,
♟ Barossa, South Australia, £4.99–£5.99 Budgens

If you want to get legless and smiley, look for Grenache on the label. This is 14.5% alcohol and is absurdly drinkable, with mild red plum and strawberry fruit, glyceriny texture with a whiff of herbs. *Also at Booths, Oddbins, Tesco, Vin du Van*

㉔ 2005 Sauvignon Blanc Reserve, Montes,
♀ Curico Valley, Chile, £5.49, Tesco

You used to have to catch this Montes Sauvignon in the first year or so of its life, because it began to fade. But now it's got a screw-cap it can stay fresh much longer and this, despite coming from a warmer part of Chile, has good coffee bean, green pepper and nettle fruit to go with its soft but fresh texture.

㉕ 2005 Cabernet Sauvignon, Fairtrade,
♟ Western Cape, South Africa, £4.99, Co-op

It's good to find rich, ripe fruit in a Cape Cabernet for only a fiver, because too often they're a little bit tough. This one is juicy and ripe, with a slightly surprising scent of apples but rather more of that booming volcanic hot lava flow smoke which could be too much – but the ripe black plum and squashy banana fruit copes with it easily.

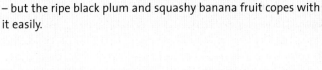

A little rosé

Suddenly pink is popular. We're all buying 50 per cent more rosé than we were a year ago. And it's not those pale, tired old orange things, vaguely sweet and tasting of a footballer's off-season kitbag. These are bright, vibrant, purpley pink – they look gorgeous in your glass, and are fresh as can be. Chill 'em down and they're fantastic party wines, with or without food.

❶ 2005 Merlot rosé, Firebird Legend, Moldova, £4.99, Waitrose

Lovely stuff, from Moldova of all places. They say Moldova's vineyards are potentially some of the best in Europe. Well, this is packed with strong red plum and strawberry syrup ripeness, leafy freshness and nice dry acidity. Well done Moldova. What else can you do?

❷ 2005 Cabernet Sauvignon rosé, Santa Rita, Maipo Valley, Chile, £5.99, Majestic, Oddbins

Chile never lets you down if you want to taste wines with lots of fruit. This has got so much ripe blackcurrant fruit and eucalyptus scent it could almost be a red. But no, it's bright pink, soft, fresh and gagging to be glugged back.

❸ 2005 Domaine de Pellehaut rosé, Vin de Pays des Côtes de Gascogne, South-West France, £5.29, Waitrose

Mmm. Yum. Lovely green leaf freshness, cranberry juice acidity and a gentle scented fruit like rosehip syrup. Gascogne white has been a favourite tangy thirst-quencher for years, so it's great to see they do lovely pinks as well.

❹ 2005 Navarra rosé, Agramont, Spain, £3.99, Sainsbury's

This is from Navarra in northern Spain, where they've been throwing their Garnacha grapes into full-bodied juicy dry rosés for as long as I can remember. They're still at it, and this is fun, fresh pink in colour, with a nice green apple acidity and full stewed red plums fruit.

5 **2005 Rosé d'Anjou, Anjou Bougrier,**
Loire Valley, France, £4.99, Oddbins
Rosé d'Anjou? Recommended? Who'da thought it? But this is what pink Anjou should taste like and rarely does – off-dry, nicely fat, but fresh, with an apple, strawberry and banana compote of fruit flavours and a streak of stony minerality.

6 **2005 Cabernet-Merlot rosé, St Donalus,**
Balatonlelle, Hungary, £4.10, Wines of Westhorpe
Quite a heavy pink, but there's lots of flavour here and it is fresh. It's got an intriguing mix of squashy apple and strawberry fruit and good glycerine texture nicely balanced by bright acidity.

7 **2005 Tempranillo rosé, El Prado,**
La Mancha, Spain, £3.99, Tesco
Good, full, juicy pink, not subtle and with a nice chubby feel to it that marries well with the strawberry and the vaguely bruised apple acidity.

8 **2005 Utiel-Requena, Bobal Rosado, Viña Decana ,**
Spain, £2.99, Aldi
Aldi's bargain buys are on song this year, making good use of the high-quality grapes from the 2005 vintage. This is big, powerful stuff for a pink; a good juicy pink cup of apple peel, strawberries and a few grapes all served in a glycerine-smooth bowl.

9 **2004 Shiraz rosé, Vin de Pays d'Oc, Co-op Selection**
Languedoc-Roussillon, France, £3.99, Co-op
Very nice, straight-talking, refreshing rosé. Super strawberry fruit, a little apple crunchiness and attractively mouth-watering acidity.

For more wine recommendations see Oz Clarke's Wine Style Guide, pages 136–145

Bargain basement

We've upped the price limit in our bargain basement this year from £2.99 to £3.99. There is still decent grog to be had for less than 3 quid, and we've included the best in this selection, but only when they can cut the mustard among a whole crowd of decent £3.99ers. However, I'd rather try to persuade you to trade up a quid, so I've raised the quality bar – and found a lot of very tasty party wine for not a lot of dosh.

❶ 2005 Garnacha-Tempranillo, Gran López, Campo de Borja, Spain, £3.99, Waitrose

If I'd had to bet my house on what our best bargain red would be, I'd have said Garnacha or Tempranillo from the as yet unsung areas to the south of trendy Rioja in Spain. And this is it. Old-fashioned vines and modern winemaking produce an utterly gluggable cocktail of syrupy soft strawberry fruit, bright refreshing acidity and a nice swish of herbs.

❷ 2004 Chardonnay Reserve, Bushland (Hope Estate), Hunter Valley, New South Wales, Australia, £3.99, Aldi

This is unbelievably good stuff for £3.99, so long as you like the fat, full-blown, funky, Aussie Hunter Valley style. It's not the coolest wine style on the planet, with its mix of pastry and yeast richness and knocked-about dry peach and apple fruit, but it's a helluva mouthful for not very much.

❸ 2004 Côtes du Rhône-Villages, Rhône Valley, France, £3.98, ASDA

They've made some really serious wines in the southern Rhône in 2004 – powerful, aggressive, but monumentally tasty if you've got enough slabs of blood-red meat on the barbie. This beast needs to be tamed, but it's piled high with plum and cherry fruit and resinous herbs and hot stones all cursing and struggling with the tannins. Fire up that barbie.

Award-winning wine seller.

Philippe Michel Brut Crémant Du Jura

£5.49

Winner

Ile La Forge Merlot 2004

£4.99

Bushland Reserve Shiraz 2005

£3.99

Highly Commended

Bushland Reserve Chardonnay 2005

£3.99

Gold Country Cabernet Sauvignon 2004

£3.49

Viña Decana Crianza 2001

£3.29

Short-listed

Viña Decana Rosé 2004

£2.99

We're rather proud of our wines. Not just because of all the awards they win. Not just because of the wide range of quality red, white and rosé wines our specialist wine buyers have sourced from all over the world. And, oddly for us, it's got nothing to do with our typically sober prices. It's just because they taste so good. Why not add one or two to your cellar?

Spend a little Live a lot

Had this at a BBQ it seemed "flat" compared to Stormhoek S.B & Moncaro

4 2005 Sauvignon-Semillon, Delor,
♀ Bordeaux, France, £3.99, Waitrose

Bordeaux does this sharp, crackling dry white style at a keen price better than anyone in Europe, yet I wonder whether most of us drink even a single glass of white Bordeaux from one year to the next. Well, just try this. It's really good, full, dry stuff with a pepper and coffee bean scent and a fresh crunchy flavour like iceberg lettuce and ripe green apples.

5 2004 Chardonnay, Felsö-Magyarországi, Budavár,
♀ Hungary, £2.69, Aldi

Spot-on basic Chardonnay. And what a price! Hungary would love to sell its wines more expensively but we don't seem willing to pay a lot – yet. So while the price remains this low, enjoy a delightful, fresh, apple and peach flavoured wine with just a hint of blossom scent and good stone-dry acidity.

6 2004 Argentine Malbec,
❢ San Juan, Argentina, £3.99, Co-op

Good powerful stuff, an overachiever at this price. Lots of ripe damson and red plum, but it's quite a sturdy wine too, so the savoury creamy texture, like tarragon and chervil mashed together in a herb butter, is very welcome. Fine, ripe glugger.

7 2004 Grenache, Fruits of France, Vin de Pays d'Oc,
❢ Languedoc-Roussillon, France, £3.99, Waitrose

Really pleasant, easygoing, mild, midweight glugger. It has a very attractive, quite rich strawberry fruit flavour, a surprising but welcome floral scent and just a nip of tannin to remind us not to drink it too fast.

8 2005 Sauvignon Blanc, Riverview,
♀ Hungary, £3.99, Waitrose

This is one of the most reliably tasty bargain whites on the market. We really should be paying more for it – as so often with Hungary – so while the price is this low, let's reward them by buying loads and loads of their wine. This is really snappy, quite aggressive, full but with lots of acidity, lemon and apple peel and the mineral scrape of pebbles on your tongue.

⑨ 2003 Shiraz Reserve, Bushland (Hope Estate), Hunter Valley,
❢ New South Wales, Australia, £3.99, Aldi

This is another Aldi special, a proper, classy Hunter Valley Shiraz for about half the price you'd expect it to be. This isn't dense – I don't really want it to be – but it's rich and syrupy with loads of smoky plum and blackcurrant fruit, leathery, herby scent and a real sensation that you've had a very serious mouthful for a lot less money than you should have paid.

⑩ 2005 Cinsault-Shiraz, Fairtrade,
❢ (Du Toitskloof), Western Cape, South Africa, £3.99, Co-op

This is from one of the most encouraging Fairtrade/Black Empowerment projects in South Africa, and for that alone we should support it. But if we are to support Fairtrade in the long term the wine must be good – and it is. The Cinsault gives a glyceriny, fat, strawberry jam juiciness, and the Shiraz adds leafy blackcurrant freshness, some plummy fruit and pepper spice.

⑪ 2005 Cuvée de Richard, Vin de Pays de l'Aude,
❢ Languedoc-Roussillon, France, £3.15, Majestic

Year in, year out, this is one of the most consistently pleasurable basic reds on the market. It's mostly made from the lovely juicy Grenache grape, and it has lots of syrupy strawberry and raspberry fruit with just enough pepper and herbs and tannin to keep it honest.

⑫ 2005 Chardonnay, Nagyréde Estate,
♀ Hungary, £3.99, Waitrose

Very pleasant, fresh, bright, clean Chardonnay: dry and acid, balanced with gentle soft apple fruit and a definite hint of springtime apple blossom. Once again, you can't beat Hungary for value.

⑬ 2004 Malbec-Bonarda, St Lucas,
❢ Mendoza, Argentina, £3.29, Aldi

This is what bargain-priced commercial red should taste like. This isn't dilute sugar-water, this is very enjoyable, characterful, soft, bright, juicy red, syrup-soft fruit and a lovely mix of damsons and wild strawberries. Malbec and Bonarda are excellent grape varieties and make good blending buddies. This is a top introduction.

*The ancient Greek temple of Segesta
overlooks vines in western Sicily*

**⑭ 2005 Grillo, Serenata,
♀ Sicily, Italy, £3.99, Budgens**
Sicily is proving itself to be a very
exciting wine area. You 'might have
thought it was so far south, so close
to Africa, it would be too hot to
make decent whites, but Grillo is a
variety perfectly suited to the semi-
African conditions. This is a really
interesting, soft, fresh glugger
tasting of melon flesh and fluffy
apples, a sort of lemon sorbet
acidity, and with a gruff reminder of
rocky minerality.

**⑮ 2005 Cuvée Pecheur, Vin de
♀ Pays de Comté Tolosan, France,
£3.39, Waitrose**
The grapes that make up this blend
are really brandy grapes, Ugni and
Colombard. But the great thing
about them is that they give a very acidic juice which, when carefully
handled, can create a delightfully tangy apple flesh, lemon sherbet and
summer dust flavour for not very much money.

**⑯ 2005 Sauvignon Blanc-Semillon, Falling Star,
♀ Trapiche, Mendoza, Argentina, £3.99, Morrisons**
This is the blend of grapes that makes the most famous of white wines in
the Bordeaux region of France. This isn't so ambitious, but it's got a nice,
fresh, direct lemon and apples taste with a bit of a scraping, stony
minerality, and it shows that Mendoza, despite being very hot, can make
attractive bright whites.

**⑰ 2004 Cabernet Sauvignon, Budavár,
🍷 Thracian Valley, Hungary, £2.69, Aldi**

Hungary finds it more difficult to ripen reds than whites – so does its
neighbour Austria – but I like this: it's a very pleasant, surprisingly full-bodied,
juicy plum-flavoured red with a good stony dry mineral background.
Impressive for £2.69.

**⑱ 2005 Vieille Fontaine, Vin de Pays du Gers,
🍷 Producteurs Vignoble de Gascogne, South-West France, £2.99, Tesco**

The Gers is true 'la France profonde' country and traditionally it used to make
brandy, not wine. As demand for brandy declined, the acidic, sharp brandy
grapes had to find other uses, and for some years now we've been getting
sharp, leafy, lemony, green apple whites like this at bargain prices.

**⑲ 2005 Vieille Fontaine, Vin de Pays du Comté
🍷 Tolosan, Producteurs Vignoble de Gascogne, South-West
France, £2.99, Tesco**

And here's the red! This tastes like a half-decent basic Bordeaux at
less than half the price. It's got good, quite stewy black plum fruit
and quite a lot of depth, a bit of tannin and a very pleasant
mouthwatering style that cries out for some of the local duck,
roasted and served in chunks on a platter.

**⑳ 2004 Bordeaux, Château Selection, Château
🍷 Limouzin, Bordeaux, France, £3.29, Aldi**

This is an example of why basic Bordeaux vineyards should be
making whites, not reds. This is very pleasant appley stuff, with
some lemon acidity and a good yeast lees softness.

**㉑ 2005 Cuvée Chasseur, Vin de Pays de l'Hérault,
🍷 Languedoc-Roussillon, France, £2.99, Waitrose**

Another of those relentlessly reliable bargain reds that we
can all praise the Lord for when party time comes round.
Bright, ripe, simple strawberry fruit and apple acidity and a
sort of pebbly cleansing dryness with a touch of leafy scent.

Fizz

My tastings this year show that you simply don't have to shell out on Champagne to get top-class bubbly. Of my top five fizzes this year, only one comes from Champagne, two come from England, one from New Zealand and one – for an extremely keen price – comes from the Jura mountains of France, where they grow the same grapes as Champagne, use the same methods to make the wine sparkle, yet only charge half the price. I wonder how that is.

❶ 1999 Nyetimber Blanc de Blancs, Première Cuvée,
♀ West Sussex, England, £21.99, Waitrose

No one who tastes the thrilling sparkling wines now appearing from the South of England can think they're just a flash in the pan. English wine – especially English sparkling wine – is now a very serious business, and as global warming continues its relentless march, the UK – at least in the short to medium term – will be able to benefit massively on the chalk and greensand Downlands which dominate the landscape in Kent, Sussex and Surrey. At West Sussex's Nyetimber they make two different cuvées, and in the 1999 vintage the 100% Chardonnay Blanc de Blancs is clearly better. As soon as you see the intense golden colour in the glass and the busy foam fretting at the rim, you know that this will be no normal mouthful of fizz. It isn't. That intensity carries through to an intensity of acidity – that's typically English – which scours your palate till it gleams, but which is shot through with so much richness you realize the wine's in perfect balance. It needs to be, because that yeasty richness is custardy, chocolaty, as yeasty as Marmite yet as reassuring as cocoa powder and Ovaltine sprinkled on rice pudding. And there *is* fruit too: ripe apples, medlars and quince. It's an exceptional wine, and as the flavours linger on and on after you've swallowed it, you'll realize we're exceptionally lucky to have such wonderful conditions for sparkling wine in this country. *Also at many independent retailers*

Nyetimber Manor is mentioned in the Domesday Book; today it produces some of England's top sparkling wine

2 **1996 Champagne Blanc de Blancs, Cuvée Orpale,**
♀ **France, £34.99, Marks & Spencer**

Balance and maturity and a caressing soft-edged foam are what make this fizz
such a delight. Good Champagne really does need bottle age – 10 years is often
about right – but so often nowadays it's drunk far too young. Drunk too young,
most Champagne just tastes of green apples and the steel blade you peeled
them with. But give them time, and those apples transform themselves into
sweet Christmastime loft-stored apples, or big Bramley apples baked with
brown sugar and dates, and the wine gets creamy too, tasting of hazelnuts and
milk chocolate bars. And I detect a whiff of pheromones – do pheromones have
a smell? – dancing in the bubbles at the rim of the glass.

3 **2004 Camel Valley Brut,**
♀ **Cornwall, England, £14.99 Waitrose and
from www.camelvalley.com**

Nyetimber and Ridgeview in West Sussex both
make remarkable fizz from the same grapes, and
grown on the same types of soil, as those of Champagne. Camel Valley is
completely different. It doesn't use the Champagne grapes – this 2004 is
three-quarters Seyval Blanc and a quarter Reichensteiner – and the flavour is
magnificently, quintessentially English. There's a gust of hedgerow scent to lift
your spirits sky high and the oh-so-English perfume of elderflower wafts up as
the bubbles race energetically to the surface of the wine. There's also
something defiantly stony at the heart of the flavour and I decided it was
nothing less than the defiant outcrops of the rocky Cornish cliffs.

4 **NV Pelorus, Cloudy Bay,**
♀ **New Zealand, £17.99 (£11.99 3 for 2),
Thresher, Wine Rack**

Cloudy Bay's tangy, nettly Sauvignon Blanc is so
famous that it's easy to overlook the fact that
Cloudy Bay makes other wines too, and makes them extremely well. Their
Pelorus has been a favourite of mine for years. It tastes like good Champagne
used to taste before so much of it was taken over by marketing men and the
grape growers and winemakers were relegated to the backroom. Creamy, nutty

For more wine recommendations see Oz Clarke's Wine Style Guide, pages 136–145

yeastiness is terribly important to give a soft bed of flavour so that the bubbles tumble across your palate rather than attack it with spears. Pelorus is beautifully creamy, beautifully nutty, beautifully balanced. Cloudy Bay is owned by the people who make Veuve Clicquot Champagne. Every time I taste them together I prefer Pelorus – and save myself a ton of money into the bargain. *Also at Majestic and many independent retailers*

⑤ 2004 Crémant du Jura, Philippe Michel,
♀ **Jura, France, £5.49, Aldi**
You're a bit short on the readies this week, but really fancy a bottle of decent fizz to cheer you up. Don't despair. Help is at hand. Aldi's Crémant du Jura is a smasher and brilliant value for money. It's creamy, it's elegant, it's fresh and scented, and tasted with my eyes shut I'd say this has to be Champagne. But it's not. Don't let that worry you. Don't be a label snob. This is better than a lot of Champagne at more than twice the price.

⑥ NV Champagne Blanc de Blancs Brut,
♀ **France, £18.99, Waitrose**
This is regularly one of my favourite own-label Champagnes. There are cheaper ones on the market, but this one offers sheer class, and I suppose class does cost. It's six years old now – and will improve for another five – and spent two and a half years sitting on the yeast sediment caused by the second fermentation, and this has imparted a delightful nutty toastiness like a piece of white bread toast still hot from the grill. The acidity is as pure as green apple flesh and the bubbles foam lazily in the glass.

⑦ 2003 Bloomsbury, Ridgeview,
♀ **Sussex, England, £16.99, Waitrose**
Ridgeview's Bloomsbury was so successful last year that they sold out two complete vintages and had to release the 2003 rather earlier than planned. It *was* a bit young last year, but it's now had time to begin developing in the bottle, though it will happily improve for another five years – that's if there's enough left after the Queen had it at her 80th birthday bash. It's a lighter style than Nyetimber (see page 104) – it always is – but is very direct and refreshing. You can almost taste the chalk in the wine, rubbing against the appley fruit and the gradually deepening nutty, creamy flavours from the yeast. *Also at The Wine Society*

⑧ 2000 Champagne, Vintage, Tesco,
♀ France, £16.94, Tesco

This is made by the giant Union Avize co-operative in the Côte des Blancs area of Champagne, where all the best Chardonnay is grown. We're lucky it's a good co-op because they seem to make about half of all our supermarket own-labels – which could mean they're making about half of all the Champagne we drink. What a responsibility. Fortunately Tesco seems to like producing own-label Champagne that tastes better than a lot of big-brand rivals, and this is no exception. It's full but nicely balanced, the six years of maturity are starting to turn the 100% Chardonnay flavours into that nutty pheromonal richness that is the joy of good Champagne – and there's just a lick of honey there too to keep it from being bone dry.

⑨ NV The Society's Exhibition Blanc de Blancs Champagne,
♀ France, £25, The Wine Society

Wine Society Champagne is always good because they get one of the most traditional, quality-conscious producers to make it for them. Alfred Gratien is a tiny producer who still uses small oak barrels to ferment the basic wine – virtually everyone else uses stainless steel vats. And Gratien keeps the wine on its second fermentation yeast deposits for 30 months to create that nutty, creamy flavour and texture that I love. This has a smell almost like rice pudding – my mum's, which was top stuff – and that creamy richness transfers to the wine where it needs to marry with some quite assertive green apple peel acidity and blend into a lovely flavour of honey and baked apples and hazelnuts.

⑩ 2000 Champagne Brut, De Saint Gall Grand Cru
♀ France, £22.99, Marks & Spencer

This is still pretty young – some other 2000s, like Tesco's (see above), are approaching maturity – but the class is very evident. I'd ideally give it one or two more years aging, but already it has a delightful soft flavour of ripe apple and pear flesh and you can taste a creaminess that will get much more pronounced and delicious over the next couple of years.

⑪ NV Champagne Brut, Prince William Premier Cru,
♀ **France, £14.99, Somerfield**

Somerfield's Prince William is another product of the giant Union Avize co-op – and it is always good. This Premier Cru selection is particularly tasty, with a lovely foaming texture, ripe apple fruit and some very attractive hazelnut, brioche and toast richness making itself felt. Serious, classy Champagne that'll be even better in a couple of years.

⑫ 2000 Cava Brut Vintage,
♀ **Spain, £6.99, Somerfield**

The word is that you always have to drink Cava young. Well, that depends on how good the Cava is. They say it won't improve with age. Yes it will – *if* it's good enough. And this one is. It's now fully mature at six years old, and has an intriguing flavour of sweet apples sharpened up by lemon sherbet and fleshed out with a little cream and honey. Cava won't age, my eye.

⑬ NV Champagne, Sainsbury's Blanc de Noirs,
♀ **France, £13.99, Sainsbury's**

This is made entirely from black Pinot grapes, which should create an altogether weightier type of fizz. Indeed it does. There's nothing twinkle-toed and feather-light about this, but it manages to be full-bodied and refreshing at the same time, with a delightful flavour of brioche and fresh bread crust just out of the oven, mild apple flesh fruit and good acidity holding it all together.

⑭ 2000 Château Vincent Extra Brut,
♀ **Hungary, £7.43, Wines of Westhorpe**

I didn't know that Vincent was a Hungarian name – in fact, I'm sure it's not, it's much too pronounceable. But this wine is Hungarian, made by the traditional Champagne method and in a dumpy bottle that rather resembles Krug. It doesn't taste like Krug. But then it doesn't cost like Krug either. It's quite weighty, with good loft apple and hazelnut fruit and a green apple peel bite which isn't a bad idea because it keeps in check a waxy, lanoliny texture that otherwise might just prove a bit strong.

🍷 NV Cava Brut Rosé, Spain, £6.99, Somerfield

Somerfield have really got their fizz sorted this year: their Champagnes and their Cavas are in fine form. This is exactly what pink fizz should be like, with enough colour to make you realize it's pink – some pink Champagne is so pale you'd think it was a trick of the light – and some pink flavour. This tastes of strawberries. Delightful! Many pink fizzes just take life too seriously. But this is creamy, foaming, full of fruit – and full of fun.

🍷 NV Champagne Brut, De Saint Gall Blanc de Blancs, France, £19.99, Marks & Spencer

Well, what do you know. Here's another wine from that Union Avize crew. But each supermarket's blends do taste different. This one is softly foaming, very fresh but gentle, with no intrusive acidity and a good deal of nutty cream. Very pleasant easy-going fizz.

🍷 NV Champagne Brut, Premier Cru, Tesco, France, £14.79, Tesco

Guess what? Another success from the Union Avize co-op. Actually, this is a really important wine for them and Tesco – and they make a serious amount of it – because it's the Premier Cru that regularly knocks spots off more expensive glitzy rivals. I can see why. It's very direct, with a fresh appley fruit, nice acidity and the beginnings of a creamy texture from its yeast. I'd like it a bit older, but Avize's fruit sources are so good they can make the wine very attractive when it's barely out of short trousers.

🍷 NV Champagne Brut, De Saint Gall Premier Cru France, £19.99, Marks & Spencer

Is it just me, or is everything suddenly Premier Cru? This is a reasonably mature one, and if anything it's lost just a bit of freshness as its flavours head towards a slightly mushroomy creaminess. But it's still attractive because there's good apple fruit there and the creaminess is like a really sumptuous mushroom cream sauce.

Please bear in mind that wine is not made in infinite quantities – some of these may well sell out, but the following year's vintage should then become available.

⑲ NV Cava Reserva, Rosado
🍷 **Spain, £6.99, Marks & Spencer**

Nice bright strawberry pink colour doesn't quite lead on to a juicy strawberry flavour, because this is just a little drier and leaner than I'd expected. But it's well balanced and refreshing and the fruit is fresh and appley with just a squeeze of lemon and a twist of pepper.

⑳ NV Cava Brut, Blanc de Blancs
🍷 **Spain, £4.99, Somerfield**

You don't often see Cava labelled as Blanc de Blancs, even though the grapes they use are generally white. For a Cava, this has quite good brioche toastiness – that's more the mark of a decent Champagne – and there's a hint of cake spice and a flicker of pepper which makes for an attractive glass of fizz.

Sweeties

I would not be being fair with you if I said sweet wines are coming back into fashion. They're not. And as I swan around the wine-drinking world I really do wonder who's drinking them. But someone must be – or all wine merchants are barmy – because I've discovered some pretty exciting stuff this year. They're the kind of wines that you don't have to have with dessert – they're so good, you have them instead of dessert.

❶ 1999 Muskateller Eiswein, Darting Estate,
♀ Dürkheimer Hochbenn, Pfalz, Germany, £13/half bottle, Marks & Spencer

This is fantastic stuff. I know it's a lot of money, but the guy who made it, Helmut Darting, is one of southern Germany's top growers. And it's an Eiswein. This is a bizarre but brilliant category of wine for which they leave the grapes on the vine to freeze way into November and December. This freezing massively concentrates the sugar sweetness and the acidity. It's a Muscat. This is pretty rare in Germany, but of all the grapes that are used to make wine, the one that gives the grapiest, most scented flavour is Muscat. And it's a 1999. That's seven years old, and the extra age really magnifies the flavour of the wine. So you'll have got the idea that I like it, right? Sure do. It's not intensely, overbearingly sweet, so it's not the kind of sweetness for rich desserts: this is one to drink by itself. It has a most astonishing flavour of lime juice acidity and lime marmalade, pure honey, soft creamy custard that seems rich yet savoury as though made with salted butter, and a fascinating whiff of putty just applied to a window frame.

❷ Pedro Ximénez, Fernando de Castilla Antique,
♀ Andalucía, Spain, £17.50 Amey's Wines, £19.99/50cl, Thresher, Wine Rack

You want sweet? It doesn't come any sweeter. You could stand the spoon up in this. In fact, drink it by the spoonful and you could be licking the spoon for a full minute after you've swallowed the sticky nectar and the spoon would still

The Goldtropfchen vineyard just to the west of Piesport in the Mosel Valley; some German winemakers leave the grapes to freeze on the vines in order to make Eiswein

reek of the treacly richness of this wine. Quite simply, this is the sheer essence of the ripest, ooziest, syrupiest grapes known to man. They pick the Pedro Ximénez grapes super-ripe, then they lay them on mats in the midday sun until there's virtually no liquid left in them, and then they find a yeast powerful enough to ferment the stuff into wine. Well, the yeasts don't get far before they doze off and you're left with absurdly indulgent alcoholic treacle. Oh, by the way, pour some over good vanilla ice-cream. Heaven in a pudding bowl.

❸ 2001 Vin Santo, Il Colombaio di Cencio, Sassodoro, Tuscany, Italy, ♀ £12.92/50cl, Lea and Sandeman

Vin Santo is one of the most abused of all Italy's wine styles. The problem is, it's so damned easy to sell to tourists. Every knick-knack shop in Tuscany has gaudy bottles of vaguely golden liquid on sale for not very much, or dusty bottles fetched from the bowels of the shop by an ancient crone and selling for a lot more. Most of them contain sweet, baked rubbish only saleable because the name Vin Santo implies that the local bishop or saint or whatever has blessed it. But just occasionally you find a real Vin Santo like this one and you realize there's no wine quite like it. This is a heavenly wine. It has a classic, creamy, yeasty, nutty depth, with an acidity just staying the right side of dangerous, and a gorgeous sweetness of old brown autumn fruit when the wasps have had enough, as well as the caramel of buttered brazils.

❹ 2003 Riesling Eiswein, Schneiderberg, ♀ Weinrieder, Austria, £25/half bottle, Waterloo Wine Company

Eiswein needs very particular conditions to make it successfully. The grapes have to be ripe, then they have to be left to hang on the vines well into winter without them rotting. Germany and Canada, not surprisingly, are the two masters of this game, but Austria is another top performer. The acidity isn't so fierce as in German or Canadian examples, but the flavours are fantastic. This is so rich it almost has the texture of pure honey swirled with cream, but the flavour is much more dense – the richness is almond paste as much as honey, the fruit is cling peaches in syrup, and it has a glittering mineral quality as though someone has sprinkled the barrel with quartz dust.

⑤ 1999 Tokaji Aszú 5 Puttonyos, Royal Tokaji Wine Co,
♀ **Hungary, £8.99/250ml, Waitrose, £9.50, Tanners**

Tokaji is strange, disturbing but wonderful stuff, always marked by a powerful, sometimes piercing, acidity, and a mineral depth that makes me think of rocks seared by a mighty flame. The fruit here is not so much crystallized pineapple chunks as crystallized grapefruit chunks – if they make such things. Well, there is pineapple sweetness too, and powerful lime acidity rolled with tobacco. This is intense, almost painful, but very good.

⑥ 2003 Torcolato, Maculan,
♀ **Breganze, Veneto, Italy, £14.59/half bottle, Oddbins**

Magical, marvellously original wine from north-east Italy. The scent – tired, care-worn but beautiful – reminds me of some Victorian beauty disappointed in love and gradually shrivelling through age and loneliness. Not Miss Havisham – younger, still lovely. This has the strangest and most haunting of scents – old jasmine, lilies and tea roses past their best – and a fruit density like leftovers from a market stall – old strawberries, squashed and messy, apricots and peaches withered yet still sweet – and through all this a certain freshness of honey and mixed fruit marmalade and a texture like Oil of Olay struggles to hold on.

⑦ 2002 Botrytis Semillon, Hermits Hill, Riverina, New South Wales,
♀ **Australia (De Bortoli), £5.99/half bottle, Marks & Spencer**

Australia's Riverina area is a dustbowl way off in the outback; if there weren't this whopping great river called the Murrumbidgee cascading down out of the Great Dividing Range of mountains and sloshing off into the desert, there'd be nothing happening here at all. As it is, the place grows a fantastic amount of fruit and veg and makes loads of wine – Yellowtail comes from here, for instance. But it's best at two things: marijuana and intensely sweet wine in the style of Sauternes. In fact, in a blind tasting, I'd probably think this was Sauternes. It's rich, with a dense pineapple, barley sugar, quince jelly and honey depth, it's got mouth-coating texture like beeswax and lanolin, and it has a fairly evident acidity, with just a hint of cider vinegar. It's a good price too.

⑧ 2002 Sauternes, Château Doisy Daëne,
♀ Bordeaux, France, £11.99/half bottle, Waitrose

This is from the personal property of one of Bordeaux's greatest white wine experts, Professor Denis Dubourdieu. He spends most of his time making dry whites and consulting all over the region, but when the autumn mists begin to fall, he hurries back to Doisy Daëne to bring in his grapes and craft this delightfully rich, beeswaxy wine, swimming in peach and apple syrup, streaked with lemon and slightly spiced with oak.

⑨ 2003 Sauternes, Château Liot,
♀ Bordeaux, France, £9.99/half bottle, Waitrose

Beautiful, classic, unctuous Sauternes. Sauternes is rarely the sweetest of dessert wines, but it has a lush texture which no other wines quite match. The flavour is of a delightful rich sugary brioche smeared with barley sugar, pineapple chunks and honey, and the texture is beeswax and lanolin coating your mouth as the wine drifts down your throat.

⑩ 2002 Beerenauslese, Tinhof,
♀ Burgenland, Austria, £11.95/half bottle, Savage Selection

Austria makes marvellous sweet wines in relatively large quantities around the Neusiedlersee lake on the Hungarian border. This is such a shallow lake that you can almost walk across it and during the summer it heats up so much that half of it evaporates, creating an incredibly humid, sticky atmosphere on the lake shore. Which may not be good for your car – the local town is called Rust and car body shops do a roaring trade – but these are perfect conditions for intensifying the sweetness in grapes. This one has a delicious flavour of fresh, super-ripe apples, golden peaches and crystallized pineapple all soaked in gooey syrup. And yet it isn't at all cloying. Excellent.

⑪ 2001 Riesling Eiswein, Ruppertsberger,
♀ Pfalz, Germany, £14.99/half bottle, Sainsbury's

Rich, deep, dense and syrupy, with a powerful acidity holding together the thickly spun strands of honey and peachy syrup. Yet there's more. It's as though someone has thrown some flowers into the syrup too, creating a delightful rosewater scent to lighten the lusciousness.

⑫ 2004 Sauternes, Château Guiraud,
♀ **Bordeaux, France, £8.99/half bottle, Sainsbury's Taste the Difference**
It's reassuring when a big supermarket group goes to a really top producer for own-label stuff. This comes from Château Guiraud, one of the smartest properties in Sauternes and it shows in this wine – sheer class. All that lovely lanolin and beeswax smoothness, no, unctuousness, along with sweet pineapple fruit and a creamy quality almost like butterscotch, from its time spent aging in new oak barrels.

⑬ 2005 Moscato d'Asti, Nivole, Michele Chiarlo,
♀ **Piedmont, Italy, £5.59/half bottle, Oddbins**
The youngest wine in my selection; it will only fade as months pass by, so drink it now, for the delightful, simple pleasure of mildly fizzy grape juice and peach peel and pear juice dusted with mineral chalk. Don't wait. There'll be a new vintage along soon enough. *Also at Averys, Booths*

⑭ 2003 Sauternes, Maison Sichel,
♀ **Bordeaux, France, £8.99/50ml, Morrisons**
This is rich and sweet for an own-label Sauternes, with a really ripe peach and pear syrupiness that seeks out and exploits every missed appointment with the dentist. But you might accept the pain for the flavour, which is a big, unsubtle blast of fruit sweetness, rich and direct.

⑮ 2004 Orange Muscat & Flora, Brown Brothers,
♀ **Milawa, Victoria, Australia, £5.99/half bottle, Budgens**
This is an old favourite; some vintages are better than others. Well, 2004 is a good one, with a really delightful blood orange acidity, bright and fresh, which balances the fat grapy richness of the Muscat grape. It's not massively sweet, but it's good. *Widely available*

Please bear in mind that wine is not made in infinite quantities – some of these may well sell out, but the following year's vintage should then become available.

Fortified wines

I've noticed a slight dropping off of quality among the own-label ports this year. I worry that they're being made a bit milder, that some idiot in the marketing department has decided we're not adult enough for an adult drink and so has dumbed them down. I do hope it ain't so, because if it is, I shall simply stop buying the stuff. And so will hordes of other adult-type human beings. There are exceptions, though, and you'll find them in the next couple of pages. I've also noticed a gradual increase in the number of fortified wines from southern France – good, gutsy, almost port-like in style. So I've shoved a couple of those in here along with the ports and sherries.

MANZANILLA
LA GITANA

❶ Manzanilla la Gitana, Hidalgo,
🍷 Spain, £4.95/50cl, Savage Selection,
£6.49/75cl Majestic, Sainsbury's, Thresher, Waitrose
and independent retailers
I've so often read that Manzanilla sherry tastes of salt, but it hardly ever does. And then I taste this – wonderfully, appetizingly, palate-fresheningly salty! The thing is, they make this sherry right down on the Atlantic coast in south-west Spain and some of the sherry cellars are only a few hundred yards from the beach, where the rollers crash in and spray salt water all over the promenade. Certainly the air is salty, seawatery. Could it affect the sherry? Well, yes it could, because dry sherry is such a fragile wine and has so little flavour before it begins its aging process that it really could pick up salt from the air over a year or two in the vat. And it could end up like this: bone dry, with a savouriness almost like a salty crust on a grilled rump steak, but with a gentleness of soft new bread and hazelnuts and a fruity flicker of apple peel.

Does taste salty
Good.

❷ Manzanilla Pastrana, Hidalgo,
🍷 Spain, £8–9, Majestic, Savage Selection, Tanners, The Wine Society
I couldn't resist putting in another Hidalgo sherry. This is browner and deeper and nuttier than La Gitana, but it's still got the wonderful, tongue-scouring dryness and the softness of bread yeast, as well as a woodiness like very old

dusty stairs at the top floor of a spinster aunt's house. This is a true original, because it's from a single vineyard – very rare in sherry –and it's made in conjunction with one of the brilliant young Turks of the port world, Cristiano van Zeller. It's wonderful how a fresh perspective on an old wine can create a completely new style.

❸ Palo Cortado, Waitrose Solera Jerezana
♀ (Diego Romero), Spain, £6.99, Waitrose
A strange but delicious 'neither one thing nor the other' sherry style. It's rich but it's bone dry. It has a great wodge of buttered brazils, hazelnut and caramel richness and even a flavour of macaroons, but it's refreshingly, totally dry. Well done Waitrose for stocking such a delightful oddity. Now *we* have to buy it, or they'll de-list it.

❹ Manzanilla, Extra Dry Sherry
♀ (Williams & Humbert), Spain, £5.99, Marks & Spencer
This isn't as salty as the Hidalgo (see previous page), but it's still very good bone dry sherry, with a dry, dusty floorboard woodiness, some bread yeast softness fattened by cream but sharpened with apple core fruit, and a quite marked acidity like a bruised Bramley apple bathed briefly in balsamic vinegar.

❺ 2001 The Society's Late Bottled Vintage Port
❗ (Symington Family Estates), Portugal, £9.95, The Wine Society
I've been fretting about the dumbing down of own-label ports recently, but the Wine Society is still doing a proper job of its Late Bottled Vintage. It's got good deep blackberry fruit, nice kitchen spice and a rich yet challenging texture.

❻ Maury, 1928 Solera, les Vignerons de Maury
❗ Roussillon, France, £14.95/50cl, Averys
What a wonderful idea. You fill up some barrels with wine in 1928 and each year you draw off a bit, see how it tastes, maybe sell some, and top up the barrel with new wine. This is how they make the unique, unbelievably concentrated, dark Oloroso sherries in Spain. The lovely thing is that even today there will be a little – maybe not much, but a bit – of the original 1928 wine in the bottle, and a dash of pretty much every vintage in between, so the flavour eventually becomes a cavalcade of the whole history of the wine, in

this case 78 years. And you can taste the history: this lovely wine smells of a ripe essence of sweet nuts, deep and old and silent; there's a dark date and fig syrup richness; there's the sweet caramel nuttiness of buttered brazils; and you never quite lose a sense of dust drifting in through the cellar window over the generations.

⑦ 2001 Maury, Vendange Mise Tardive, Domaine Pouderoux, ♀ Roussillon, France, £11.49/50cl, Waitrose

A totally different style of Maury to the 1928 Solera (see above). This is dense, strong, muscular stuff, young and assertive. The fruit is dark and edged with bitterness, the texture is as chewy as an ox's haunch and the sweetness is of blackberry syrup and glycerine.

⑧ 10 Year Old Aged Tawny Port, ♀ Portugal, £10.99, Marks & Spencer

Attractive, soft, mellow port, which is just what you want from a tawny style. It's spent 10 years in a barrel, softening, smoothing out rough edges and losing its angry colour so that just a russet blush remains. The long oak aging hasn't quite got rid of a slight blackcurrant leafiness, but there's enough rich plum and honey, hazelnuts and brown sugar syrup for the leafiness to be quite welcome.

⑨ Dow's Crusted Port, bottled 2000, ♀ Portugal, £12.99, Waitrose

Crusted port is such a wonderful style, allowing you a glimpse of the majesty and furious power of vintage port yet at a fraction of the price. This isn't quite as good as usual. It's still a classy drink, it still has a little scent, a streak of lime and green leaf acidity and pretty good dark fruit, but it lacks a little oomph. I still like it, I just don't like it quite so much.

⑩ Finest Reserve Port, ♀ Portugal, £7.99, Marks & Spencer

High-falutin' terms like Finest Reserve don't mean much on port bottles: this is good, solid, basic ruby port, with perhaps a bit more age than you often get. Chunky blackberry and loganberry fruit, a decent peppery bite and a sense that on a cold winter's day a draught of this will make you not mind you forgot to turn the heating on.

Everyday Bordeaux

Red Bordeaux doesn't have to be expensive, serious, demanding 15 to 20 years in the cellar before being carefully decanted, tasted and discussed in reverential tones. The majority of the 800 million bottles produced each year are meant for everyday enjoyment. Their place is at the table, to accompany pâtés, cheese, sausages and stews. All red Bordeaux is basically a blend of Cabernet Sauvignon, Cabernet Franc and Merlot grapes – a few other varieties occasionally creep in – but French wine law means they're not supposed to name the grapes on the label. I've picked some of my favourites at around £7 to £15.

The wines below are listed in alphabetical order.

✪ 2002 Château de l'Abbaye de Sainte-Ferme, Bordeaux Supérieur, £6.49, Majestic
Very attractive, leafy, crunchy style. Everyday Bordeaux is at its best when the fruit is appetizing, dry yet tasty, and you can almost imagine the grapes' juice squirting in your mouth.

✪ 2003 Château Barreyres, Haut-Médoc, £8.49, Sainsbury's
Sainsbury's have stocked this for as long as I can remember. Which is fine by me because it consistently delivers good, firm Haut-Médoc style, and nowadays has added attractively ripe fruit as well.

✪ 2003 Château Bauduc Clos de Quinze, Premières Côtes de Bordeaux, £8.25, Château Bauduc, tel: 0800 316 3676
This is a beautiful château run by London rat-race exiles Angela and Gavin Quinney. They make excellent red, white and rosé, all marked by their sheer

---

A NOTE ON PRICES

Prices are for one bottle inclusive of VAT, unless otherwise stated. Remember that some retailers sell only by the case; others offer a better price by the case than for a single bottle.

The vintages, retailers and prices are given as examples: the same wine may be available from a number of retailers, and prices may vary.

For advice about buying Bordeaux for the long term see pages 152–5.

See also the retailers directory beginning on page 156.

drinkability and by their true sense of Bordeaux style. Affordable, approachable, Bordeaux needs another 100 Bauducs – and fast.

☺ 2001 Château Bel Air, Haut-Médoc, £8.45, Haynes Hanson & Clark
Good, satisfying, proper old-style claret, with a bit of edge, a bit of rustic grunt, but also attractive dry blackcurrant fruit and a ripe tannin that courteously cleanses your palate, rather like a butler removing crumbs from the tablecloth.

☺ 2001 le Blason d'Issan, Margaux, £14.95, Savage Selection
Lovely bright blackcurrant scent, slightly coarsened by a savoury earthiness and volatile lift – but Issan is all about sweet fruit and perfume and they easily win out.

☺ 2003 Château Clos Renon, Bordeaux Supérieur, £9.99, Tesco
This vineyard is right on the edge of the Graves and you can taste the characteristic pebbles in the wine. This is dense, ripe and rich, cut through by stones.

☺ 2002 Le Haut-Médoc de Giscours, £12.99, Waitrose
Unofficially, this is the 'third wine' of the famous Château Giscours in Margaux: the grapes that don't get selected for the first and second wines are blended to make this classy red, at a fraction of the price. Deep red and black fruit, some leafy freshness and a streak of graphite mineral – that's good Haut-Médoc.

✪ **2001 Château Grand Village, Bordeaux Supérieur, £7.45, Armit**
This comes from the edge of the Fronsac region and the proprietors also own some very smart outfits in Pomerol. I'm sure the class rubs off, because this is very well made, with full black fruit, leafy freshness and an earthy rasp of tannin to make you salivate.

✪ **2003 Château les Grangeaux, Bordeaux Supérieur, £5.99, Nicolas**
This is what used to be known as 'luncheon claret' – light, mouthwatering, crying out for a plate of lamb or beef – but it's very attractive in its own right, with soft strawberry fruit and mellow texture.

✪ **2001 Château La Gurgue, Margaux, £10.99, Magnum Fine Wines (www.magnum.co.uk, tel: 020 7839 5732)**
This offers a great chance to discover Margaux class and elegance and not break the bank. The vineyard is next to that of Château Margaux; the site couldn't be better. This is dark, full of lush, scented black fruit, but finely balanced and dry and appetizing.

✪ **2003 Château Pey la Tour, Bordeaux Supérieur, £8.75, The Wine Society**
They had to change the name of this château from Clos de la Tour in 2003, but they didn't change its barnstorming style: rich, focused, full of plum and cherry fruit and sweet, warming oak. Excellent example of how good these unknown châteaux can be with investment and commitment.

✪ **2000 Château Peyrabon, Haut Médoc, £15.00 Millésima**
Peyrabon has been making extremely consistent wines for several years now, on good soils just inland from Pauillac. Fresh ripe black plum fruit with a dash of blackcurrant, grainy tannin and light oak make for a very satisfying Haut-Médoc.

✪ **2002 Château Pierrail, Bordeaux Supérieur, £5.99, Booths**
This is just about the last property in Bordeaux before the appellation boundary in the east. Somehow it's got 14% alcohol. I want to say that's too

much, but in fact this deep, oaky, blackberryish wine is remarkably balanced and integrated.

✪ 2002 Château Potensac, Médoc, £15.99, Morrisons

Potensac is usually well over £20, but because the 2002 vintage isn't a popular one, this deep, cedary, marvellously structured classic claret comes in at just under £16.

✪ 2004 Château Robin (Sichel), Lussac-St-Emilion, £7.99, Morrisons

Lussac-St-Emilion doesn't go in for subtle wines, and this isn't subtle. But satisfying, yes – full of rather stewy red plum fruit, a mouthfilling earthiness, a hint of mint and enough tannin to let you age it a bit.

✪ 2002 Château Ribeyrolles, Bordeaux Supérieur, £6.99, Laithwaites

Very nice, easy, juicy style. This has a particularly attractive mint perfume and a taste of sour cherries slightly like a Tunes throat pastille.

✪ 2004 Averys Fine St-Emilion, £9.95, Averys

Averys has traditionally been one of Britain's greatest shippers of Bordeaux, so it's reassuring that they've gone to such a star as Hubert de Boüard of Château Angélus for their St-Emilion. He's done them proud: this is lovely plummy scented red, full, dry, balanced, with a sense of the rocky limestone in the vineyard.

✪ 2004 Château Segonzac, Premières Côtes de Blaye, £7.99, Waitrose

Blaye is an area to look if you like soft but dry Bordeaux. There's a new generation determined to make the best of their limestone clay soils and Merlot-dominated vines to produce gentle, soft round wines like this, just touched by oak.

✪ 2004 Seigneurs d'Aiguilhe, Côtes de Castillon, £7.99, Waitrose

Year after year this is one of the stars of the high street; it has now become so deservedly popular that Waitrose's allocation is sold out long before a new vintage is available. The wine is spicy, dense, beautifully ripe and sensitively enriched with oak.

Discover the secrets of wine tasting
at the Bordeaux Wine School

From discovery to proficiency. The Bordeaux Wine School is adapted to all levels of wine appreciation, anchored in practical tasting experience.

INTENSIVE COURSES
Total immersion for rapid comprehension: 4 levels, each with vineyard visits. Courses of 3 to 4 consecutive days.

SATURDAYS AT SCHOOL
Familiarise yourself with Bordeaux wines in one day. Discover the diversity of Bordeaux or concentrate on one appellation.

2-HOUR COURSES
Everyday from Monday - Saturday from May 1st to November 4th.

BORDEAUX
L'ECOLE DU VIN

ECOLE DU VIN DE BORDEAUX
1, cours du XXX juillet - 33075 Bordeaux cedex - FRANCE
TEL: 33 5 56 00 22 88 - FAX: 33 5 56 00 99 30
Further information:

http://ecole.vins-bordeaux.fr - Email: ecole@vins-bordeaux.fr

l'Agence 2.com réf. 7287-01

✪ 2004 Château Tire Pé, Bordeaux, £8.99, Bennetts

A hard-charging over-achiever from the Bordeaux hinterland, this time down by the banks of the Garonne. This has buckets of blackberry fruit and a nice earthy rasp.

✪ 2003 Château Villars, Fronsac, £9.80, Justerini & Brooks

Fronsac rarely manages to add perfume to its broad ripe fruit and chunky frame, but Villars combines blackcurrant and plum with a typical Fronsac metallic streak and the promise of orchard perfume to come.

✪ 2003 Château Villepreux, Bordeaux Supérieur, £5.99, Waitrose

Dense, surprisingly dark wine from vineyards just off the main Bordeaux–Libourne road. It's got powerful black fruit, stony perfume and fair tannin. You could age this for 2–4 years.

Freshly picked Cabernet Sauvignon grapes

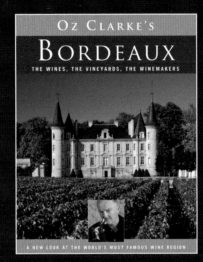

Oz Clarke's

BORDEAUX

THE WINES, THE VINEYARDS, THE WINEMAKERS

A NEW LOOK AT THE WORLD'S MOST FAMOUS WINE REGION

Oz Clarke's

BORDEAUX

Publication Date: 2 November 2006
Price: £18.99

A New Look at the World's Most Famous Wine Region

In his new book Oz Clarke returns to his wine roots and reveals the
world's most famous and glamorous wine region in a state of flux.

Storing, serving, tasting

Wine is all about enjoyment, so don't let anyone make you anxious about opening, serving, tasting and storing it. Here are some tips to help you enjoy your wine all the more.

THE CORKSCREW

The first step in tasting any wine is to extract the cork. Look for a corkscrew with an open spiral and a comfortable handle. The Screwpull brand is far and away the best, with a high-quality open spiral. 'Waiter's friend' corkscrews – the type you see used in restaurants – are good too, once you get the knack.

Corkscrews with a solid core that looks like a giant woodscrew tend to mash up delicate corks or get stuck in tough ones. A simple non-levered screw can require a heroic effort. And try to avoid those 'butterfly' corkscrews with the twin lever arms and a bottle opener on the end; they tend to leave cork crumbs floating in the wine.

CORKS

Don't be a cork snob. The only requirements for the seal on a bottle of wine are that it should be hygienic, airtight, long-lasting and removable. Real cork is environmentally friendly, but is prone to shrinkage and infection, which can taint the wine. Synthetic closures modelled on the traditional cork are common in budget wines and are increasingly used by high-quality producers, as are screwcaps, or Stelvin closures.

THE WINE GLASS

The ideal wine glass is a fairly large tulip shape, made of fine, clear glass, with a slender stem. This shape helps to concentrate the aromas of the wine and to show off its colours and texture. For sparkling wine choose a tall, slender glass, as it helps the bubbles to last longer.

Look after your glasses carefully. Detergent residues or grease can affect the flavour of any wine and reduce the bubbliness of sparkling wine. Ideally, wash glasses in very hot water and don't use detergent at all. Rinse glasses thoroughly and allow them to air-dry. Store wine glasses upright to avoid trapping stale odours.

DECANTING

Transferring wine to a decanter brings it into contact with oxygen, which can open up the flavours. You don't need to do it ages before serving and you don't need a special decanter: a glass jug is just as good. And there's no reason why you shouldn't decant the wine to aerate it, then pour it back into its bottle to serve it.

Mature red wine is likely to contain sediment and needs careful handling. Stand the bottle upright for a day or two to let the sediment fall to the bottom. Open the wine carefully, and place a torch or candle beside the decanter. As you pour, stand so that you can see the light shining through the neck of the bottle. Pour the wine into the decanter in one steady motion and stop when you see the sediment reaching the neck of the bottle.

OZ CLARKE
connoisseur range

Electric Corkscrew   Wine Chiller   Ice Shaver   Drinks Maker

TEMPERATURE

The temperature of wine has a bearing on its flavour. Heavy reds are happy at room temperature, but the lighter the wine the cooler it should be. Juicy, fruity young reds, such as wines from the Loire Valley, are refreshing served lightly chilled; I'd serve Burgundy and other Pinot Noir reds at cool larder temperature.

Chilling white wines makes them taste fresher, but also subdues flavours, so bear this in mind if you're splashing out on a top-quality white – don't keep it in the fridge too long. Sparkling wines, however, must be well chilled to avoid exploding corks and fountains of foam.

For quick chilling, fill a bucket with ice and cold water, plus a few spoonfuls of salt if you're in a real hurry. This is much more effective than ice on its own. If the wine is already cool a vacuum-walled cooler will maintain the temperature.

KEEPING LEFTOVERS

Exposure to oxygen causes wine to deteriorate. It lasts fairly well if you just push the cork back in and stick the bottle in the fridge, but you can also buy a range of effective devices to help keep oxygen at bay. Vacuvin uses a rubber stopper and a vacuum pump to remove air from the bottle. Others inject inert gas into the bottle to shield the wine from the ravages of oxidation.

WINE STORAGE

The longer you keep wine, the more important it is to store it with care. If you haven't got a cellar, find a nook – under the stairs, a built-in cupboard or a disused fireplace – that is cool, relatively dark and vibration-free, in which you can store the bottles on their sides to keep the corks moist (if a cork dries out it will let air in and spoil the wine).

Wine should be kept cool – around 10–15°C/50–55°F. It is also important to avoid sudden temperature changes or extremes: a windowless garage or outhouse may be cool in summer but may freeze in winter. Exposure to light can ruin wine, but dark bottles go some way to protecting it from light.

Learn About Wine

The Wine & Spirit Education Trust (WSET) is an independent, not-for-profit charity founded in 1969 to provide training in wines and spirits to those in the trade and for the general public.

Five levels of qualification courses are available, starting with a one-day Foundation Certificate in Wines through to an Honours Diploma in Wines and Spirits. Consumer events also cater for those that just want to understand a bit more about wine whilst having a fun evening out. These include food and wine workshops along with a variety of tastings that include anything from a focus on Chardonnay to prestigious tastings of cult wines from across the globe; all expertly tutored by leaders in their field.

Call 020 7089 3800
Visit www.wset.co.uk
www.wsetinternational.com

"...thanks to the Wine & Spirit Education Trust, my education in wine at least started out in a miraculously methodical manner. My experience of (their) courses between 1976 and 1978 gave me a sure foundation in this wonderful world of wine." JANCIS ROBINSON MW

How to taste wine

If you just knock your wine back like a cold beer, you'll be missing most of whatever flavour it has to offer. Take a bit of time to pay attention to what you're tasting and I guarantee you'll enjoy the wine more.

Read the label

There's no law that says you have to make life hard for yourself when tasting wine. So have a look at what you're drinking and read the notes on the back label if there is one. The label will tell you the vintage, the region and/or the grape variety, the producer and the alcohol level.

Look at the wine

Pour the wine into a glass so it is a third full and tilt it against a white background so you can enjoy the range of colours in the wine. Is it dark or light? Is it viscous or watery? As you gain experience the look of the wine will tell you one or two things about the age and the likely flavour and weight of the wine. As a wine ages, whites lose their springtime greenness and gather deeper, golden hues, whereas red wines trade the purple of youth for a paler brick red.

Swirl and sniff

Give the glass a vigorous swirl to wake up the aromas in the wine, stick your nose in and inhale gently. This is where you'll be hit by the amazing range of smells a wine can produce. Interpret them in any way that means something to you personally: it's only by reacting honestly to the taste and smell of a wine that you can build up a memory bank of flavours against which to judge future wines.

Take a sip

At last! It's time to drink the wine. So take a decent-sized slurp – enough to fill your mouth about a third full. The tongue can detect only very basic flavour elements: sweetness at the tip, acidity at the sides and bitterness at the back. The real business of tasting goes on in a cavity at the back of the mouth which is really part of the nose. The idea is to get the fumes from the wine to rise up into this nasal cavity. Note the toughness, acidity and sweetness of the wine, then suck some air through the wine to help the flavours on their way. Gently 'chew' the wine and let it coat your tongue, teeth, cheeks and gums. Jot down a few notes as you form your opinion and then make the final decision... Do you like it or don't you?

Swallow or spit it out

If you are tasting a lot of wines, you will have to spit as you go if you want to remain upright and retain your judgement. Otherwise, go ahead and swallow and enjoy the lovely aftertaste of the wine.

Wine Faults

If you order wine in a restaurant and you find one of these faults you are entitled to a replacement. Many retailers will also replace a faulty bottle if you return it the day after you open it, with your receipt. Sometimes faults affect random bottles, others may ruin a whole case of wine.

- **Cork taint** – a horrible musty, mouldy smell indicates 'corked' wine, caused by a contaminated cork
- **Volatile acidity** – pronounced vinegary or acetone smells
- **Oxidation** – sherry-like smells are not appropriate in red and white wines
- **Hydrogen sulphide** – 'rotten eggs' smell.

Watchpoints

- Sediment in red wines makes for a gritty, woody mouthful. To avoid this, either decant the wine or simply pour it gently, leaving the last few centilitres of wine in the bottle.
- White crystals, or tartrates, on the cork or at the bottom of bottles of white wine are both harmless and flavourless.
- Sticky bottle neck – if wine has seeped past the cork it probably hasn't been very well kept and air might have got in. This may mean oxidized wine.
- Excess sulphur dioxide is sometimes noticeable as a smell of a recently struck match; it should dissipate after a few minutes.

Wine style guide

When faced with a shelf – or a screen – packed with wines from around the world, where do you start? Well, if you're after a particular flavour, my guide to wine styles will point you in the right direction.

RED WINES
Juicy, fruity reds

The definitive modern style for easygoing reds. Tasty, refreshing and delicious with or without food, they pack in loads of crunchy fruit while minimizing the tough, gum-drying tannins that characterize most traditional red wine styles. Beaujolais (made from the Gamay grape) is the prototype, and the 2005 vintage in the shops at the moment delivers juicy fruit by the bucketful. And if you're distinctly underwhelmed by the very mention of the word 'Beaujolais', remember that the delightfully named Fleurie, St-Amour and Chiroubles also come from the Beaujolais region. Loire reds such as Chinon and Saumur (made from Cabernet Franc) pack in the fresh raspberries. Italy's Bardolino, from the Veneto, is light and refreshing. Nowadays, hi-tech producers all over the world are working the magic with a whole host of grape varieties. Carmenère, Malbec and Merlot are always good bets, and Grenache/Garnacha and Tempranillo usually come up with the goods. Italian grapes like Bonarda, Barbera and Sangiovese seem to double in succulence under Argentina's blazing sun. And at around £5 even Cabernet Sauvignon – if it's from somewhere warm like Australia, South America, South Africa or Spain – or a vin de pays Syrah from southern France, will emphasize the fruit and hold back on the tannin.

- 2004 Garnacha-Tempranillo, La Riada, **Campo de Borja, Spain, £4.99 (£3.33 3 for 2),** Thresher
- 2005 Merlot, Sunrise, Concha y Toro, **Central Valley, Chile, £4.99,** Waitrose
- 2005 Beaujolais, Domaine Chatelus de la Roche, **France, £7.15,** Roger Harris
- 2005 Chiroubles, Georges Duboeuf, **Beaujolais, France, £7.99,** Waitrose
- 2004 Saumur-Champigny, Domaine Filliatreau, **Loire Valley, France, £8.50,** Yapp Bros

Silky, strawberryish reds

Here we're looking for some special qualities, specifically a gorgeously smooth texture and a heavenly fragrance of strawberries, raspberries or cherries. We're looking for soft, decadent, seductive wines. One grape – Pinot Noir – and one region – Burgundy – stand out and prices are high to astronomical. Good red Burgundy is addictively hedonistic and all sorts of strange decaying aromas start to hover around the strawberries as the wine ages. Pinot Noirs from New Zealand, California, Oregon and, increasingly, Australia come close, but they're expensive, too; Chilean Pinots are far more affordable. You can get that strawberry perfume (though not the silky texture) from other grapes in Spain's Navarra, Rioja and up-coming regions like La Mancha and Murcia. Southern Rhône blends can deliver if you look for fairly light examples of Côtes du Rhône-Villages or Costières de Nîmes.

- 2004 Pinot Noir, Porta Select Reserve, Viña Porta, Bío-Bío, Chile, £6.49 (£4.33 3 for 2) Thresher, £6.99 Oddbins
- 2004 Pinot Noir, Las Brisas Vineyard, Viña Leyda, Leyda Valley, Chile, £7.95 Wine Society, £8.99 Sainsbury's
- 2004 Lacrima di Morro d'Alba, Rubico, Marotti Campi, Marche, Italy, £7.99, Oddbins
- 1999 Rioja Reserva, Viña Ardanza, La Rioja Alta, Spain, £16.95, Laymont and Shaw
- 2003 Pinot Noir, Rippon, Central Otago, New Zealand, £22.75, Lea and Sandeman

Intense, blackcurranty reds

Firm, intense wines which often only reveal their softer side with a bit of age; Cabernet Sauvignon is the grape, on its own or blended with Merlot or other varieties. Bordeaux is the classic region but there are far too many overpriced underachievers there. And Cabernet's image has changed. You can still choose the austere, tannic style, in theory aging to a heavenly cassis and cedar maturity, but most of the world is taking a fruitier blackcurrant-and-mint approach. Chile does the fruity style par excellence. New Zealand can deliver Bordeaux-like flavours, but in a faster-maturing wine. Australia often adds a medicinal eucalyptus twist or a dollop of blackcurrant jam. Argentina and South Africa are making their mark too.

- 2002 Coonawarra Cabernet (Katnook Estate), Australia, £6.99, Sainsbury's Taste the Difference
- 2002 Cabernet Sauvignon, Peñalolen, Maipo Valley, Chile, £7.49, Oddbins

Please bear in mind that wine is not made in infinite quantities – some of these may well sell out, but the following year's vintage should then become available.

- 2004 Côtes de Castillon, Seigneurs d'Aiguilhe, Bordeaux, France, £7.99, Waitrose
  - 2002 Cabernet Sauvignon, The Willows, Barossa Valley, South Australia, £10.99, Australian Wine Club
  - 2003 Catharina, Steenberg, Constantia, South Africa, £12.98, Armit

Spicy, warm-hearted reds

Australian Shiraz is the epitome of this rumbustious, riproaring style: dense, rich, chocolaty, sometimes with a twist of pepper, a whiff of smoke, or a slap of leather. But it's not alone. There are southern Italy's Primitivo and Nero d'Avola, California's Zinfandel, Mexico's Petite Sirah, Argentina's Malbec, South Africa's Pinotage, Toro from Spain and some magnificent Greek reds. In southern France the wines of the Languedoc often show this kind of warmth, roughed up with hillside herbs. And if you want your spice more serious, more smoky and minerally, go for the classic wines of the northern Rhône Valley.

- 2004 Corbières, Château Pech-Latt, Languedoc, France, £5.99, Waitrose
- 2001 Primitivo-Aglianico, Dorio, Puglia, Italy, £6.99, Oddbins
- 2004 Clos de los Siete, Mendoza, Argentina, £10.99, Oddbins, Waitrose
- 2004 Shiraz-Grenache, Blueprint, Tim Smith Wines, Barossa Valley, South Australia, £11.99, Oz Wines

Mouthwatering, sweet-sour reds

Sounds weird? This style is the preserve of Italy, and it's all about food: the rasp of sourness cuts through rich, meaty food, with a lip-smacking tingle that works equally well with pizza or tomato-based pasta dishes. But there's fruit in there too – cherries and plums – plus raisiny sweetness and a herby bite. The wines are now better made than ever, with more seductive fruit, but holding on to those fascinating flavours. You'll have to shell out up to a tenner for decent Chianti; more for Piedmont wines (especially Barolo and Barbaresco, so try Langhe instead). Valpolicella can be very good, but choose with care. Portugal can deliver something of the same character with its sour-cherries reds. Oddball grapes like Chambourcin often have these flavours.

- 2004 Jumilla, Monastrell, Casa de la Ermita, **Spain, £6.79, Oddbins**
- 2004 Shiraz-Sangiovese Il Briccone, **Primo Estate, South Australia, £9.99, Australian Wine Club, Direct Wine Shipments, Noel Young Wines**
- 2003 Chianti Classico, Villa Cafaggio, **Tuscany, Italy, £9.99, Tesco (190 stores)**
- 2003 Amarone, **Valpantena, Veneto, Italy, £10.99, Sainsbury's Taste the Difference**
- 2003 Teroldego Rotaliano, Vigneto Lealbere, Roberto Zeni, **Trento, Italy, £12.50, Bat & Bottle**
- 2003 Langhe Rosso Serrapiù, Gianni Voerzio, **Piedmont, Italy, £21.95, Lay & Wheeler**

Delicate (and not-so-delicate) rosé

Dry rosé can be wonderful, with flavours of strawberries and maybe herbs. Look for wines made from sturdy grapes like Cabernet, Syrah or Merlot, or go for Grenache/Garnacha or Tempranillo from Spain and the Rhône Valley. South America is a good, flavoursome bet for this style of wine. *See also pages 96–7.*

- 2005 Merlot rosé, La Palma, **Chile, £3.99, Sainsbury's**
- 2005 Costières de Nîmes rosé, **Château Guiot, Rhône Valley, France, £5.99, Majestic Wine**
- 2005 Shiraz rosé, Jacob's Creek, **South-Eastern Australia, £5.99, Tesco**
- 2005 Bordeaux rosé, Domaine de Sours, **Bordeaux, France, £5.99, Sainsbury's**
- 2005 Corbières rosé, Château de Caraguilhes, **Languedoc-Roussillon, France, £7.99, Waitrose**

WHITE WINES

Bone-dry, neutral whites

Neutral wines exist for the sake of seafood or to avoid interrupting you while you're eating. It's a question of balance, rather than aromas and flavours, but there will be a bit of lemon, yeast and a mineral thrill in a good Muscadet sur lie or a proper Chablis. Loads of Italian whites do the same thing, but Italy is increasingly picking up on the global shift towards fruit flavours and maybe some oak. Basic, cheap South African whites are often a good bet if you want something thirst-quenching and easy to drink. Colombard and Chenin are fairly neutral

grape varieties widely used in South Africa, often producing appley flavours, and better examples add a lick of honey.

- 2004 Viña Sol, Torres, Cataluña, Spain, £4.43, ASDA
- 2005 Muscadet Sèvre et Maine sur lie, (Domaine Jean Douillard), Loire Valley, France, £4.99, Sainsbury's Taste the Difference
- 2005 Chenin Blanc, Peter Lehmann, Barossa Valley, South Australia, £5.99, Budgens, Waitrose
- 2004 Muscadet Sèvre et Maine sur lie Réserve, Château du Cléray, Loire Valley, France, £7.30, Christopher Piper
- 2005 Pinot Grigio, La Prendina Estate, Alto Mincio, Veneto, Italy, £7.49, Marks & Spencer
- 2005 Chablis, Sainte Céline (Jean-Marc Brocard), Burgundy, France, £7.99, Sainsbury's Taste the Difference
- 2004 Pinot Grigio, Colli Orientale del Friuli, Sirch, Friuli-Venezia Giulia, Italy, £8.30, Tanners

Green, tangy whites

For nerve-tingling refreshment, Sauvignon Blanc is the classic grape, full of fresh grass, gooseberry and nettle flavours. I always used to go for New Zealand versions, but I'm now more inclined to reach for an inexpensive bottle from Chile, South Africa or Hungary. Or even a simple white Bordeaux, because suddenly Bordeaux Sauvignon is buzzing with life. Most Sancerre and the other Loire Sauvignons are overpriced. Austria's Grüner Veltliner has a peppery freshness. From north-west Iberia, Galicia's Albariño grape has a stony, mineral lemon zest sharpness; the same grape is used in Portugal, for Vinho Verde. Alternatively, look at Riesling: Australia serves it up with aggressive lime and mineral flavours, and New Zealand and Chile give milder versions of the same style. Alsace Riesling is lemony and dry, while German Rieslings go from bone-dry to intensely sweet, with the tangiest, zestiest, coming from the Mosel Valley.

- 2005 Colombard, Vin de Pays des Côtes de Gascogne, Calvet Limited Release, South-West France, £4.99, Waitrose
- 2005 Vinho Verde, Quinta de Simaens, Portugal, £5.49, Waitrose
- 2005 Riesling, Cono Sur, Bío-Bío Valley, Chile, £7.99, Majestic Wine
- 2004 Riesling, Forster, J L Wolf, Pfalz, Germany, £7.99, Tesco (90 stores)

- 2005 Sauvignon Blanc, Springfield Estate, Robertson, South Africa, £8.99, Sainsbury's
- 2005 Sauvignon Blanc, Jackson Estate, Marlborough, New Zealand, c.£8.49–£10, Booths, Majestic Wine, Oddbins, Wright Wine Co

Intense, nutty whites

The best white Burgundy from the Côte d'Or cannot be bettered for its combination of soft nut and oatmeal flavours, subtle, buttery oak and firm, dry structure. Prices are often hair-raising and the cheaper wines rarely offer much Burgundy style. For £6 or £7 your best bet is oaked Chardonnay from an innovative Spanish region such as Somontano or Navarra. You'll get a nutty, creamy taste and nectarine fruit with good oak-aged white Bordeaux or traditional white Rioja. Top Chardonnays from New World countries – and Italy for that matter – can emulate Burgundy, but once again we're looking at serious prices.

- 2004 Rioja Blanco, Cune Monopole, barrel-fermented, Companía Vinícola del Norte de Espana, Spain, £6.49, Waitrose
- 2004 Pessac-Léognan, Château Tour-Léognan (Château Carbonnieux), Bordeaux, France, £7.99, Waitrose
- 2004 Bourgogne, Vieilles Vignes, Le Chat Blanc, Bruno Fèvre, Burgundy, France, £9.95, Irma Fingal-Rock
- 2004 Graves, Clos Floridène, Bordeaux, France, £13.45, Anthony Byrne
- 2004 Puligny-Montrachet, Vieilles Vignes, Vincent Girardin, Burgundy, France, £23.79, Berkmann Wine Cellars

Ripe, tropical whites

Aussie Chardonnay conquered the world with its upfront flavours of peaches, apricots and melons, usually spiced up by the vanilla, toast and butterscotch richness of new oak. This winning style has now become a standard-issue flavour produced by all sorts of countries, though I still love the original. You'll need to spend a bit more than a fiver nowadays if you want something to relish beyond the first glass. Oaked Australian Semillon can also give rich, ripe fruit flavours. If you see the words 'unoaked' or 'cool-climate' on an Aussie bottle, expect an altogether leaner drink.

- 2004 Chardonnay, Capitana, Viña La Rosa, Cachapoal Valley, Chile, £6.99, Somerfield
- 2004 Chardonnay, Windy Peak, De Bortoli, Victoria, Australia, £6.99, Sainsbury's
- 2004 Semillon, Denman Vineyard Estate Reserve, Hunter Valley, New South Wales, Australia, £7.99, Tesco Finest
- 2003 Chardonnay, Rustenberg, Stellenbosch, South Africa, £11.50, Savage Selection
- 2003 Chardonnay, Wild Boy, Au Bon Climat, Santa Barbara, California, USA, £12.95, Berry Bros & Rudd

Aromatic whites

Alsace has always been a plentiful source of perfumed, dry or off-dry whites: Gewurztraminer with its rose and lychee scent or Muscat with its floral, hothouse grape perfume. A few producers in New Zealand, Australia, Chile and South Africa are having some success with these grapes. Floral, apricotty Viognier, traditionally the grape of Condrieu in the northern Rhône, now appears in vins de pays from all over southern France and also from California and Australia. Condrieu is expensive (£20 will get you entry-level stuff and no guarantee that it will be fragrant); vin de pays wines start at around £5 and are just as patchy. For aroma on a budget grab some Hungarian Irsai Olivér or Argentinian Torrontes.

- 2005 Irsai Olivér, Budai, Nyakas, Buda, Hungary, £4.82, Wines of Westhorpe
- 2005 Alsace Gewurztraminer, Cave de Turckheim, Alsace, France, £6.99, Marks & Spencer
- 2004 Viognier, Domaine de Coudoulet, Vin de Pays d'Oc, Languedoc, France, £7.45, Berry Bros & Rudd
- 2004 Gewurztraminer, Winemaker's Lot, Concha y Toro, Chile, £7.49, Oddbins
- 2005 Viognier-Pinot Gris, Heartland, Langhorne Creek, South Australia, £8.95, Great Western Wine,
- 2000 Gewurztraminer, Herrenweg, Zind-Humbrecht, Alsace, France, £16.99, Tesco (90 stores)

Golden, sweet whites

Good sweet wines are difficult to make and therefore expensive: prices for Sauternes and Barsac (from Bordeaux) can go through the roof, but near-neighbours Monbazillac, Loupiac, Saussignac and Ste-Croix-du-Mont are more affordable. Sweet Loire wines such as Quarts de Chaume, Bonnezeaux and some Vouvrays have a quince aroma and a fresh acidity that can keep them lively for decades, as do sweet Rieslings, such as Alsace Vendange Tardive, German and Austrian Beerenauslese (BA), Trockenbeerenauslese (TBA) and Eiswein. Canadian icewine is quite rare over here, but we're seeing more of Hungary's Tokaji, with its sweet-sour, marmalade flavours.

- 2002 Beerenauslese, Tinhof, Burgenland, Austria, £11.95/half bottle, Savage Selection
- 2001 Sainte-Croix-du-Mont, Château La Rame Sublime, Bordeaux, France, £12.99/50cl, Waitrose
- 2002 Sauternes, Château Suduiraut, Bordeaux, France, £19.99, Tesco (190 stores)
- 1999 Muskateller Eiswein, Darting Estate, Dürkheimer Hochbenn, Pfalz, Germany, £13/half bottle, Marks & Spencer
- 2002 De Bortoli Noble One Botrytis Semillon, New South Wales, Australia, c.£12–14.95/half bottle, Lea and Sandeman, Majestic Wine, Oddbins, Frank Stainton, Wright Wine Co
- 2003 Torcolato, Maculan, Veneto, Italy, £14.59/half bottle, Oddbins

SPARKLING WINES

Champagne can be the finest sparkling wine on the planet, but fizz made by the traditional Champagne method in Australia, New Zealand or California – often using the same grape varieties – is often just as good and cheaper. It might be a little more fruity, where Champagne concentrates on bready, yeasty or nutty aromas, but a few are dead ringers for the classic style. Fizz is also made in other parts of France: Crémant de Bourgogne is one of the best. England is beginning to show its potential. Spain's Cava is perfect party fizz available at bargain basement prices in all the big supermarkets.

CHAMPAGNE
BILLECART-SALMON

www.champagne-billecart.fr

- NV Jansz, Australia, £10.99, Oddbins
- NV Pelorus, Cloudy Bay, Marlborough, New Zealand, c.£11.39–17.99, Connolly's, Majestic Wine, Thresher, Wright Wine Co
- 1999 Blanc de Blancs, Nyetimber, England, £22–23, Berry Bros & Rudd, Waitrose, Noel Young Wines
- NV Champagne Blanc de Blancs Grand Cru Brut, Le Mesnil, France, £19–20, Waitrose, Noel Young Wines
- Champagne Mise en Cave 2001, Charles Heidsieck, France, £25.99, Booths, Tesco, Villeneuve, Waitrose
- 1996 Champagne Cuvée Nicolas François Billecart, Billecart-Salmon, c.£50, Ballantynes, Berry Bros & Rudd, Lay & Wheeler, James Nicholson, Oddbins

FORTIFIED WINES
Tangy, appetizing fortified wines
To set your taste buds tingling, fino and manzanilla sherries are pale, perfumed, bone dry and bracingly tangy. True amontillado, dark and nutty, is also dry. Dry oloroso adds deep, raisiny flavours. Palo cortado falls somewhere between amontillado and oloroso, and manzanilla pasada is an older, nuttier style of manzanilla.

The driest style of Madeira, Sercial, is steely and smoky; Verdelho Madeira is a bit fuller and richer, but still tangy and dry.

Finding vegetarian and vegan wine

Virtually all wine is clarified with 'fining' agents, many of which are animal by-products. Although they are not present in the finished wine, they are clearly not acceptable for strict vegetarians and vegans. Non-animal alternatives such as bentonite clay are widely used and vegan wines rely solely on these; vegetarian wines can use egg whites or milk proteins.

• **Specialist merchants** Organic specialists such as Vinceremos and Vintage Roots assess every wine on their lists for its vegetarian or vegan status.

• **Supermarkets** Most supermarkets stock some vegetarian and vegan wines and identify own-label ones with a symbol, such as the 'V' logo used by Somerfield and Marks & Spencer.

• **Other outlets** Check the labels. Some producers, such as Chapoutier, use a 'V' symbol to indicate vegetarian wines.

- Manzanilla San Léon, Herederos de Argüeso, c £4.95/half bottle, Butlers Wine Cellar, D Byrne, les Caves de Pyrene, Philglas & Swiggot, Christopher Piper, Frank Stainton
- Fino Inocente, Valdespino, £6.25/half bottle, Lea and Sandeman, Noel Young Wines
- Amontillado Del Duque, González Byass, £11.99/half bottle, Fortnum & Mason, Harvey Nichols, Sainsbury's (selected stores), Threshers (selected stores)
- Oloroso Solera 1842, Valdespino, £11.99/half bottle, Waitrose
- 10 Year Old Sercial Madeira, Henriques & Henriques, £11.99–16.99/50 cl, Majestic Wine, Noel Young Wines

Rich, warming fortified wines

Raisins and brown sugar, dried figs and caramelized nuts – do you like the sound of that? Port is the classic dark sweet wine, and it comes in several styles, from basic ruby, to tawny, matured in cask for 10 years or more, to vintage, which matures to mellowness in the bottle. The Portuguese island of Madeira produces fortified wines with rich brown smoky flavours and a startling bite of acidity: the sweet styles to look for are Bual and Malmsey. Decent sweet sherries are rare; oloroso dulce is a style with stunningly concentrated flavours. In southern France, Banyuls and Maury are deeply fruity fortified wines. Marsala, from Sicily, has rich brown sugar flavours with a refreshing sliver of acidity. The versatile Muscat grape makes luscious golden wines all around the Mediterranean, but also pops up in orange, black, and the gloriously rich, treacly brown versions that Australia does superbly.

- 2003 Mas Amiel, Roussillon, France, £9.95/50 cl, Lea and Sandeman
- Pedro Ximénez, Fernando de Castilla Antique, Spain, £19.99/50 cl, Thresher, Wine Rack
- Oloroso Viejo Matusalem, González Byass, Spain, £11.99/half bottle, Fortnum & Mason, Harvey Nichols, Sainsbury's (selected stores), Selfridges, Somerfield (selected stores)
- Madeira, Alvada, Blandy's, £9.99, Waitrose
- Rutherglen Grand Muscat, Chambers Rosewood Vineyards, Victoria, Australia, £21.95/half bottle, Lay & Wheeler
- 1983 Vintage Port, Graham's, Portugal, c.£30–50, Berry Bros & Rudd, Farr Vintners

Out and about

We're lucky in the UK to have a huge choice of wines right on our doorstep – or just a phone call or mouse-click away. But if you're anything like me, sometimes the spirit of adventure will take hold, and you'll just have to stride out and explore the world of wine for yourself.

Many of us visit France, Spain and Italy on holiday, and I can think of few greater pleasures for wine lovers than tasting wine in the place it's made. It's a wonderful way to learn about wine and who knows, you might come across something that even *we* haven't discovered. If you're an independent traveller you probably already have a smattering of the language; a bit of swotting up on local wine styles will help, too.

SPECIALIST WINE TOURS
Specialist wine tours are a fantastic way to learn about wine in a way you'll never forget, and it's all done for you – visits planned, experts to show you around, translators on hand. Established companies such as Arblaster & Clarke have the experience to help you get the most out of your visit.

WHERE TO GO
Alsace, Burgundy and the Loire are perhaps the most delightful regions for the wine lover, but wherever vines are grown in France you're likely to see signs by the roadside saying *'dégustation et vente'* (tasting and sales) or *'vente directe'* (direct sales). Follow the sign and you might end up at a château, a barn next to a private house, or an industrial-looking co-operative. In Bordeaux, by all means visit the famous châteaux, but it's the less famous ones that will welcome you in, and even then you'll be shocked at the prices. In Champagne, most of the big houses in Reims and Epernay do guided tours.
 Cantinas (wine cellars) can be found all over Italy, but Piedmont, Tuscany and the Veneto are the regions that have been at it longest, and are most geared up for tourists. The local *consorzio* (group of growers) might organize wine tours – check at the town tourist office. If you're on the road, look for signs saying *vendita diretta* (direct sales) or *degustazione* (tasting).

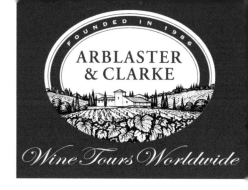

Arblaster & Clarke Wine Tours

The leading specialist in Wine Tours world wide

Quality visits to a mix of rising stars, famous names and some of our own discoveries, including invitations to wine cellars, tastings with the wine makers, not usually available to the public

Destinations include: Burgundy, Alsace, Tuscany, Piemonte, Rioja, Chile & Argentina, New Zealand, South Africa & Pacific North West

Exclusive tours are accompanied by well known wine guides and include stays at private wine chateaux such as Château Suduiraut & Château Pichon
Vineyard Walks in Douro, Rhone, Burgundy, Mosel & Languedoc
Annual Wine Cruises
Private & Incentive Wine Tours
Champagne Weekends & Coach Tours

Arblaster & Clarke Wine Tours, Farnham Road, West Liss, U.K. GU33 6JQ
sales@winetours.co.uk   www.arblasterandclarke.com
Tel: 01730 893344

In Spain you'll find bodegas set up to welcome tourists in three main regions: Rioja, about 90 km (60 miles) south-east of Bilbao; Penedès, 30 km (20 miles) inland from Barcelona, the most important region for the production of cava fizz; and down in Andalucía you'll find it hard to avoid visiting at least one sherry bodega in the town of Jerez.

TASTING TIPS

Don't expect to find an English speaker, but a few words of the local language go a long way. In France it's good manners when entering a room to greet people with '*Bonjour, Monsieur/ Madame*'. Don't feel you have to buy, even if you taste – just say *merci beaucoup* before you leave.

In Italy a liberal use of *buon giorno* (good day), *bella* (beautiful) and *grazie* (thank you) will win friends.

In Spain, smooth your path with *buenos días* (good morning), *buenas tardes* (good afternoon), *gracias* (thank you); *vino tinto* means red wine.

Remember that lunchtimes are important in Europe: the French often close for 2 hours, and the Italians and Spanish for even longer.

THE LONG HAUL

Wine tourists in South Africa, Australia, New Zealand and California are well catered for, by friendly people who speak our language.

Cape Town is a great base from which to explore South Africa's most important vineyard regions: Stellenbosch, Paarl and Constantia.

In Australia the big cities of Adelaide, Sydney and Melbourne all have top wine destinations within easy reach. Most famous of all is the Hunter Valley

Websites for wine tourism

- www.englishwineproducers.co.uk – contains useful maps and details for visitors.
- www.australia.com – features an overview of Australian wine and links to detailed regional websites.
- www.newzealand.com/travel – search 'Michael Cooper' to find introductions to all NZ wine regions, including touring information and festival dates.
- www.wosa.co.za – includes maps and touring routes for all South Africa's wine regions.
- www.travelenvoy.com/wine/siteindex.htm – details for just about every winery in the USA.

near Sydney. Melbourne has the Yarra Valley and Mornington Peninsula within an hour or so's drive. Adelaide is the best wine city, with Barossa Valley and McLaren Vale to the north and south and Adelaide Hills to the east.

In New Zealand's important regions, such as Hawkes Bay, Martinborough and Marlborough, the wineries are fairly close together. Look for a magazine called *Cuisine Wine Country*, which has maps and all the details you need to visit over 400 wineries, plus places to eat and stay.

California's Napa Valley is well set up for tourists, but is not cheap. Just over the mountains to the west is Sonoma County, which is less commercialized, more friendly, and has a wider range of wines. If you're feeling adventurous, head for Amador County, the old gold-mining region nestling in the Sierra Nevada mountains.

CLOSE TO HOME
There are some 350 vineyards in England and Wales. English wine is getting better and better; our sparkling wines in particular are beginning to challenge Champagne for quality. The very hot 2003 vintage and the

beautifully ripe 2005 produced some super whites and reds – and 2004 wasn't bad either. Get down to your local vineyard and see for yourself.

DAY TRIPPER

Cross-Channel wine shopping is hugely popular with us Brits – and no wonder, when UK duty is £1.29 on a bottle of still wine, while in France it's negligible (the difference is even greater on sparkling wines) – there are fantastic savings to be made.

Calais accounts for around 80% of all our booze-buying in France: it has the widest choice of sea crossings, four hypermarkets, numerous supermarkets and wine warehouses, some of them in the huge Cité d'Europe shopping complex next to the Eurotunnel terminal.

There are no limits on the amount of wine you can bring back, as long as it is for personal consumption – you can fill a van for a party, but you may be questioned at customs if you try to bring back more than 90 litres (10 cases of 12 bottles). Wine bottles are heavy, so don't overload your car.

Calais

If you're mainly looking to save money, the UK store outlets have the advantage of familiarity. Use their websites to check out what's available before you go. You can also pre-order online and collect on the day, giving you more time for lunch or stocking up on French cheeses. Some are closed on Sunday.

- Majestic has 3 French outlets called Wine & Beer World **www.wineandbeer.co.uk**
- **www.oddbins.com/storelocator**
- **www.sainsburys.co.uk**/calais
- **www. tesco.com**/vinplus
- **www.day-tripper.net** has masses of information on cross-Channel shopping for visitors to Calais.

Buying for the long term

Most of this book is about wines to drink more or less immediately – that's how modern wines are made, and that's what you'll find in most High Street retail outlets. If you're looking for a mature vintage of a great wine that's ready to drink – or are prepared to wait 10 years or more for a great vintage to reach its peak – specialist wine merchants will be able to help; the internet's another good place to look for mature wines. Here's my beginners' guide to buying wine for drinking over the longer term.

AUCTIONS

A wine sale catalogue from one of the UK's auction houses will have wine enthusiasts drooling over names they certainly don't see every day. Better still, the lots are often of mature vintages that are ready to drink. Before you go, find out all you can about the producer and vintages described in the catalogue. My *Pocket Wine Book* is a good place to start, or Michael Broadbent's *Vintage Wines* for old and rare wines, and the national wine magazines (*Decanter, Wine & Spirit*) run regular features on wine regions and their vintages. You can also learn a lot from tutored tastings – especially 'vertical' tastings, which compare different vintages. This is important – some merchants take the opportunity to clear inferior vintages at auction.

The drawbacks? You have no guarantee that the wine has been well stored, and if it's faulty you have little chance of redress. As prices of the most sought-after wines have soared, so it has become profitable either to forge the bottles and their contents or to try to pass off stock that is clearly out of condition. But for expensive and mature wines, I have to say that the top auction houses nowadays make a considerable effort to check the provenance and integrity of the wines. Don't forget that there will often be a commission, or buyers premium, to pay, so check out the small print in the sale catalogue. Online wine auctions have similar pros and cons.

If you've never bought wine at an auction before, a good place to start would be a local auctioneers such as Straker Chadwick in Abergavenny (tel: 01873 852624, www.strakerchadwick.co.uk) or Morphets in Harrogate (tel: 01423 530030, www.morphets.co.uk); they're less intimidating than the famous London houses of Christie's and Sotheby's and you may come away with some really exciting wine.

BUYING EN PRIMEUR

En primeur is a French term for wine which is sold before it is bottled, sometimes referred to as a 'future'. In the spring after the vintage the Bordeaux châteaux – and a few other wine-producing regions – hold tastings of barrel samples for members of the international wine trade. The châteaux then offer a proportion of their production to the wine merchants (*négociants*) in Bordeaux, who in turn offer it to wine merchants around the world at an opening price.

The advantage to the châteaux is that their capital is not tied up in expensive stock for the next year or two, until the wines are bottled and ready to ship. Traditionally merchants would buy *en primeur* for stock to be sold later at a higher price, while offering their customers the chance to take advantage of the opening prices as well. The idea of private individuals investing rather than institutions took off with a series of good Bordeaux vintages in the 1980s.

WINE FOR THE FUTURE

There is a lot to be said for buying *en primeur*. For one thing, in a great vintage you may be able to find the finest and rarest wines far more cheaply than they will ever appear again. This was especially true of the 1990 vintage in Bordeaux; this, in turn, primed the market for the exceptional vintages of 1999 in Burgundy and 2000 in Bordeaux. Equally, when a wine – even a relatively inexpensive one – is made in very limited quantities, buying *en primeur* may be practically your only chance of getting hold of it.

In the past, British wine merchants and their privileged customers were able to

Clarke's canny picks

2005 is being hyped to the skies, with good reason, as it's one of the best vintages ever; prices are also sky-high, and I doubt whether I'll be buying any. What I will be buying is 2004; there are some seriously good wines around – some of these should become collectors' classics:

- Château d'Angludet (Margaux)
- Château Batailley (Pauillac)
- Château Canon la Gaffelière (St-Émilion)
- Château Ferrière (Margaux)
- Château Grand-Puy-Lacoste (Pauillac)
- Château Haut Marbuzet (St-Estèphe)
- Château Haut-Bages Libéral (Pauillac)
- Château Pontet-Canet (Pauillac)
- Château Siran (Margaux)
- Château Sociando-Mallet (Haut-Médoc)
- Château du Tertre (Margaux)

'buy double what you want, sell half for double what you paid, and drink for free', but as the market has opened up to people more interested in making a quick buck than drinking fine wine, the whole process has become more risky.

Another potential hazard is that a tasting assessment is difficult at an early date. There is a well-founded suspicion that many barrel samples are doctored (legally) to appeal to the most powerful consumer critics, in particular the American Robert Parker and the *Wine Spectator* magazine. The wine that is finally bottled may or may not bear a resemblance to what was tasted in the spring following the vintage. In any case, most serious red wines are in a difficult stage of their evolution in the spring, and with the best will in the world it is possible to get one's evaluation wrong. However, the aforementioned Americans, and magazines like *Decanter* and *Wine & Spirit*, will do their best to offer you accurate judgements on the newly offered wines, and most merchants who make a primeur offer also write a good assessment of the wines. You will find that many of them quote the Parker or *Wine Spectator* marks. Anything over 90 out of 100 risks being hyped and hiked in price. Many of the best bargains get marks between 85 and 89, since the 90+ marks are generally awarded for power rather than subtlety. Consideration can be given to the producer's reputation for consistency and to the general vintage assessment for the region.

Prices can go down as well as up. They may easily not increase significantly in the few years after the campaign.

Some popular vintages are offered at ridiculously high prices – some unpopular ones too. It's only about twice a decade that the combination of high quality and fair prices offers the private buyer a chance of a good, guaranteed profit. Interestingly, if one highly touted vintage is followed by another, the prices for the second one often have to fall because the market simply will not accept two inflated price structures in a row. Recent Bordeaux examples of this are the excellent 1990 after the much hyped 1989 and the potentially fine 2001 after the understandably hyped 2000.

2003 was hot and dry in Bordeaux: the heavier, less classic – but more water-retentive – clay soils of the northern Médoc made many of the best wines, at reasonable prices. Well-known Haut-Médoc wines, St-Émilions and Pomerols are more patchy in quality – but it is already too late to invest in 2003 for profit.

2004 wines will soon be arriving on these shores – so your wine can be delivered within a week. It was a bigger, more classic, but more erratic vintage than 2003 in Bordeaux; the good news is that prices dropped by a third. A lot of people didn't buy the 2004 and it will be overshadowed by the 2005, but don't overlook it – there's some absolutely smashing stuff at very reasonable prices (see box, left).

The superlative 2005 vintage is certainly one of the best ever – but the prices are some of the highest ever, as I said in my introduction to this book (page 4).

SECURE CELLARAGE

Another worry is that the merchant you buy the wine from may not still be around to deliver it to you two years later. Buy from a merchant you trust, with a solid trading base in other wines.

Once the wines are shipped you may want your merchant to store the wine for you; there is usually a small charge for this. If your merchant offers cellarage, you should insist that (1) you receive a stock certificate; (2) your wines are stored separately from the merchant's own stocks; and (3) your cases are identifiable as your property and are labelled accordingly. All good merchants offer these safeguards as a minimum service.

CHECK THE SMALL PRINT

Traditional wine merchants may quote prices exclusive of VAT and/or duty: wine may not be the bargain it first appears.

A wine quoted *en primeur* is usually offered on an ex-cellars (EC) basis; the price excludes shipping, duties and taxes such as VAT. A price quoted in bond (IB) in the UK includes shipping, but excludes duties and taxes. Duty paid (DP) prices exclude VAT. You should check beforehand the exact terms of sale with your merchant, who will give you a projection of the final 'duty paid delivered' price.

Retailers' directory

All these retailers have been chosen on the basis of the quality and interest of their lists. From each list we've picked out a few wines for you to try. If you want to find local suppliers, retailers are listed by region in the Who's Where directory on page 223.

The following services are available where indicated:
C = cellarage G = glass hire/loan M = mail order T = tastings and talks

A & B Vintners

Little Tawsden, Spout Lane, Brenchley, Kent TN12 7AS (01892) 724977
FAX (01892) 722673
E-MAIL info@abvintners.co.uk
WEBSITE www.abvintners.co.uk
HOURS Mon–Fri 9–6 CARDS MasterCard, Visa DELIVERY Free 5 cases or more, otherwise £11.75 per consignment UK mainland MINIMUM ORDER 1 mixed case EN PRIMEUR Burgundy, Languedoc, Rhône. C M T
✪ Star attractions *Specialists in Burgundy, the Rhône and southern France, with a string of top-quality domaines from all three regions.*
• 2003 Côtes du Rhône, Les Arbousiers, Domaine La Réméjeanne, Rhône Valley, France, £8.80

• 2003 Vin de Pays des Côtes Catalanes Blanc, Calcinaires, Domaine Gauby, Roussillon, France, £9.80
• 1999 Chambolle-Musigny, Domaine Ghislaine Barthod, Burgundy, France, £23
• 2002 Chassagne-Montrachet Premier Cru Vergers, Domaine Marc Morey, Burgundy, France, £27.40

Adnams

HEAD OFFICE & MAIL ORDER
Sole Bay Brewery, Southwold, Suffolk IP18 6JW (01502) 727222
FAX (01502) 727223
E-MAIL wines@adnams.co.uk
WEBSITE www.adnamswines.co.uk
SHOPS The Wine Cellar & Kitchen Store, Victoria Street, Southwold, Suffolk IP18

Please bear in mind that wine is not made in infinite quantities – some of these wines may well sell out, but the following year's vintage should then become available.

All prices listed are per bottle inclusive of VAT, unless otherwise stated. The prices are those which applied in summer 2006. When comparing prices remember that some retailers only sell by the case. In this instance we have arrived at a bottle price by dividing the VAT-inclusive price of a single case by 12. Retailers who sell by the case will often sell cases of mixed bottles and many retailers offer case discounts of around 5%.

When clubs have both members and non-member prices we have used the non-member prices.

6JW • The Wine Shop, Pinkney's Lane, Southwold, Suffolk IP18 6EW • Adnams Wine Cellar & Kitchen Store, The Old School House, Park Road, Holkham, Wells-next-the-Sea, Norfolk NR23 1AB (01328) 711714 **HOURS** (Orderline) Mon–Fri 9–8, Sat 9–5; Wine Cellar & Kitchen Store and Wine Shop: Mon–Sat 9–6 (Norfolk 10–6), Sun 11–4 **CARDS** MasterCard, Maestro, Visa, Delta **DISCOUNTS** 5% for 5 cases or more **DELIVERY** Free for orders over £125 in most of mainland UK, otherwise £7.50 **MINIMUM ORDER** (mail order) 1 case **EN PRIMEUR** Bordeaux, Burgundy, Rhône. **G M T**
✪ **Star attractions** *Extensive list of personality-packed wines from around the world, chosen by a team of enthusiasts. Plenty from France, of course, but there's good stuff from Spain too, and Telmo Rodríguez, one of Spain's top winemakers, is well represented. New World wines include Ridge and Saintsbury from California, Forrest Estate and Martinborough Vineyards from New Zealand.*
• **2004 Mâcon-Chardonnay, The Adnams Selection White Burgundy, Paul Talmard, Burgundy, France, £6.99**
• **2002 l'Orangerie de Carignan Premières Côtes de Bordeaux, Château Carignan, Bordeaux, France, £7.75**
• **2001 Kuyen, Alvaro Espinoza, Maipo Valley, Chile, £8.99**
• **2001 Costières de Nîmes, Domaine Les Perrières, Languedoc, France, £9.99**

Aldi Stores
PO Box 26, Atherstone, Warwickshire CV9 2SH; 300 stores **STORE LOCATION LINE** 08705 134262 **WEBSITE** www.aldi-stores.co.uk **HOURS** Mon–Wed 9–6, Thurs–Fri 9–7, Sat 8.30–5.30, Sun 10–4 (selected stores) **CARDS** Switch, Visa (debit only)
✪ **Star attractions** *Aldi have some terrific bargains from around the world, with lots of wines available under £3, but can also push the boat out for decent claret.*
• **2004 Malbec-Bonarda, St Lucas, Mendoza, Argentina, £3.29**
• **2004 Chardonnay Reserve, Bushland, Hunter Valley, New South Wales, Australia, £3.99**
• **2004 Crémant du Jura, Philippe Michel, Jura, France, £5.49**
• **2001 Les Allées de Cantemerle, Château de Cantemerle, Bordeaux, France, £8.99**

Amey's Wines
83 Melford Road, Sudbury, Suffolk CO10 1JT (01787) 377144 **HOURS** Tue–Fri 9–5; Sat 9–4 **CARDS** AmEx, MasterCard, Switch, Visa **DISCOUNTS** 10% for a mixed dozen, 15% for 5 or more mixed cases **DELIVERY** Free within 10 miles of Sudbury for orders over £60. **G M T**
✪ **Star attractions** *Well-chosen and wide-ranging list of around 500 characterful wines from around the world.*
• **2005 Pinot Gris Santa Celina, Bodegas J and F Lurton, Mendoza, Argentina, £6.00**

- 2002 Maranges Premier Cru Clos des Loyères, Domaine Vincent Girardin, Burgundy, France, £13.40
- NV Champagne Grand Réserve Brut, Vilmart, Champagne, France, £21.50
- 1995 Grange, Penfolds, Barossa Valley, South Australia, £110.00

armit

5 Royalty Studios, 105 Lancaster Road, London W11 1QF (020) 7908 0600 **FAX** (020) 7908 0601 **E-MAIL** info@armit.co.uk **WEBSITE** www.armit.co.uk **HOURS** Mon–Fri 9–5.30 **CARDS** MasterCard, Switch, Visa **DELIVERY** Free for orders over £180, otherwise £15 delivery charge **MINIMUM ORDER** 1 case **EN PRIMEUR** Bordeaux, Burgundy, Italy, Rhône, New World. **C M T**
✪ **Star attractions** *Classy merchant with a star-studded list that's particularly strong on wines to go with food – they supply some top restaurants – from Italy, Burgundy and the Rhône, with some gems from Germany, Spain and the New World. For everyday drinking there's an own-label range from some top winemakers.*

- 2004 Grüner Veltliner Strasse Hasel, Weingut Eichinger, Kamptal, Austria, £7.54
- 2001 Armit Bordeaux Supérieur, Christian Moueix, Bordeaux, France, £7.80
- 2003 Dolcetto d'Alba Rochettevino, Gianni Voerzio, Piedmont, Italy, £10.79
- 2005 Sauvignon Blanc, Seresin, Marlborough, New Zealand, £11.67

ASDA

HEAD OFFICE Asda House, Southbank, Great Wilson Street, Leeds LS11 5AD (0113) 243 5435 **FAX** (0113) 241 8666 **CUSTOMER SERVICE** (0500) 100055; 320 stores **WEBSITE** www.asda.co.uk **HOURS** Selected stores open 24 hrs, see local store for details **CARDS** MasterCard, Switch, Visa **DISCOUNTS** Buy 6 bottles, save 10%; case deals: 10% off price including delivery **DELIVERY** Selected stores. **T**
✪ **Star attractions** *Good-value basics – lots under a fiver – and the range now includes some interesting wines at £7+.*
- 2004 Côtes du Rhône-Villages, Rhône Valley, France, £3.98
- 2004 Viña Sol, Torres, Cataluña, Spain, £4.43
- 2004 Pinot Noir, Cono Sur, Chile, £5.49
- 2005 Chardonnay ASDA Extra Special, McLaren Vale, South Australia, £6.98

L'Assemblage

Pallant Court, 10 West Pallant, Chichester, West Sussex PO19 1TG (01243) 537775 **FAX** (01243) 538644 **E-MAIL** sales@lassemblage.co.uk **WEBSITE** www.lassemblage.co.uk **HOURS** Mon–Fri 9.30–6 **CARDS** MasterCard, Switch, Visa **DELIVERY** Free for orders over £500 **MINIMUM ORDER** 1 mixed case or by arrangement **EN PRIMEUR** Bordeaux, Burgundy, Port, Rhône. **C M T**
✪ **Star attractions** *A fascinating list of fine wines, mostly from classic regions of France, especially Burgundy. The list specializes in one-off cases of wine, mostly sold by the case, so if you want*

COMPETITIVE EN PRIMEUR OFFERS

Including Bordeaux 2005

* Classic vintage wines from **1900** to **2005**
* Expert advice, Investments and Cellar Management
* The **best** prices for your surplus fine wine
* World-wide, well packed delivery service

Please call for a full list or visit our web-site
Tel: + 44 (0)1243 537775
Fax: + 44 (0)1243 538644

sales@lassemblage.co.uk www.lassemblage.co.uk

to find a wine to celebrate a special anniversary, or indulge in a truly mature wine, have a look at this list.

- **2000 Ruber Merlot-Cabernet Sauvignon, Stonewall, Stellenbosch, South Africa, £7.50**
- **2002 Puligny-Montrachet, Paul Pernot, Burgundy, France, £18.00**
- **2003 Château Malartic-Lagravière rouge, Pessac-Léognan, Bordeaux, France, £18.58**
- **1977 Vintage Port, Taylor's, Portugal, £73.00**

Australian Wine Club

MAIL ORDER PO Box 3079, Datchet, Slough SL3 9L2 0800 856 2004
FAX 0800 856 2114
E-MAIL orders@australianwine.co.uk
WEBSITE www.australianwine.co.uk
HOURS Mon–Fri 8am–9pm, Sat–Sun 9–6 **CARDS** AmEx, MasterCard, Switch, Visa, Diners **DELIVERY** £5.99 anywhere

in UK mainland **MINIMUM ORDER** 1 mixed case. **M T**
✪ **Star attractions** *The original mail-order Aussie wine specialist, buzzing with top names.*
- **2003 Shiraz-Petit Verdot, Westend Wines, Griffith, New South Wales, Australia, £7.65**
- **2005 Pinot Gris, Tim Adams, Clare Valley, South Australia, £9.99**
- **2002 Shiraz, Rufus Stone, Tyrrell's, Heathcote, Victoria, Australia, £13.99**
- **Joseph Sparkling Red, Primo Estate, South Australia, £27**

Averys Wine Merchants

4 High Street, Nailsea, Bristol BS48 1BT (08451) 283797 **FAX** (01275) 811101
E-MAIL sales@averys.com **WEBSITE** www.averys.com • Shop and Cellars, 9 Culver Street, Bristol BS1 5LD (0117) 921 4146 **FAX** (0117) 922 6318
E-MAIL cellars@averys.com
HOURS Mon–Fri 9–7, Sat 9.30–5.30, Sun 10–4; Shop Mon–Sat 9–7
CARDS AmEx, MasterCard, Switch, Visa
DISCOUNTS Monthly mail order offers, Discover Wine with Averys 13th bottle free **DELIVERY** £5.95 per delivery address **EN PRIMEUR** Bordeaux, Burgundy, Port, Rhône.
C G M T
✪ **Star attractions** *A small but very respectable selection from just about everywhere in France, Italy, Spain and Germany. Italy looks particularly promising and there's some good New World stuff, such as Felton Road from New Zealand and Hamilton Russell from South Africa.*

- 2005 Colección Malbec, Michel Torino, Cafayate, Argentina, £5.50
- 2004 Costières de Nîmes Tradition, Château de Campuget, Languedoc, France, £5.95
- 2003 Vouvray, Château Gaudrelle, Loire Valley, France, £8.95
- 2001 Vougeot Blanc Clos du Prieuré, Domaine de la Vougeraie, Burgundy, France, £29.95

Bacchus Wine

Warrington House Farm Barn, Warrington, Olney, Bucks MK46 4HN (01234) 711140 **FAX** (01234) 711199 **E-MAIL** wine@bacchus.co.uk **WEBSITE** www.bacchus.co.uk **HOURS** Mon–Fri 11–6.30, Sat 10.30–2 **CARDS** AmEx, Diners, MasterCard, Switch, Visa **DELIVERY** £5 per mixed case. Free for 2 or more cases **MINIMUM ORDER** 1 case. **G M T** ✪ Star attractions *France and Italy have the broadest coverage, but there are some gems from Argentina, Australia, Austria and South Africa— and you'll find many wines under £10.*

- 2004 Grüner Veltliner, Lois, Loimer, Austria, £6.95
- 2003 Benventano Aglianico, Vesevo, Campania, Italy, £7.95
- 2004 Lugana, Ca' dei Frati, Piedmont, Italy, £9.50
- 2003 Shiraz G.A.M., Mitolo, McLaren Vale, South Australia, £19.95

Ballantynes Wine Merchants

211–17 Cathedral Road, Cardiff, CF11 9PP (02920) 222202 **FAX** (02920) 222112

E-MAIL richard@ballantynes.co.uk **WEBSITE** www.ballantynes.co.uk **HOURS** Mon–Sat 9.30–7 **CARDS** MasterCard, Switch, Visa, Access **DISCOUNTS** 8% per case **DELIVERY** £9.99 for first case; £4.99 for subsequent cases **EN PRIMEUR** Bordeaux, Burgundy, Italy, Rhône. **C G M T** ✪ Star attractions *Italy, Burgundy, Rhône and Languedoc-Roussillon are stunning, most regions of France are well represented, and there's some terrific stuff from Australia, New Zealand and Spain. Plenty to choose from under £10.*

- 2004 Lirac, La Reine des Bois, Domaine de la Mordorée, Rhône Valley, France, £16.99
- 2001 Meursault, Jean-Philippe Fichet, Burgundy, France, £21.99
- 2001 Triolet, Mount Mary, Yarra Valley, Victoria, Australia, £36.99
- 1999 Sammarco, Castello dei Rampolla, Tuscany, Italy, £47.00

Balls Brothers

313 Cambridge Heath Road, London E2 9LQ (020) 7739 1642 **FAX** 0870 243 9775 **DIRECT SALES** (020) 7739 1642 **E-MAIL** wine@ballsbrothers.co.uk **WEBSITE** www.ballsbrothers.co.uk **HOURS** Mon–Fri 9–5.30 **CARDS** AmEx, Diners, MasterCard, Switch, Visa **DELIVERY** Free 1 case or more locally; £8 1 case, free 2 cases or more, England, Wales and Scottish Lowlands; islands and Scottish Highlands phone for details. **G M T**

✪ **Star attractions** *French specialist –
you'll find something of interest from
most regions – with older vintages
available. Spain and Australia are also
very good. Many of the wines can be
enjoyed in Balls Brothers' London wine
bars and restaurants.*
- **Chilean Cabernet Sauvignon, Viña
Carmen, Maipo Valley, Chile, £7.25**
- **2002 Rioja Tinto, Marqués de
Cacéres, Rioja, Spain, £7.50**
- **2002 Montagny Premier Cru les
Loges Vieilles Vignes, Cave Co-
operative de Buxy, Côte Chalonnaise,
Burgundy, France, £10.00**
- **NV Champagne Cuvée Royale Brut,
Joseph Perrier, Champagne, France,
£21.00**

H & H Bancroft Wines
1 China Wharf, 29 Mill Street, London
SE1 2BQ (020) 7232 5450
FAX (020) 7232 5451 **E-MAIL**
sales@handhbancroftwines.com
WEBSITE www.bancroftwines.com
HOURS Mon–Fri 9–5.30 **CARDS** Delta,
MasterCard, Switch, Visa **DISCOUNTS**
Negotiable **DELIVERY** £11.75 for 1–2
cases in mainland UK; free 3 cases or
more **MINIMUM ORDER** 1 case
EN PRIMEUR Bordeaux, Burgundy,
Rhône. **C M T**
✪ **Star attractions** *Bancroft are UK
agents for an impressive flotilla of
French winemakers: Burgundy, Rhône,
Loire and some interesting wines from
southern France. Italy looks promising,
too. A separate fine wine list includes
Bordeaux back to 1945, plus top names
from Burgundy and the Rhône.*

- **2005 Chardonnay Finca La Linda,
Luigi Bosca, Mendoza, Argentina,
£5.50**
- **Rioja Crianza, Bodegas Lan, Spain,
£7.75**
- **2002 Chianti Classico, San Giusto a
Rentennano, Tuscany, Italy, £10.95**
- **2004 Côteaux du Languedoc La
Falaise, Château de la Negly,
Languedoc, France, £11.95**

Bat & Bottle
MAIL ORDER 24d Pillings Road,
Oakham, Rutland LE15 6QF
(0845) 108 4407 /01572 759735
FAX (0870) 458 2505
E-MAIL post@batwine.co.uk
WEBSITE www.batwine.co.uk **HOURS**
Mon–Thurs 9–5, Fri 9–7, Sat 10–5
CARDS MasterCard, Switch, Visa. **G M T**
✪ **Star attractions** *Ben and Emma
Robson specialize in Italy, and in
characterful wines from small
producers discovered on their regular
visits to the country. An inspired and
inspiring list.*
- **2005 Verdicchio dei Castelli di Jesi
Classico, Mancinelli, Marche, Italy,
£7.85**
- **2004 Sciaglin, Emilio Bulfon, Friuli-
Venezia Giulia, Italy, £10.75**
- **2003 Teroldego Rotaliano Vigneto
Lealbere, R Zeni, Trento, Italy, £12.50**
- **2003 Cento, Castel di Salve, IGT
Salento, Puglia, Italy, £15.00**

Bennetts Fine Wines
High Street, Chipping Campden, Glos
GL55 6AG (01386) 840392
FAX (01386) 840974 **E-MAIL**

enquiries@bennettsfinewines.com
WEBSITE www.bennettsfinewines. com
HOURS Tues–Fri 10–6, Sat 9.30–6
CARDS MasterCard, Switch, Visa, Access
DISCOUNTS On collected orders of 1 case
or more **DELIVERY** £6 per case, minimum
charge £12, free for orders over £200 **EN
PRIMEUR** Burgundy, California, Rhône,
New Zealand. **G M T**
✪ Star attractions *Given the calibre of
the producers, the prices are very fair:
there's certainly lots to choose from at
around £10. France and Italy have the
lion's share, but Germany, Spain and
Portugal look good too. New World
wines are similarly high up the quality
scale, with the likes of Kumeu River and
Isabel Estate from New Zealand,
Plantagenet and Cullen from Australia,
Seghesio from California and Domaine
Drouhin from Oregon.*
• **2005 Garganega, Alpha Zeta, Veneto,
Italy, £5.10**
• **2003 Valpolicella Classico, Corte
Sant'Alda, Veneto, Italy, £9.85**
• **2004 Zinfandel, Seghesio, Sonoma
County, California, USA, £15.75**
• **1996 Château Gloria, St-Julien,
Bordeaux, France, £24.50**

Berkmann Wine Cellars

10–12 Brewery Road, London N7 9NH
(020) 7609 4711 **FAX** (020) 7607 0018
• Brunel Park, Vincients Road, Bumpers
Farm, Chippenham, Wiltshire SN14 6NQ
(01249) 463501
• Brian Coad Wine Cellars, 41b Valley
Road, Plympton, Plymouth, Devon PL7
1RF (01752) 334970 **FAX** (01752) 346540
• Pagendam Pratt Wine Cellars, 16

Marston Moor Business Park, Rudgate,
Tockwith, N. Yorks YO26 7QF (01423)
337567 **FAX** (01423) 357568
• T M Robertson Wine Cellars, Unit 12,
A1 Industrial Estate, 232 Sir Harry Lauder
Road, Portobello, Edinburgh EH15 2QA
(0131) 657 6390 **FAX** (0131) 657 6389
FAX (01249) 463502
E-MAIL info@berkmann.co.uk
WEBSITE www.berkmann.co.uk
HOURS Mon–Fri 9–5.30 **CARDS**
MasterCard, Switch, Visa **DISCOUNTS** £3
per unmixed case collected **DELIVERY**
Free for orders over £120 to UK
mainland (excluding the Highlands)
MINIMUM ORDER 1 mixed case. **C G M**
✪ Star attractions *Wow! Where do you
start on a list that includes Mexico,
Corsica and India? Italy, perhaps, since
Berkmann is the UK agent for, among
others, Antinori, Maculan,
Mastroberardino, Masi and Tasca
d'Almerita, so there are some fab Italian
wines here. Spain has Marqués de
Griñon, Portugal has Casa Ferreirinha.
New World wines include some top stuff
from Australia, New Zealand, South
Africa and California. But France hasn't
been forgotten: affordable claret and
Burgundy, Alsace, Beaujolais, Loire …
need I go on?*
• **2004 Syrah, Finca Antigua, La Mancha,
Spain, £7.39**
• **2005 Vernaccia di San Gimignano
(organic), Teruzzi & Puthod, Tuscany,
Italy, £8.49**
• **2003 Norton Privada, Norton,
Mendoza, Argentina, £9.99**
• **2003 Nebbiolo d'Alba Occheti,
Prunotto, Piedmont, Italy, £12.59**

Berry Bros. & Rudd

3 St James's Street, London SW1A 1EG
(020) 7396 9600 FAX (020) 7396 9611
ORDERS OFFICE 0870 900 4300 (lines
open Mon–Fri 9–6, ORDERS FAX 0870
900 4301
• Berrys' Wine Shop, (Sat 10-4) Hamilton
Close, Houndmills, Basingstoke, Hants
RG21 6YB (01256) 323566
E-MAIL orders@bbr.com
WEBSITE www.bbr.com
HOURS St James's Street: Mon–Fri 10–6,
Sat 10–4; Berrys' Wine Shop: Mon–Thur
10–6, Fri 10–7, Sat 10–4 CARDS AmEx,
Diners, MasterCard, Switch, Visa
DISCOUNTS Variable
DELIVERY Free for orders of £200 or
more, otherwise £10
EN PRIMEUR Bordeaux, Burgundy, Rhône.
C G M T
✪ Star attractions *The shop in
St James's is the very image of a
traditional wine merchant, but Berry
Bros. also has one of the best websites
around. The Blue List covers old, rare fine
wines while the main list is both classy
and wide-ranging: there's an emphasis
on the classic regions of France; smaller
but equally tempting selections from
just about everywhere else. Not
everything is expensive: Berrys' Own
Selection is extensive, with wines made
by world class producers, e.g. Alain
Vauthier of Château Ausone fame makes
the Berry's St-Émilion.*
• Berry's Good Ordinary Claret, Borie-
Manoux, Bordeaux, France, £5.50
• 2003 Crozes-Hermitage, Les Trois
Chênes, Domaine Emmanuel
Darnaud, Rhône Valley, France, £13.95
• Berry's St-Émilion, Château de Fonbel,
Bordeaux, France, £15.95
• 1999 Brunello di Montalcino, Casisano
Colombaio, Tuscany, Italy, £24.50

Bibendum Wine

113 Regents Park Road, London
NW1 8UR (020) 7449 4120
FAX (020) 7449 4121 E-MAIL
sales@bibendum-wine.co.uk WEBSITE
www.bibendum-wine.co.uk HOURS
Mon–Fri 9–6 CARDS MasterCard,
Switch, Visa DELIVERY Free throughout
mainland UK for orders over £250,
otherwise £15 EN PRIMEUR Bordeaux,
Burgundy, New World, Rhône, Port. M T
✪ Star attractions *Bibendum looks for
wines that nobody else is shipping –
although that's not to say you won't
find them elsewhere, since Bibendum
supply the trade as well as private
customers. Equally strong in the Old
World and the New: Huet in Vouvray and
Lageder in Alto Adige are matched by
d'Arenberg and Katnook from Australia
and Catena Zapata from Argentina.*
• 2004 Riesling, Howard Park, Margaret
River, Western Australia, £9.35
• 2004 Pinot Noir, Wither Hills,
Marlborough, New Zealand, £13.61
• NV Caballo Loco, Valdevieso, Curicó,
Chile, £16.67
• 2002 Alta Malbec, Catena Zapata,
Mendoza, Argentina, £21.92

Booths Supermarkets

E H Booth & Co, Booths Central Office,
Longridge Road, Ribbleton, Preston PR
5BX (01772) 693800 FAX (01772)
693893; 26 stores across the North of

Cephas
picture library

The world's foremost collection of wine photography

Images available for all uses

Whenever I start on a new book, the first phone call I make is to Cephas. Their photographs inspire me when I'm writing and bring my words to life when you're reading them

Oz Clarke

www.cephas.com 020 8979 8647

England **E-MAIL** admin@booths-supermarkets.co.uk **WEBSITE** www.booths-supermarkets.co.uk and www.booths-wine.co.uk **HOURS** Office: Mon–Fri 8.30–5; shop hours vary **CARDS** AmEx, Electron, MasterCard, Maestro, Solo, Visa **DISCOUNTS** 5% off any 6 bottles. **G T**
✪ **Star attractions** *A list for any merchant to be proud of, never mind a supermarket. There's plenty under £5, but if you're prepared to hand over £7–9 you'll find some really interesting stuff.*
- 2005 Viognier Otra Vida, Trivento/ Concha y Toro, Mendoza, Argentina, £4.99
- 2004 Nero d'Avola, Inycon, Settesoli, Sicily, Italy, £4.99
- 2003 Trincadeira Grand'Arte, DFJ Vinhos, Ribatejo, Portugal, £6.99
- 2004 Semillon, Steenberg, Constantia, South Africa, £7.99

Bordeaux Index

MAIL ORDER 6th Floor, 159–173 St John Street, London EC1V 4QJ (020) 7253 2110 **FAX** (020) 7490 1955 **E-MAIL** sales@bordeauxindex.com **WEBSITE** www.bordeauxindex.com **HOURS** Mon–Fri 8.30–6 **CARDS** AmEx, MasterCard, Switch, Visa, JCB (transaction fees apply) **DELIVERY** (Private sales only) free for orders over £2,000 UK mainland; others at cost **MINIMUM ORDER** £500 **EN PRIMEUR** Bordeaux, Burgundy, Rhône, Italy. **C T**
✪ **Star attractions** *A serious list for serious spenders. Pages and pages of red Bordeaux and, in spite of the company*

name, stacks of top Burgundies and Rhônes. Italy and Australia are looking increasingly interesting. And if you're looking to blow that bonus, get a few friends round to share a jeroboam of 1990 Cristal.
- 2003 Château les Ormes de Pez, St-Estèphe, Bordeaux, France, £13.21
- 1988 Château La Lagune, Haut-Médoc, Bordeaux, France, £29.37
- 1998 Château Canon-la-Gaffelière, St-Émilion Grand Cru Classé, Bordeaux, France, £34.27
- 1990 Louis Roederer Cristal, Champagne, France £3525.00 (jeroboam)

Budgens Stores

HEAD OFFICE Musgrave House, Widewater Place, Moorhall Road, Harefield, Uxbridge, Middlesex UB9 6PE (0870) 050 0158 **FAX** (0870) 050 0159, for nearest store call 0800 526002; 210 stores mainly in Southern England and East Anglia **E-MAIL** info@ budgens.co.uk **WEBSITE** www.budgens.co.uk **HOURS** Vary according to size and location (55 stores open 24 hours); usually Mon–Sat 8–8, Sun 10–4 **CARDS** MasterCard, Solo, Switch, Visa. **G**
✪ **Star attractions** *These days you can feel reasonably confident of going into a Budgens store and coming out with some wine you'd actually like to drink, at bargain-basement prices upwards.*
- 2005 Grillo, Serenata, Sicily, Italy, £3.99
- 2004 Cabernet Sauvignon Casillero del Diablo, Concha y Toro, Chile, £5.99

- 2005 Sauvignon Blanc Private Bin, Villa Maria, Marlborough, New Zealand, £7.99
- 2001 Rioja Reserva Coleccion Personal, Marqués de Griñon, Spain, £8.35

The Butlers Wine Cellar

247 Queens Park Road, Brighton BN2 9XJ (01273) 698724 **FAX** (01273) 622761 **E-MAIL** henry@butlers-winecellar.co.uk **WEBSITE** www.butlers-winecellar.co.uk **HOURS** Tue–Wed 10–6, Thur–Sat 10–7 **CARDS** Access, AmEx, MasterCard, Switch, Visa **DELIVERY** Free locally 1 case or more; free UK mainland 3 cases or more **EN PRIMEUR** Bordeaux. **G M T**

✪ Star attractions *The regular list is full of fascinating stuff, all personally chosen by Henry Butler; Italy and Spain look strong,and there's Breaky Bottom from England and other top-quality fizz from local Sussex vineyards. But it's the bin end list that's the main point, guaranteed to delight Bordeaux enthusiasts. Prices are affordable – you can get some great surprises here for only £20 – and although the risk is there, you could get a very good bottle: you'll only find out by buying it. You want a 35-year-old wine for only £25? Here's where to come. And – in smaller numbers – there's excellent Burgundy, Rhône, Loire and Germany. You'll need to look at the website or join the mailing list, as these odds and ends change all the time.*
- 2004 Rosso Piceno Superiore, Saladini Pilastri, Marche, Italy, £6.99
- 2003 Pinot Noir Special Reserve, Anakena, Chile, £7.25
- 2004 Grüner Veltliner, Loimer, Langenlois, Austria, £8.99
- 1996 Sparkling Brut, Breaky Bottom, Sussex, England, £18.00

Anthony Byrne

MAIL ORDER Ramsey Business Park, Stocking Fen Road, Ramsey, Cambs PE26 2UR (01487) 814555 **FAX** (01487) 814962 **E-MAIL** anthony@abfw.co.uk or claude@abfw.co.uk **WEBSITE** www.abfw.co.uk **HOURS** Mon–Fri 9–5.30 **CARDS** None **DISCOUNTS** available on cases **DELIVERY** Free 5 cases or more, or orders of £250 or more; otherwise £12 **MINIMUM ORDER** 1 case **EN PRIMEUR** Bordeaux, Burgundy, Rhône. **C M T**

✪ Star attractions *A serious list of Burgundy; Loire from top growers such as Serge Dagueneau; and from Alsace there are enough Zind-Humbrecht wines to sink a ship. Interesting French wines also come from Provence (Château de Pibarnon) and the Rhône (Alain Graillot). Increasing coverage of South Africa.*
- 1998 Alsace Gewurztraminer Clos Windsbuhl, Zind-Humbrecht, Alsace, France,£9.96 (37.5 cl)
- 2000 Premières Côtes de Bordeaux, Château Reynon, Bordeaux, France, £9.98
- 2004 Crozes-Hermitage La Guiraude, Alain Graillot, Rhône Valley, France, £16.04
- 1999 Clos de la Roche Grand Cru, Armand Rousseau, Burgundy, France, £37.58

D Byrne & Co

Victoria Buildings, 12 King Street,
Clitheroe, Lancs BB7 2EP (01200)
423152 HOURS Mon–Sat 8.30–6 CARDS
MasterCard, Switch, Visa DELIVERY
Free within 50 miles; nationally £10 1st
case, £5 subsequent cases EN PRIMEUR
Bordeaux, Burgundy, Rhône, Germany.
G M T
❂ Star attractions *One of northern
England's best wine merchants, with a
hugely impressive range. Clarets back
to 1982, stacks of Burgundy, faultless
Loire and Rhône, Germany, Spain, USA
(not just California) and many, many
more. I urge you to go and see for
yourself, or at least send for the lists.*
- 2004 Gewürztraminer, Enate,
  Somontano, Aragón, Spain, £9.79
- 2004 Riesling, Howard Park,
  Margaret River, Western Australia,
  £9.89
- 2001 Château Bournac, Médoc,
  Bordeaux, France, £9.89
- 2002 Syrah, Bonny Doon, California,
  USA, £10.59

Cape Wine and Food

77 Laleham Road, Staines,
Middx TW18 2EA (01784) 451860 FAX
(01784) 469267 E-MAIL
ross@capewineandfood.com WEBSITE
www.capewineandfood.com
HOURS Mon–Sat 10–6, Sun 10–5 CARDS
AmEx, MasterCard, Switch, Visa
DISCOUNTS 10% mixed case. G M T
❂ Star attractions *South African wines
from 80 estates, including top names
such as Graham Beck, Iona, Thelema
and Vergelegen.*

- 2005 Sauvignon Blanc, Vergelegen,
  Stellenbosch, South Africa, £8.49
- 2004 Mourvedre, Spice Route,
  Stellenbosch, South Africa, £9.50
- 2000 Shiraz, Stellenzicht,
  Stellenbosch, South Africa, £11.29
- 2002 Pinotage, L'Avenir,
  Stellenbosch, South Africa, £13.35

Les Caves de Pyrene

Pew Corner, Old Portsmouth Road,
Artington, Guildford GU3 1LP (office)
(01483) 538820 (shop) (01483) 554750
FAX (01483) 455068 E-MAIL
sales@lescaves.co.uk
WEBSITE www.lescaves.co.uk HOURS
Mon–Fri 9–5 CARDS MasterCard,
Switch, Visa DELIVERY Free for orders
over £180 within M25, elsewhere at
cost DISCOUNTS negotiable MINIMUM
ORDER 1 mixed case EN PRIMEUR
South-West France. G M T
❂ Star attractions *Excellent operation,
devoted to seeking out top wines from
all over southern France. Other areas of
France, especially the Loire, are equally
good. And there's Armagnac dating
back to 1893!*
- 2004 Côtes du Roussillon Villages, Le
  Roc des Anges, Domaine Segna de
  Cor, Languedoc-Roussillon, France,
  £8.75
- NV Vouvray Brut, Domaine
  Champalou, Loire Valley, France, £8.75
- 2002 Madiran, Cuvée Charles de
  Batz, Domaine Berthoumieu, South-
  West France, £9.85
- 2002 Jurançon Sec, Vitatge Vielh de
  Lapeyre, Jean-Bernard Larrieu,
  South-West France, £10.25

ChateauOnline

MAIL ORDER BP68, 39602 Arbois Cedex, France (0033) 3 84 66 42 21 **FAX** (0033) 1 55 30 31 41 **CUSTOMER SERVICE** 0800 169 2736 **WEBSITE** www.chateauonline.com **HOURS** Mon–Fri 8–11.30, 12.30–4.30 **CARDS** AmEx, MasterCard, Switch, Visa **DELIVERY** £7.99 per consignment **EN PRIMEUR** Bordeaux, Burgundy, Languedoc-Roussillon.

✪ **Star attractions** *French specialist, with an impressive list of over 2000 wines. Easy-to-use website with a well-thought-out range of mixed cases, frequent special offers and bin end sales.*

- 2004 Cuvée Simone Descamps, Château de Lastours, Languedoc, France, £8.99
- 2002 Château Ladouys, St-Estèphe, Bordeaux, France, £9.59
- 2002 Vacqueyras Clos Montirius, Domaine Saurel, Rhône Valley, France, £9.59
- 2002 Chablis Premier Cru, Cuvée Première, Laroche, Burgundy, France, £13.99

Cockburns of Leith (incorporating J E Hogg)

Cockburn House, Unit 3, Abbeyhill Industrial Estate, Abbey Lane, Edinburgh EH8 8HL (0131) 661 8400 **FAX** (0131) 661 7333
• 382 Morningside Road, Edinburgh EH10 5HX (0131) 446 0700 **E-MAIL** sales@winelist.co.uk **WEBSITE** www.winelist.co.uk **HOURS** Mon–Fri 9–6; Sat 10–5 **CARDS**

MasterCard, Switch, Visa **DELIVERY** Free 12 or more bottles within Edinburgh; elsewhere £7 1–2 cases, free 3 cases or more **EN PRIMEUR** Bordeaux, Burgundy. **G T**

✪ **Star attractions** *Clarets at bargain prices – in fact wines from all over France, including plenty of vins de pays. Among other countries New Zealand looks promising, and there's a great range of sherries.*

- 2002 Corbières, Château La Bastide, Languedoc, France, £7.15
- 2005 Semillon-Sauvignon Blanc, Ferngrove, Frankland River, Western Australia, £7.20
- 2002 Stark Shiraz, Stark-Condé, Stellenbosch, South Africa, £14.45
- 2002 Beaune Vieilles Vignes, Champy, Burgundy, France £16.50

Connolly's Wine Merchants

Arch 13, 220 Livery Street, Birmingham B3 1EU (0121) 236 9269/3837 **FAX** (0121) 233 2339
E-MAIL sales@connollyswine.co.uk **WEBSITE** www.connollyswine.co.uk **HOURS** Mon–Fri 9–5.30, except Thurs 9–7, Sat 10–4 **CARDS** AmEx, MasterCard, Switch, Visa **DELIVERY** Surcharge outside Birmingham area **DISCOUNTS** 10% for cash & carry **EN PRIMEUR** Burgundy. **G M T**

✪ **Star attractions** *There's something for everyone here. Burgundy, Bordeaux and the Rhône all look very good; and there are top names from Germany (Dr Loosen, Selbach-Oster), Italy (Isole e Olena, Allegrini), Spain (Artadi, Marqués de Riscal) and California (Bonny Doon,*

Saintsbury, Ridge). Monthly tutored tastings and winemaker dinners.

- **2004 Soave Classico Superiore, Prà, Veneto, Italy, £8.29**
- **2002 Bourgogne Rouge, Nicolas Potel, Burgundy, France, £9.85**
- **2003 Grüner Veltliner Alte Reben Oberfeld, Dr Unger, Kremstal, Austria, £12.05**
- **1990 Champagne Bollinger RD, Champagne, France, £77.50**

The Co-operative Group

HEAD OFFICE New Century House, Manchester M60 4ES Freephone 0800 068 6727 for stock details **FAX** (0161) 827 5117; approx. 3,000 licensed stores **E-MAIL** customer relations@co-op.co.uk **WEBSITE** www.co-op.co.uk **HOURS** Variable **CARDS** Variable • **ONLINE WINE STORE** www.co-opdrinks2u.com **TELEPHONE** 0845 090 2222 **CARDS** AmEx, MasterCard, Solo, Switch, Visa **DELIVERY** Within 7 days mainland UK £4.99 (UK islands and N. Ireland £23); Saturday delivery (major towns only) £26
✪ **Star attractions** *Champions of Fairtrade and organic wines. South Africa, Australia, Chile and Argentina all deliver tasty wine for around £5.*

- **2004 Argentine Malbec, San Juan, Argentina, £3.99**
- **2005 Cape Sauvignon Blanc, Fairtrade, South Africa, £4.99**
- **2005 Chardonnay-Viognier, Anakena, Chile, £4.99**
- **2003 Grenache-Shiraz, d'Arry's Original, d'Arenberg, McLaren Vale, South Australia, £8.99**

Corney & Barrow

HEAD OFFICE No. 1 Thomas More Street, London E1W 1YZ (020) 7265 2400 **FAX** (020) 7265 2539
• 194 Kensington Park Road, London W11 2ES (020) 7221 5122
• Corney & Barrow East Anglia, Belvoir House, High Street, Newmarket CB8 8DH (01638) 600000 • Corney & Barrow (Scotland) with Whighams of Ayr, 8 Academy Street, Ayr KA7 1HT (01292) 267000, and Oxenfoord Castle, by Pathhead, Mid Lothian EH37 5UD (01875) 321921
E-MAIL wine@corbar.co.uk
WEBSITE www.corneyandbarrow.com
HOURS Mon–Fri 8–6 (24-hr answering machine); Kensington Mon–Fri 10.30–9, Sat 9.30–8; Newmarket Mon–Sat 9–6; Edinburgh Mon–Fri 9–6; Ayr Mon–Fri 9–6, Sat 9.30–5.30 **CARDS** AmEx, MasterCard, Maestro, Visa **DELIVERY** Free 24 or more bottles within M25 boundary, elsewhere free 36 or more bottles or for orders above £200. Otherwise £9 + VAT per delivery. For Scotland and East Anglia, please contact the relevant office **EN PRIMEUR** Bordeaux, Burgundy, Champagne, Rhône, Italy, Spain. **C G M T**
✪ **Star attractions** *If you want certain Pomerols like Pétrus, Trotanoy, la Fleur-Pétrus and Latour à Pomerol, Corney & Barrow, by Royal Appointment, is where you have to come. At least, if you want them en primeur. Burgundy kicks off with Domaine de la Romanée-Conti and proceeds via names like Domaine Trapet and Domaine Leflaive. The rest*

of Europe is equally impressive; with Australia, South Africa and South America hot on their heels. Wines in every price bracket; try them out at Corney & Barrow wine bars in London.

- **2004 Chenin Blanc, Old Vines, Wine Cellar, Stellenbosch, South Africa, £6.93**
- **2004 Château de Sours Rosé, Bordeaux, France, £8.81**
- **2002 Bourgogne Blanc, Domaine Trapet, Burgundy, France, £12.57**
- **2003 Bolgheri, Poggio Al Moro, Enrico Santini, Tuscany, Italy, £13.25**

Croque-en-Bouche

Groom's Cottage, Underdown, Gloucester Road, Ledbury, HR8 2JE (01531) 636400 **FAX** (08707) 066282 **E-MAIL** mail@croque-en-bouche.co.uk **WEBSITE** www.croque-en-bouche. co.uk **HOURS** By appointment 7 days a week **CARDS** MasterCard, Switch, Visa **DISCOUNTS** 3% for orders over £500 if paid in cash or by Switch or Delta **DELIVERY** Free locally; elsewhere £5 per consignment; free in England and Wales for orders over £500 if paid by credit card **MINIMUM ORDER** 1 mixed case. **M**
✪ **Star attractions** *A wonderful list, including older wines. Mature Australian reds from the 1990s; terrific stuff from the Rhône – Château Beaucastel's Châteauneuf-du-Pape going back to 1979; some top clarets; and a generous sprinkling from other parts of the world. Sweet wines include marvellously mature Sauternes and Loire wines.*

- **2000 St-Chinian, Renaud de Valon, Languedoc, France, £8.00**
- **2005 Sauvignon Blanc, St Clair, Marlborough, New Zealand, £9.50**
- **2000 Alsace Riesling Gueberschwihr, Zind-Humbrecht, Alsace, France, £14.00**
- **1995 Mount Edelstone Shiraz, Henschke, Eden Valley, Australia, £51.00**

deFINE Food & Wine

Chester Road, Sandiway, Cheshire CW8 2NH (01601) 882101 **FAX** (01606) 888407 **E-MAIL** office@definefoodandwine.com **WEBSITE** www.definefoodandwine.com **HOURS** Mon–Sat 10–8; Sun 12–6 **CARDS** MasterCard, Maestro, Switch, Visa **DISCOUNTS** 5% off 6 bottles or more **DELIVERY** Free locally, otherwise £10 UK **MINIMUM ORDER** 1 mixed case. **C G**
✪ **Star attractions** *Wine shop and delicatessen, with British cheeses and food from Italy and Spain. Excellent, if conservative stuff from Bordeaux and the Loire; less conservative choices from elsewhere – including a white Chacoli from the Basque region of Spain – with New Zealand and South Africa looking good.*

- **2001 Old Vine Zinfandel, Bogle, California, USA, £10.99**
- **2003 Pinot Gris, Isabel Estate, Marlborough, New Zealand, £11.49**
- **2001 Alsace Gewurztraminer, Grand Cru Brand, Cave de Turckheim, Alsace, France, £11.99**
- **2000 The Vergelegen, Vergelegen, Stellenbosch, South Africa, £24.99**

Some of Champagne's best vineyard sites are on the slopes of the Montagne de Reims, south of the city of Reims

Devigne Wines

Maes Y Coed, 13 Llanerchydol
Park, Welshpool SY21 9QE (01938)
553478 **FAX** (01938) 556831
E-MAIL info@devignewines.co.uk
WEBSITE www.devignewines.co.uk
HOURS Mon–Fri 10–6 (telephone 7
days) **CARDS** MasterCard, Switch, Visa
DISCOUNTS selected mixed cases at
introductory rate **DELIVERY** free for
orders over £300, otherwise £6.50 per
consignment **M**
✪ **Star attractions** *Small list specializing
in French wines: traditional-
(Champagne) method sparkling wines
from all over France, 12 different rosés,
red Gaillac from the South-West and a
range of Languedoc reds.*

- 1999 Jurançon Moelleux, Ballet
  d'Octobre, Domaine Cauhapé,
  South-West France, £7.75 (37.5 cl)
- 2001 Coteaux du Languedoc-Pic St-
  Loup, Vieilles Vignes, Château de
  Lancyre, Languedoc, France, £8.80
- 2003 Coteaux du Languedoc Pic St-
  Loup Rosé, Bergerie de l'Hortus,
  Languedoc, France, £8.80
- Anjou Méthode Traditionelle Rouge,
  Domaine de Montgilet, Loire Valley,
  France, £9.30

Direct Wine Shipments

5–7 Corporation Square, Belfast,
N Ireland BT1 3AJ (028) 9050 8000
FAX (028) 9050 8004
E-MAIL shop@directwine.co.uk
WEBSITE www.directwine.co.uk
HOURS Mon–Fri 9–6.30 (Thur 10–8),
Sat 9.30–5.30 **CARDS** Access,
MasterCard, Switch, Visa **DISCOUNTS**

10% in the form of complementary
wine with each case **DELIVERY** Free N
Ireland 1 case or more, variable
delivery charge for UK mainland
depending on customer spend
EN PRIMEUR Bordeaux, Burgundy,
Rhône. **C M T**
✪ **Star attractions** *Rhône, Spain,
Australia and Burgundy look
outstanding, Italy and Germany are
not far behind, and from Chile there's
Santa Rita and Miguel Torres. In fact
there's good stuff from pretty well
everywhere. Wine courses, tastings and
expert advice.*

- 2004 Caprice des Colombelles
  Colombard, Producteurs Plaimont,
  South-West France, £5.99
- 2001 Côtes du Rhône Villages-
  Rasteau, Domaine Santa Duc, Rhône
  Valley, France, £9.99
- 2003 Priorat, Creu Celta, Viñedos
  McAlindon e Hijos, Cataluña, Spain,
  £14.99
- 2003 St-Aubin Premier Cru Les
  Cortons, Domaine Larue, Burgundy,
  France, £16.99

Nick Dobson Wines

38 Crail Close, Wokingham, Berkshire
RG41 2PZ (01189) 771545
FAX (0870) 460 2358
E-MAIL
nick.dobson@nickdobsonwines.co.uk
WEBSITE www.nickdobsonwines.co.uk
HOURS Mon–Sat 9–5 **CARDS** Access,
MasterCard, Switch, Visa **DELIVERY** £7
1 case, £5.50 2 or more cases. **M T**
✪ **Star attractions** *Mail order outfit
specializing in wines from Switzerland,*

Austria and Beaujolais. It's really encouraging to find an independent company seeking out jewels that are usually hidden to the British consumer. Choose a pre-mixed case or create your own from a terrific list that includes plenty of wines at under £10.

- **2004 Graacher Domprobst Riesling Kabinett Trocken, Weingut Philipps-Eckstein, Mosel, Germany, £8.95**
- **2005 Fendant de Chamoson, F & D Giroud, Valais, Switzerland, £9.95**
- **2004 Fleurie, Grille Midi Vieilles Vignes, Domaine La Madone, Beaujolais, France, £12.95**
- **2003 Grüner Veltliner Alte Reben, Nigl, Kremstal, Austria, £17.50**

Domaine Direct

8 Cynthia Street, London N1 9JF (020) 7837 1142 **FAX** (020) 7837 8605 **E-MAIL** mail@domainedirect.co.uk **WEBSITE** www.domainedirect.co.uk **HOURS** 8.30–6 or answering machine **CARDS** MasterCard, Switch, Visa **DELIVERY** Free London; elsewhere in UK mainland 1 case £12, 2 cases £16.90, or more free **MINIMUM ORDER** 1 mixed case **EN PRIMEUR** Burgundy. M T
✪ Star attractions *Sensational Burgundy list. From Australia you'll find wines from the Leeuwin Estate; from California there's Spottswoode, Etude, Nalle and Ridge.*

- **2003 Savigny-lès-Beaune Rouge, Jean-Marc Pavelot, Burgundy, France, £13.57**
- **2004 St-Aubin Blanc Premier Cru Les Frionnes, Hubert et Olivier Lamy, Burgundy, France, £17.61**

- **2001 Pinot Noir Carneros, Etude, California, USA, £24.67**
- **2003 Chardonnay Art Series, Leeuwin Estate, Margaret River, Western Australia, £34.66**

Farr Vintners

220 Queenstown Road, Battersea, London SW8 4LP (020) 7821 2000 **FAX** (020) 7821 2020 **E-MAIL** sales@farrvintners.com **WEBSITE** www.farrvintners.com **HOURS** Mon–Fri 10–6 **CARDS** Access, Mastercard, Switch, Visa **DELIVERY** London £1 per case (min £14); elsewhere at cost **MINIMUM ORDER** £500 + VAT **EN PRIMEUR** Bordeaux. C M T
✪ Star attractions *A fantastic list of the world's finest wines. The majority is Bordeaux, but you'll also find top stuff and older vintages of white Burgundy and red Rhône, Italy (Gaja, Sassicaia), Australia and California (Araujo, Dominus).*

- **2001 Château Villa Bel-Air, Graves, Bordeaux, France, £8.80**
- **2003 Gnarly Dudes Shiraz, Two Hands, South Australia £11.26**
- **1999 Vacqueyras Vieilles Vignes, Tardieu-Laurent, Rhône Valley, France, £19.09**
- **1990 Château du Tertre, Margaux, Bordeaux, France, £27.37**

Fine Wines of New Zealand

MAIL ORDER PO Box 476, London NW5 2NZ (020) 7482 0093 **FAX** (020) 7267 8400 **E-MAIL** sales@fwnz.co.uk or info@fwnz.co.uk **WEBSITE**

www.fwnz.co.uk **HOURS** Mon–Sat 9–6
CARDS Access, MasterCard, Switch, Visa
DISCOUNTS 6 or more cases **DELIVERY**
Free for 1 mixed case or more UK
mainland **MINIMUM ORDER** 1 mixed
case. **M**
○ Star attractions *Some great New
Zealand wines: Ata Rangi, Hunter's,
Kumeu River, Pegasus Bay, Te Motu,
Aotea, Redwood Valley, plus Bordeaux-
style Larose from Stonyridge.*
• 2004 Pinot Noir, Hunter's
  Marlborough, New Zealand, £12.00
• 2004 Pinot Gris Lismore, Ata Rangi,
  Wairarapa, New Zealand, £12.90
• 2005 Sauvignon Blanc-Semillon,
  Pegasus Bay, Waipara, New Zealand,
  £14.00
• 2003 Syrah, Winemaker's Collection,
  Aotea, New Zealand, £15.00

Irma Fingal-Rock

64 Monnow Street, Monmouth NP25
3EN **TEL & FAX** 01600 712372
E-MAIL tom@pinotnoir.co.uk
WEBSITE www.pinotnoir.co.uk
HOURS Mon 9.30–1.30, Thurs & Fri
9.30–5.30, Sat 9.30–5 **CARDS**
MasterCard, Switch, Visa **DISCOUNTS** 5%
for at least 12 bottles collected from
shop, 7.5% for collected orders over
£500, 10% for collected orders over
£1,200 **DELIVERY** Free locally (within 30
miles); orders further afield free if over
£100. **G M T**
○ Star attractions *A merchant who
knows the highways and byways of
French wine better than most. The list's
great strength is Burgundy, from some
very good growers and priced between*

*£6 and £34. Small but tempting
selections from other French regions, as
well as Italy, Spain, Portugal and the New
World. Two local (yes, Welsh) producers
are also represented.*
• 2000 Douro, Vega, DFJ Vinhos,
  Portugal, £6.50
• 2002 Bourgogne Ordinaire Pinot Noir,
  Clos Toulmin, Burgundy, France, £8.55
• 2002 Pinot Noir, Bannockburn,
  Victoria, Australia, £16.85
• 2001 Château Haut-Bages-Libéral,
  Pauillac, Bordeaux, France, £22.50

Flagship Wines

417 Hatfield Road, St Albans,
Hertfordshire AL4 0XP (01727) 865309
E-MAIL info@flagshipwines.co.uk
WEBSITE www.flagshipwines.co.uk
HOURS Tues–Thurs 11–6, Fri 11–7.30, Sat
10–6 **CARDS** MasterCard, Switch, Visa
DELIVERY Free within 5 miles of St
Albans; £3.50 in Herts, Beds, Bucks; £7.50
per case elsewhere in UK mainland.
G M T
○ Star attractions *Well-run independent
whose prices can match those of the
supermarkets – and you get the friendly,
well-informed advice of boss Julia Jenkins
thrown in. Good Chilean and French
basics, interesting Italians, and strongest
in Spain, Australia and Portugal.*
• 2004 Cheverny, Domaine des
  Marnières, Loire Valley, France, £7.49
• 2002 Cigales Museum Crianza, Baron
  de Ley, Castilla y León, Spain, £8.49
• 2004 Santorini, Hatzidakis, Greece,
  £9.25
• 2001 Il Briccone, Primo Estate,
  Adelaide Plains, South Australia, £9.89

Le Fleming Wines

MAIL ORDER 19 Spenser Road,
Harpenden, Hertfordshire AL5 5NW
(01582) 760125 **E-MAIL** cherry@
leflemingwines.co.uk **WEBSITE**
www.leflemingwines.co.uk
HOURS 24-hour answering machine
DISCOUNTS 5% on large orders **DELIVERY**
Free locally **MINIMUM ORDER** 1 case. **G**
✪ **Star attractions** *Australia looks terrific
here, with lots of serious and not so
serious wines. South Africa, too, is good,
with wines from Hamilton Russell and
Thelema. The list is basically the New
World and France, plus short but focused
selections from Italy and Spain.*
- **2002 Tryst, Nepenthe, Adelaide Hills,
  South Australia, £6.50**
- **2002 Merlot Reserve, Montgras, Chile,
  £7.69**
- **2003 Sauvignon Blanc, Thelema
  Mountain Vineyard, Stellenbosch,
  South Africa, £10.54**
- **1999 Alsace Riesling Turkheim,
  Domaine Zind-Humbrecht, Alsace,
  France, £16.24**

The Flying Corkscrew

Leighton Buzzard Road, Water End,
Nr Hemel Hempstead, Hertfordshire
HP1 3BD
(01442) 412311 **FAX** (01442) 412313
E-MAIL sales@flyingcorkscrew.com
WEBSITE www.flyingcorkscrew.com
HOURS Mon–Wed 10–7, Thurs–Fri 10–8,
Sat 10–7, Sun 11–5 **CARDS** AmEx,
MasterCard, Switch, Visa **DISCOUNTS**
10% on case **DELIVERY** Free locally, £15
per case UK mainland, free on online
orders over £100 **G M T**

THE FLYING CORKSCREW
THE VERY INDEPENDENT WINE MERCHANT

Independent
WINE MERCHANT OF THE YEAR 2003

Central England
WINE MERCHANT OF THE YEAR 2003

Runner up – Eastern England
WINE MERCHANT OF THE YEAR 2004

We have loads of parking.
Comfy area with wine reference library
and toys to amuse the kids!

Our knowledgeable staff can give you
advice about wines from all
over the world.
Buy by the bottle or by the case.
10% case discount
(12 bottles – may be mixed)

Imported bottled beers
Gift ideas, chocolates, condiments etc.
Mail order - national
delivery available.

Leighton Buzzard Road, Water End
Nr. Hemel Hempstead HP1 3BD
Tel: 01442 412311
info@flyingcorkscrew.com
www.flyingcorkscrew.com

✪ **Star attractions** *A very stylish shop with friendly, knowledgeable staff and an extensive and imaginative range of wines. If you're local, look out for tastings led by experts and winemakers such as Randall Grahm of Bonny Doon, and Douro specialist Dirk Niepoort.*
- 2005 Sauvignon Blanc, Bird in Hand, Adelaide Hills, South Australia, £9.23
- 2004 Quincy, Domaine des Ballandors, Loire Valley, France, £9.45
- 2004 Pinot Gris, Isabel Estate, Marlborough, New Zealand, £11.03
- 2002 Gran Lurton Cabernet Sauvignon, Bodegas J & F Lurton, Mendoza, Argentina, £11.48

Fortnum & Mason

181 Piccadilly, London W1A 1ER (020) 7734 8040 **FAX** (020) 7437 3278 **ORDERING LINE** 0845 300 1707 **E-MAIL** info@fortnumandmason. co.uk **WEBSITE** www.fortnumand mason.co.uk **HOURS** Mon–Sat 10–6.30, Sun 12–6 (Food Hall and Patio Restaurant only) **CARDS** AmEx, Diners, MasterCard, Switch, Visa **DISCOUNTS** 1 free bottle per unmixed dozen **DELIVERY** £7 per delivery address **EN PRIMEUR** Bordeaux. **M T**
✪ **Star attractions** *Champagne, Bordeaux and Burgundy are the leaders of a very smart pack, but there are names to impress from just about everywhere, including the cream of the crop from Italy, Germany, Australia, New Zealand, South Africa and California. Impeccably sourced own-label range.*
- 2004 Riesling Kabinett, Max Ferd Richter, Mosel, Germany, £8.90
- 2003 Shiraz, Torbreck, Barossa Valley, South Australia, £12.50
- Champagne Rosé, Billecart-Salmon, Champagne, France, £12.50 (half)
- 2001 Chianti Classico, Riecine, Tuscany, Italy, £15.50

Friarwood

26 New King's Road, London SW6 4ST (020) 7736 2628 **FAX** (020) 7731 0411 • 16 Dock St, Leith, Edinburgh, EH6 6EY (0131) 554 4159 **FAX** (0131) 554 6703 **E-MAIL** sales@friarwood.com; edinburgh@friarwood.com **WEBSITE** www.friarwood.com **HOURS** Mon–Sat 10–7 **CARDS** AmEx, Diners, MasterCard, Switch, Visa, Solo, Electron **DISCOUNTS** 5% on mixed cases, 10% unmixed **DELIVERY** (London) Free within M25 and on orders over £250 in mainland UK (Edinburgh) free locally and for 2 cases or more elsewhere (under 2 cases at cost) **EN PRIMEUR** Bordeaux. **C G M T**
✪ **Star attractions** *The focus is Bordeaux, including a good selection of petits châteaux as well as classed growths; vintages available go back to 1982, or 1967 for Yquem. Burgundy and other French regions are strong too, but this year I've been particularly impressed by the wines they've chosen from independent producers in Chile (Haras de Pirque), New Zealand (Clifford Bay) and Australia (Belgravia). Armagnacs back to 1940 round off this imaginative list.*
- 2003 Festivo Malbec, Bodega Monteviejo, Uco Valley, Mendoza, Argentina, £6.50

- 2004 Single Vineyard Riesling, Clifford Bay Estate, Marlborough, New Zealand, £9.95
- 2003 Château Fonbel, St-Émilion Grand Cru, Bordeaux, France, £13.50
- 2003 Petit Manseng Sec, Vin de Pays des Pyrénées-Atlantiques, Domaine de Cabidos, South-West France, £15.50

Gauntleys

4 High Street, Exchange Arcade, Nottingham NG1 2ET (0115) 911 0555 **FAX** (0115) 911 0557 **E-MAIL** rhone@gauntleywine.com **WEBSITE** www.gauntleywine.com **HOURS** Mon–Sat 9–5.30 **CARDS** MasterCard, Switch, Visa **DELIVERY** Free within Nottingham area, otherwise 1–3 cases £9.50, 4 or more cases free **MINIMUM ORDER** 1 case **EN PRIMEUR** Alsace, Burgundy, Italy, Loire, Rhône, southern France, Spain. **M T**
✪ **Star attractions** *They've won awards for their Rhône list, but it doesn't stop there: Alsace, Loire, Burgundy, southern France, Spain and Italy are all top-notch. A few Bordeaux wines. Champagne is Vilmart's wonderfully big, rich wines.*

- 2003 Bourgogne Rouge, Domaine Dureuil-Janthial, Burgundy, France, £9.49
- 2003 Savennières, Château d'Épiré, Loire Valley, France, £10.57
- 2001 Côtes du Rhône Coudoulet Rouge, Château Beaucastel, Rhône Valley, France, £12.23
- 1998 Alsace Riesling Rangen de Thann, Clos St-Théobald, Vendange Tardive, Domaine Schoffit, Alsace, France £25.26

Goedhuis & Co

6 Rudolf Place, Miles Street, London SW8 1RP (020) 7793 7900 **FAX** (020) 7793 7170 **E-MAIL** sales@goedhuis.com **WEBSITE** www.goedhuis.com **HOURS** Mon–Fri 9–5.30 **CARDS** AmEx, MasterCard, Switch, Visa **DELIVERY** Free 3 cases or more, otherwise £15 England, elsewhere at cost **MINIMUM ORDER** 1 unmixed case **EN PRIMEUR** Bordeaux, Burgundy, Rhône. **C G M T**
✪ **Star attractions** *Fine wine specialist. Bordeaux, Burgundy and the Rhône are the core of the list, but everything is good, and if you buy your everyday wines here you'll get very good quality, plus friendly, expert advice.*

- 2004 Montepulciano d'Abruzzo, La Salare, Abruzzo, Italy, £4.91
- 2002 St-Aubin Premier Cru, Marc Colin, Burgundy, France, £10.41
- 2003 Cornas, Rochepertuis, Jean Lionnet, Rhône Valley, France, £13.25
- 2003 La Réserve de Léoville-Barton St-Julien, Château Léoville-Barton, Bordeaux, France, £13.75

Great Northern Wine

The Warehouse, Blossomgate, Ripon, N. Yorks HG4 2AJ (01765) 606767 **FAX** (01765) 609151 **E-MAIL** info@greatnorthern wine.com **HOURS** Tues–Fri 9–6, Sat 9–5.30 **CARDS** AmEx, MasterCard, Switch, Visa **DISCOUNTS** 10% on case quantities **DELIVERY** Free locally, elsewhere at cost **EN PRIMEUR** Bordeaux. **G M T**
✪ **Star attractions** *A sound list that mixes well-known and less familiar*

names, specializing in Old World wines, especially Portugal and Spain, while New World wines concentrate on South America.
- 2004 Sangiovese-Bonarda, Santa Rosa, Mendoza, Argentina, £5.49
- 2005 Garnacha, Artazuri, Navarra, Spain, £6.99
- 2005 Sauvignon Blanc, El Delirio Reserve, Botalcura, Casablanca Valley, Chile, £7.99
- 1999 Douro Reserva, Quinta do Portal, Douro, Portugal, £9.99

Great Western Wine

The Wine Warehouse, Wells Road, Bath BA2 3AP (01225) 322810 (shop) or (01225) 322800 (office) FAX (01225) 442139 E-MAIL retail@greatwesternwine.co.uk WEBSITE www.greatwesternwine. co.uk HOURS Mon–Fri 10–7, Sat 10–6 CARDS AmEx, MasterCard, Switch, Visa DISCOUNTS Negotiable DELIVERY £8.95 per case, free over £200 MINIMUM ORDER 1 mixed case EN PRIMEUR Australia, Bordeaux, Burgundy, Rioja. C G M T
○ Star attractions *Great Western brings in wines from individual growers around the world. Highlights include Bonnefond and Gilles Robin from the Rhône, Glaetzer and Heartland from Australia, Carrick from New Zealand – and this year they've ventured as far as Uruguay. Frequent events and tastings.*
- 2003 Joffre e Hijas Grand Malbec, RJ Viñedos, Uco Valley, Mendoza, Argentina, £7.95
- 2005 Viognier-Pinot Gris, Heartland, Langhorne Creek, South Australia, £8.95
- 2004 Jurançon Sec, Cuvée Casterasses, Domaine Bru-Baché, South-West France, £9.95
- 2002 Saumur Blanc, Château du Hureau, Loire Valley, France, £10.95

Peter Green & Co

37A/B Warrender Park Road, Edinburgh EH9 1HJ (0131) 229 5925 **FAX** (0131) 229 0606

E-MAIL shop@petergreenwines.com **HOURS** Tues–Thur 10–6.30, Fri 10–7.30, Sat 10–6.30

CARDS MasterCard, Switch, Visa **DISCOUNTS** 5% on unmixed half-dozens **DELIVERY** Free in Edinburgh **MINIMUM ORDER** (For delivery) 1 case. G T

✪ Star attractions *Extensive, well-chosen and adventurous list from all over the world.*

- **2005 Old Winery Verdelho, Tyrrell's, New South Wales, Australia, £6.75**
- **2002 Dry Furmint Mandolás, Bodegas Oremus, Tokaj, Hungary, £7.95**
- **2003 Douro, Quinto do Crasto, Douro, Portugal, £8.50**
- **2004 Zweigelt, Umathum, Burgenland, Austria, £10.50**

Green & Blue

38 Lordship Lane, East Dulwich, London, SE22 8HJ (020) 8693 9250 **FAX** (020) 8693 9260

E-MAIL info@greenandbluewines.com **HOURS** Mon–Tues 11–10, Wed–Sat 11–11, Sun 12–8 **CARDS** Delta, MasterCard, Switch, Visa **DISCOUNTS** 5% on unmixed half-dozens **DELIVERY** Free locally over £75, otherwise £15 outside London dependent on weight, £10 under £150. G T

✪ Star attractions *A great local wine retailer with a tempting list full of unusual, intriguing wines you really want to drink – and you can try them on the spot, in the wine bar, which serves tapas-style food. The staff are friendly and knowledgeable, and there's a waiting list for the popular tutored tastings.*

- **2004 Pacherenc du Vic-Bilh Sec, Domaine Berthoumieu, South-West France, £8.85**
- **2004 Gamay Vinifera, Domaine Henry Marionnet, Loire Valley, France, £10.75**
- **2002 Isolation Ridge Shiraz, Frankland Estate, Frankland River, Western Australia, £12.65**
- **2003 Non Confunditur, Argiano, Tuscany, Italy, £13.50**

Halifax Wine Company

18 Prescott Street, Halifax, West Yorkshire HX1 2LG (01422) 256333 **E-MAIL** andy@halifaxwinecompany.com **WEBSITE** www.halifaxwinecompany. com **HOURS** Tues–Fri 9.30–6, Sat 9–5 **CARDS** Switch, Access, MasterCard, Visa **DISCOUNTS** 8% on 12 bottles or more for personal callers to the shop, 5% and free delivery online orders above £350

DELIVERY Free locally on orders over £95; rest of UK mainland, £9.95 on online orders £100 or less, £4.95 orders up to £150, free over £150. G M T

✪ Star attractions *Exciting and extremely wide-ranging list: I don't know of many places you'd find 145 wines from Portugal and almost 100 from Spain; there are even 9 wines from Greece. Champagnes include Billecart-Salmon, and other regions of France are just as carefully chosen.*

- **2004 Cabernet-Shiraz, Simonsig Estate, Stellenbosch, South Africa, £5.95**
- **2001 Dão Quinta da Garrida, Caves Aliança, Dão, Portugal, £7.95**
- **2003 Samos Grand Cru, Samos Co-op, Samos, Greece, £7.95**
- **2003 Tokay Pinot Gris Reserve, Cave de Turckheim, Alsace, France, £7.95**

Handford Wines

12 Portland Road, Holland Park, London W11 4LE (020) 7221 9614
• 105 Old Brompton Road, South Kensington, London SW7 3LE (020) 7589 6113 **FAX** (020) 7581 2983 **E-MAIL** wine@handford.net **WEBSITE** www.handford.net **HOURS** Mon–Sat 10–8.30 **CARDS** AmEx, MasterCard, Visa **DISCOUNTS** 5% on mixed cases **DELIVERY** £8.25 for orders under £150 within UK. **EN PRIMEUR** Bordeaux **G M T**
✪ Star attractions *Two delightful London shops, absolutely packed with the sort of wines I really want to drink.*
- **2002 Chardonnay Reserve, Seresin Estate, Marlborough, New Zealand, £12.99**
- **2003 Château le Boscq, St-Estèphe, Bordeaux, France, £17.99**
- **2001 Barbera d'Asti Bricco dell'Uccellone, Braida, Piedmont, Italy, £27.95**
- **2003 Merlot, Shafer Vineyards, Napa Valley, California, USA, £33.95**

Roger Harris Wines

Loke Farm, Weston Longville, Norfolk NR9 5LG (01603) 880171 **FAX** (01603) 880291 **E-MAIL** sales@rogerharriswines.co.uk **WEBSITE** www.rogerharris wines.co.uk **HOURS** Mon–Fri 9–5 **CARDS** AmEx, MasterCard, Visa **DELIVERY** next working day UK mainland, £3 for orders up to £110, £2 up to £160, free over £160 **MINIMUM ORDER** 1 mixed case. **M**
✪ Star attractions *Beaujolais-loving family business – Britain's acknowledged experts in this area. The list also ventures into the Mâconnais, Champagne and the south of France.*
- **2005 Beaujolais, Domaine Chatelus de la Roche, Burgundy, France, £7.10**
- **2005 Beaujolais-Villages, Château de Belleverne, Burgundy, France £7.25**
- **2005 St-Véran Les Monts, Cave de Prissé, Burgundy, £9.30**
- **2005 Chiroubles, Gérard-Roger Méziat, Burgundy, France, £9.95**

Harvey Nichols

109–125 Knightsbridge, London SW1X 7RJ (020) 7235 5000 • The Mailbox, 31–32 Wharfside Street, Birmingham B1 1RE (0121) 616 6000 • 30–34 St Andrew Square, Edinburgh EH2 3AD (0131) 524 8388 • 107–111 Briggate, Leeds LS1 6AZ (0113) 204 8888 • 21 New Cathedral Street, Manchester M3 1RE (0161) 828 8888 **E-MAIL** wineshop@harveynichols.com **WEBSITE** www.harveynichols.com **HOURS** (London) Mon–Fri 10–8, Sat 10–7, Sun 12–6 (Birmingham) Mon–

Wed 10–6, Thurs 10–8,
Fri–Sat 10–7, Sun 11–5 (Edinburgh)
Mon–Wed 10–6, Thurs 10–8,
Fri, Sat 10–7, Sun 11–5 (Leeds)
Mon–Wed 10–6, Thurs–Fri 10–7,
Sat 9–7, Sun 12–6 (Manchester) Mon,
Wed, Fri 10–7, Thurs 10–8,
Sat 9–7, Sun 12–6 CARDS AmEx,
MasterCard, Switch, Visa.

✪ Star attractions *Top names from France, Italy and California, especially for sought-after producers such as Dalla Valle, Ridge and Stag's Leap.*

• 2001 La Grola, Allegrini, Veneto, Italy, £14.00
• 2003 Zinfandel, Seghesio, Sonoma County, California, USA, £15.00
• 2001 Moonambel Chardonnay, Dalwhinnie, Pyrenees, Victoria, Australia, £16.75
• NV Champagne Terre de Vertus, Blanc de Blancs, Larmandier Bernier, Champagne, France, £24.00

Haynes Hanson & Clark

Sheep Street, Stow-on-the-Wold, Glos GL54 1AA (01451) 870808
FAX (01451) 870508 • 25 Eccleston Street, London SW1W 9NP (020) 7259 0102 FAX (020) 7259 0103
E-MAIL stow@hhandc.co.uk or london@hhandc.co.uk
WEBSITE www.hhandc.co.uk
HOURS (Stow) Mon–Fri 9–6, Sat 9–5.30 (London) Mon–Fri 9–7 CARDS Access, AmEx, MasterCard, Switch, Visa
DISCOUNTS 10% unsplit case DELIVERY Free central London and Glos for 1 case or more; elsewhere 1 case £14.50, 2–3 cases £8.90 per case, 4 or more cases

£7.25 per case, free orders over £650
EN PRIMEUR Bordeaux, Burgundy.
G M T

✪ Star attractions *HH&C's preference is for subtle, elegant wines, so you won't find too many hefty blockbusters here. It's most famous for Burgundy – but there are also lovely wines from the Loire, Alsace and Rhône, Italy, Spain, Australia, New Zealand and California. Bordeaux is chosen to suit every pocket. Their house Champagne, Pierre Vaudon, is invariably a winner.*

• 2004 Côtes de St-Mont Blanc, Producteurs Plaimont, South-West France, £5.10
• 2004 Bourgogne Blanc, Les Grandes Coutures, Franck Grux, Burgundy, France, £10.50
• 2004 Salia, Finca Sandoval, Victor de la Serna, Manchuela, Spain, £12.30
• 2002 Monthélie Rouge Premier Cru Les Duresses, Annick Parent, Burgundy, France, £19.35

Hedley Wright

11 Twyford Centre, London Road, Bishop's Stortford, Herts CM23 3YT (01279) 465818 FAX (01279) 465819
• Wyevale Garden Centre, Cambridge Road, Hitchin, Herts, SG4 0JT (01462) 431110 FAX (01462) 422983
E-MAIL sales@hedleywright.co.uk
WEBSITE www.hedleywright.co.uk
HOURS Mon–Wed 9–6, Thur–Fri 9–7, Sat 10–6; Hitchin Mon–Wed 11–7, Thur–Fri 11–8, Sat 11–7, Sun 11–5 CARDS AmEx, MasterCard, Switch, Visa
DELIVERY £5 per delivery, free for orders over £100 MINIMUM ORDER 1 mixed

case **EN PRIMEUR** Bordeaux, Chile, Germany, Port. **C G M T**

○ **Star attractions** *A good all-round list that does justice to most French regions. Italy, something of a speciality, has wines from the likes of Pieropan, Allegrini and Le Pupille. Portugal, Spain, South Africa, New Zealand and Australia are packed with interesting wines, and Chile majors on the wines of Montes.*

- **2005 Sauvignon Blanc, Jackson Estate, Marlborough, New Zealand, £9.99**
- **2003 Alpha Chardonnay, Montes, Casablanca Valley, Chile, £10.95**
- **2004 Mangan, Cullen, Margaret River, Western Australia, £17.95**
- **2003 Burdese, Planeta, Sicily, Italy, £19.95**

Hicks & Don

4 Old Station Yard, Edington, Westbury, Wiltshire BA13 4NT (01380) 831234 **FAX** (01380) 831010

• Park House, North Elmham, Dereham, Norfolk NR20 5JY (01362) 668571 **FAX** (01362) 668573

E-MAIL mailbox@hicksanddon.co.uk
WEBSITE www.hicksanddon.co.uk
HOURS Mon–Fri 9–5 **CARDS** MasterCard, Switch, Visa **DISCOUNTS** Negotiable
DELIVERY Free over £100, otherwise £6 per case **MINIMUM ORDER** 1 case
EN PRIMEUR Bordeaux, Burgundy, Chile, Italy, Port, Rhône. **C G M T**

○ **Star attractions** *Subtle, well-made wines that go with food and plenty of good-value wines at around £6 for everyday drinking. The list is set out by style, regardless of origin: white Burgundies and other Chardonnays are followed by Sauvignons and Sémillons, then 'white wines of individuality' – the likes of Vin de Pays des Côtes de Gascogne, Muscadet and Pieropan's Soave Classico – then dessert wines, then Rieslings.*

- **2001 Bergerac, Château Pique-Sègue, South-West France, £7.70**
- **2001 Lirac, Château d'Aquéria, Rhône Valley, France, £9.65**
- **2002 Rully Premier Cru La Pucelle, Domaine Vincent Girardin, Burgundy, France, £14.85**
- **2002 Pinot Noir, Wither Hills, Marlborough, New Zealand, £15.44**

Jeroboams (incorporating Laytons and La Réserve)

HEAD OFFICE 43 Portland Road, London W11 4LJ (020) 7985 1560 **FAX** (020) 7229 1085 **MAIL ORDER** Jeroboams, 6 Pont Street, London SW1X 9EL (020) 7259 6716

FAX (020) 7235 7246
SHOPS 50–52 Elizabeth Street, London SW1W 9PB (020) 7730 8108 • 51 Elizabeth Street, London SW1W 9PP (020) 7823 5623

• 20 Davies Street, London W1K 3DT (020) 7499 1015

• 77–78 Chancery Lane, London WC2A 1AE (020) 7405 0552

• 96 Holland Park Avenue, London W11 3RB (020) 7727 9359

• 6 Pont Street, London SW1X 9EL (020) 7235 1612

• 29 Heath Street, London NW3 6TR (020) 7435 6845

• 56 Walton Street, London SW3 1RB
(020) 7589 2020
• Mr Christian's Delicatessen, 11 Elgin
Crescent, London W11 2JA (020) 7229
0501
• Milroy's of Soho, 3 Greek Street,
London W1D 4NX (020) 7437 2385
E-MAIL sales@jeroboams.co.uk
WEBSITEs www.jeroboams.co.uk
HOURS Offices Mon–Fri 9–6, shops
Mon–Sat 9–7 (may vary)
CARDS AmEx, MasterCard, Switch, Visa
DELIVERY Shops: free for orders of £50
or over in central London; mail order
free for orders over £235, otherwise
£11.75 delivery charge
EN PRIMEUR Bordeaux, Burgundy,
Rhône. **C G M T**
✪ **Star attractions** *Sensibly priced
everyday clarets as well as classed
growths, interesting Burgundies and a
good list from the Rhône. Other regions
of France – including Jura – are covered
too, though in less depth. Italy and
Australia – in particular Western
Australia – are also specialities here. A
wide range of fine foods, especially
cheeses and olive oils, is available in the
shops.*
• **2004 Riesling, Alkoomi, Frankland
River, Western Australia, £7.95**
• **2003 Côtes du Roussillon-Villages,
Les Millères, Domaine Gardiès,
Roussillon, France, £10**
• **2001 Savennières, Clos du Papillon,
Domaine des Baumard, Loire Valley,
France, £13**
• **2003 Syrah-Grenache-Mourvedre,
Sequillo, Sadie Family, Malmesbury,
South Africa, £15.50**

S H Jones

27 High Street, Banbury, Oxfordshire
OX16 5EW (01295) 251179 **FAX** (01295)
272352
• 9 Market Square, Bicester,
Oxfordshire OX26 6AA (01869) 322448
• The Cellar Shop, 2 Riverside, Tramway
Road, Banbury, Oxfordshire OX16 5TU
(01295) 672296 **FAX** (01295) 259560
• 121 Regent Street, Leamington Spa,
Warwickshire CV32 4NU (01926)
315609 **E-MAIL** retail@shjones.com
WEBSITE www.shjones.com
HOURS Mon–Sat 8.30–6 **CARDS**
MasterCard, Switch, Visa
DELIVERY Free within van delivery area
for 1 case or more; 'small charge'
otherwise. Elsewhere £9.50; free for
orders over £250 **EN PRIMEUR**
Bordeaux, Burgundy, Port. **C G M T**
✪ **Star attractions** *Wide-ranging list,
with good Burgundies and Rhônes;
some top-name clarets along with
'everyday' ones at around £10; and a
comprehensive and affordable
selection from across southern France.
Other good stuff from Old and New
World includes Dr Loosen from
Germany and Terrazas de los Andes
from Argentina.*
• **2004 Sauvignon Blanc, Santa Digna,
Miguel Torres, Chile, £5.74**
• **2000 Rasteau Cuvée Prestige,
Domaine la Soumade, Rhône Valley,
France, £9.90**
• **2002/03 Rully Premier Cru, H & P
Jacqueson, Burgundy, France,
£14.07**
• **2001 Merlot, Veenwouden, Paarl,
South Africa, £17.30**

Justerini & Brooks

MAIL ORDER 61 St James's Street, London SW1A 1LZ (020) 7484 6400 **FAX** (020) 7484 6499 **E-MAIL** justorders@justerinis.com **WEBSITE** www.justerinis.com **HOURS** Mon–Fri 9–5.30 **CARDS** AmEx, MasterCard, Switch, Visa **DELIVERY** Free for unmixed cases over £250, otherwise £15 UK mainland **MINIMUM ORDER** 1 case **EN PRIMEUR** Bordeaux, Burgundy, Italy, Rhône, Germany. **C G M T**

✪ **Star attractions** *Superb list of top-quality wines from Europe's classic regions. The New World, though succinct, also has some excellent drinking. And while there are some very classy – and pricy – wines here, you'll find plenty of bottles under £8.50.*

- **2004 Sancerre, Lucien Crochet, Loire Valley, France, £9.31**
- **2004 Chablis, Vincent Dauvissat, Burgundy, France, £11.86**
- **2005 Dry Riesling, Felton Road, Central Otago, New Zealand, £12.91**
- **NV Pomerol, Justerini & Brooks Bordeaux, France, £13.03**

Kwiksave

See Somerfield.

Laithwaites

MAIL ORDER New Aquitaine House, Exeter Way, Theale, Reading, Berks RG7 4PL; **ORDER LINE** 0870 444 8383 **FAX** 0870 444 8182 **E-MAIL** orders@laithwaites.co.uk **WEBSITE** www.laithwaites.co.uk **HOURS** 24-hr answering machine

CARDS AmEx, Diners, MasterCard, Switch, Visa **DISCOUNTS** On unmixed cases of 6 or 12 **DELIVERY** £5.99 per order **EN PRIMEUR** Australia, Bordeaux, Burgundy, Port, Rhône, Rioja. **C M T**

✪ **Star attractions** *Good selection including well-known names and interesting finds. France represents around 50% of the list, but you may also find wines from Uruguay, Mexico or Moldova. The lists are generally the same as those for the Sunday Times Wine Club (see page 207) although some wines are exclusive to each. User-friendly website offers excellent mixed cases, while the bin ends and special offers are good value. Added extras include wine plans offering regular delivery of hand-picked cases, and a comprehensive database for matching wine and food – from cold fresh prawns to kangaroo steaks!*

- **2004 Tempranillo, La Boqueria, Cataluña, Spain, £5.00**
- **2004 Gran Tarapacá Carmenère, Viña Tarapaca, Central Valley, Chile, £7.00**
- **2004 Montepulciano d'Abruzzo Casale Vecchio, Farnese, Abruzzo, Italy, £9.00**
- **2003 Pinot Noir, Felton Road, Central Otago, New Zealand, £19.99**

The Lay & Wheeler Group

Holton Park, Holton St Mary, Suffolk CO7 6NN 0845 330 1855 **FAX** 0845 330 4095 **E-MAIL** sales@laywheeler. com **WEBSITE** www.laywheeler.com **HOURS** (order office) Mon–Fri 8.30–5.30, Sat 9–1 **CARDS** AmEx, MasterCard, Switch, Visa **DELIVERY** £9.95; free for orders over £200 **EN PRIMEUR** Alsace, Australia,

Bordeaux, Burgundy, California, Champagne, Germany, Italy, Loire, Rhône, Spain. **C G M T**

✪ **Star attractions** *There's enough first-class Bordeaux and Burgundy to satisfy the most demanding drinker here; indeed everything is excellent. A must-have list – and if you really can't make up your mind, their mixed cases are excellent too.*

- Asti Dolce, Ca' Solare, Piedmont, Italy, £5.95
- 2000 Château Hanteillan, Haut-Médoc, Bordeaux, France, £9.95
- 2004 Monferrato Rosso, Il Bacialé, Braida, Piedmont, Italy, £12.45
- 2002 Chassagne-Montrachet Premier Cru Morgeot-Clos Pitois, Domaine Roger Belland, Burgundy, France, £27.95

Laymont & Shaw

The Old Chapel, Millpool, Truro, Cornwall TR1 1EX (01872) 270545
FAX (01872) 223005 **E-MAIL** info@laymont-shaw.co.uk
WEBSITE www.laymont-shaw.co.uk
HOURS Mon–Fri 9–5 **CARDS** MasterCard, Switch, Visa **DISCOUNTS** £5 per case if wines collected, also £1 per case for 2 cases, £2 for 3–5, £3 for 6 or more
DELIVERY Free UK mainland **MINIMUM ORDER** 1 mixed case. **C G M T**

✪ **Star attractions** *An excellent, knowledgeable list that specializes in Spain, with Portugal, Uruguay and Argentina also featuring. And when I say 'specializes', I mean that they seek out wines that you won't find in supermarkets because the quantities are too small.*

- 2003 Toro, Miralmonte Tinto Joven, Frutos Villar, Castilla y León, Spain, £5.50
- 2004 Valdeorras Valdesil, Bodegas Valdeorra, Galicia, Spain, £10
- 2002 Vinha Formal, Luis Pato, Portugal, £17
- 1994 Miserere, Costers del Siurana, Priorat, Spain, £24

Laytons

See Jeroboams.

Lea & Sandeman

170 Fulham Road, London SW10 9PR (020) 7244 0522 **FAX** (020) 7244 0533
• 211 Kensington Church Street, London W8 7LX (020) 7221 1982 • 51 High Street, Barnes, London SW13 9LN (020) 8878 8643 **E-MAIL** info@leaandsandeman.co.uk
WEBSITE www.londonfinewine.co.uk
HOURS Mon–Sat 10–8 **CARDS** AmEx, MasterCard, Switch, Visa **DISCOUNTS** 5–15% by case, other discounts on 10 cases or more **DELIVERY** £5 for less than 1 case; free 1 case or more London, and to UK mainland south of Perth on orders over £250
EN PRIMEUR Bordeaux, Burgundy, Italy. **C G M T**

✪ **Star attractions** *Burgundy and Italy take precedence here, and there's a succession of excellent names, chosen with great care. But L&S really do seek out unknown treasures wherever they go, so it's worth taking the time to study the list carefully. Bordeaux has wines at all price levels, and there are short but fascinating ranges from the*

*USA, Spain, Australia's Mornington
Peninsula and Central Otago in New
Zealand. Lea and Sandeman are also
the UK agents for Valdespino sherries.*

- 2005 Grenache-Viognier, Vin de Pays
  des Côtes de Thongue, Domaine la
  Croix Belle, Languedoc, France, £6.95
- 2005 Gruner Veltliner,
  Hochterrassen, Weingut Salomon-
  Undhof, Kremstal, Austria £6.95
- 2004 Lirac La Reine des Bois,
  Domaine de la Mordorée, Rhône
  Valley, France, £15.95
- 2003 Pinot Noir, Rippon, Central
  Otago, New Zealand, £22.75

Liberty Wines

MAIL ORDER Unit D18, New Covent
Garden Food Market, London SW8 5LL
(020) 7720 5350 **FAX** (020) 7720 6158
WEBSITE www.libertywine.co.uk
E-MAIL info@libertywine.co.uk
HOURS Mon–Fri 9–5.30 **CARDS**
MasterCard, Switch, Visa
DELIVERY Free to mainland UK
MINIMUM ORDER 1 mixed case. **M**
✪ Star attractions *Italy rules, with
superb wines and pretty well all the best
producers. Liberty are the UK agents for
most of their producers, so if you're
interested in Italian wines, this should
be your first port of call. Australia
features top producers such as Cullen,
Mount Horrocks, Charles Melton and
Plantagenet to name but a few. France,
Germany, Austria, Spain, California and
South America are not neglected.*

- 2005 Grenache, Willunga 100,
  McLaren Vale, South Australia,
  £7.99

- 2004 Soave Classico Calvarino,
  Pieropan, Veneto, Italy, £13.49
- 2003 La Grola, Allegrini, Veneto, Italy,
  £13.95
- 2004 Flors di Uis, Vie di Romans,
  Friuli-Venezia Giulia, Italy, £20.95

Linlithgow Wines

Crossford, Station Road, Linlithgow,
West Lothian EH49 6BW
TEL & FAX (01506) 848821
E-MAIL jrobmcd@aol.com
HOURS Mon–Fri 9–5.30 (please phone
first) **CARDS** none: cash, cheque or bank
transfer only **DELIVERY** Free locally;
elsewhere in UK £5 for 1 case, £4.50 for
2 or more cases. **G M T**
✪ Star attractions *Specialist in the
south of France – Languedoc, southern
Rhône and Provence – with lots around
£5–7; prices rarely exceed £20, unless
you're tempted by top names such as
Domaine de Trévallon and Châteauneuf-
du-Pape from Domaine Font de
Michelle. There's also a short list of
Chablis and Champagne to offset all
those sunny southern reds.*

- 2003 Carignan Les Centenaires, Vin
  de Pays Catalanes, Domaine Ferrer-
  Ribière, Roussillon, France, £6.37
- 2003 Minervois la Livinière, Clos
  l'Angely, Domaine Piccinini,
  Languedoc, France, £6.67
- 2003 Côtes du Rhône-Villages
  Cairanne, Coteaux des Travers,
  Domaine Brusset, Rhône Valley,
  France, £6.93
- 2000 Chablis, Premier Cru
  Fourchaume, La Chablisienne,
  Burgundy, France, £11.65

O W Loeb & Co

3 Archie Street, off Tanner Street,
London SE1 3JT (020) 7234 0385
FAX (020) 7357 0440 **E-MAIL**
brough@owloeb.com
WEBSITE www.owloeb.com
HOURS Mon–Fri 8.30–5.30 **CARDS**
MasterCard, Switch, Visa **DISCOUNTS** 3
cases and above **DELIVERY** Free 3 cases
or more and on order over £250
MINIMUM ORDER 1 case **EN PRIMEUR**
Burgundy, Bordeaux, Rhône, Germany
(Mosel). **C M T**
✪ Star attractions *Burgundy, the Rhône,
Loire and Germany stand out, with top
producers galore. Then there are Loeb's
new discoveries from Spain and the New
World, especially New Zealand and
South Africa.*
• 2003 Vin de Pays de Vaucluse,
Domaine du Pesquier, Rhône Valley,
France, £6.76
• 2003 Chinon, Cuvée Terroir, Domaine
Charles Joguet, Loire Valley, France,
£9.30
• 2002 St-Véran, Les Rochats, Domaine
de la Croix Senaillet, Burgundy,
France, £11.55
• 1998 Dorsheimer Pittermänchen
Riesling Spätlese, Schlossgut Diel,
Nahe, Germany, £15.86

Maison du Vin

Moor Hill, Hawkhurst, Kent TN18 4PF
(01580) 753487 **FAX** (01580) 755627 **E-
MAIL** kvgriffin@aol.com
WEBSITE www.maison-du-vin.co.uk
HOURS Mon 10–4, Tues, Thur, Fri 10–5,
Sat 10–6, Sun 12–4 **CARDS** AmEx,
Access, MasterCard, Switch, Visa

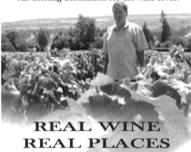

DELIVERY Free locally; UK mainland at cost **EN PRIMEUR** Bordeaux.

C G M T

✪ **Star attractions** *As the name suggests, the focus here is on French wine, at prices ranging from around £6 to £120 for a 1988 Château Latour. Also some thoughtfully chosen Italian wines. There's a monthly themed 'wine school' or you can book personal tutored tastings.*

- 2004 Rolle Vin de Pays des Coteaux de Murviel, Domaine de Coujan, Languedoc-Roussillon, France, £5.99
- 2000 Côtes du Rhône-Villages Sablet, Domaine le Souverain, Rhône Valley, France, £8.99
- 2002 Chablis Vieilles Vignes, la Chablisienne, Burgundy, France, £13.99
- 2001 Nuits-St-Georges Premier Cru les St-George, Domaine Liger-Belair, Burgundy, France, £18.99

Majestic

(see also Wine and Beer World)
HEAD OFFICE Majestic House, Otterspool Way, Watford, Herts WD25 8WW (01923) 298200
FAX (01923) 819105; 127 stores nationwide **E-MAIL** info@majestic. co.uk **WEBSITE** www.majestic.co.uk
HOURS Mon–Fri 10–8, Sat 9–7, Sun 10–5 (may vary)
CARDS AmEx, Diners, MasterCard, Switch, Visa
DELIVERY Free UK mainland
MINIMUM ORDER 1 mixed case
EN PRIMEUR Bordeaux, Port. **G M T**
✪ **Star attractions** *This has long been*

one of the best places to come for Champagne, with a good range and good discounts for buying in quantity. Elsewhere you'll find genuine stars rubbing shoulders with some interesting oddballs, and there always seem to be really worthwhile special offers. Loads of reasonably priced stuff, epecially from France and most of the New World.

- 2005 Vin de Pays du Comté Tolosan, Cuvée de Richard Blanc, Languedoc, France, £3.15
- 2005 Syrah Vin de Pays d'Oc, Camplazens, Languedoc-Roussillon, France, £6.49
- 2005 Sauvignon Blanc, Montes Limited Selection, Viña Montes, Leyda Valley, Chile, £7.99
- 1999 Château La Dominique, St-Émilion Grand Cru Classé, Bordeaux, France, £19.99

Marks & Spencer

HEAD OFFICE Waterside House, 35 North Wharf Road, London W2 1NW (020) 7935 4422 **FAX** (020) 7487 2679; 350 licensed stores **WEBSITE** www.marksandspencer.com
HOURS Variable **DISCOUNTS** Variable, Wine of the Month, 12 bottles for the price of 11. **T**
✪ **Star attractions** *M&S has clearly been beavering away in vineyards around the world, working with top producers to create their own-label wines, and the list is looking more impressive than ever this year.*

- 2005 Puglia Rosso, (Casa Girelli), Puglia, Italy, £5.49

Come and *taste* the Majestic experience

AWARD WINNING SERVICE
from friendly, knowledgeable staff

100s OF WINES ON SPECIAL OFFER

FREE TASTING
Wines open to taste, all day, every day

FREE HOME DELIVERY
of a mixed case of wine *anywhere* in mainland UK*

FINE WINES
Download price list from **majestic.co.uk/finewine**

NATIONWIDE STORES
129 stores across the UK, open 7 days a week

ORDER ONLINE
Visit Majestic Online **majestic.co.uk**

E-mail us at info@majestic.co.uk

* We're sorry that this excludes the Scottish Islands, Northern Ireland, Isles of Scilly and the Isle of Man. Mail order deliveries to these locations can be arranged for a nominal charge. Please call our Mail Order department on 01727 847935 for further information. We do not deliver to the Channel Islands and destinations outside of the UK.

majestic.co.uk

Visiting France?

Wine & Beer World is Majestic Wine Warehouses French operation offering the best value wines in the Channel ports. Wines start from only 99p and include many Majestic favourites at astonishingly low prices. With more than 100 products on Special Offer you can expect to save up to 60% on the UK price of your drinks bill. We offer a pre-ordering service, free tasting and a friendly, knowledgeable English speaking service.

Pre-order online via **wineandbeer.co.uk** or call 01923 298297 for a **free** price list and directions to our **Calais**, **Coquelles** and **Cherbourg** stores.

- 2005 Semillon-Sauvignon Blanc, (Evans & Tate), Margaret River, Western Australia, £7.99
- 1999 Muskateller Eiswein, Darting Estate, Pfalz, Germany, £13.00 (half)
- NV Champagne Blanc de Blancs Brut, De Saint Gall, Champagne, France, £19.99

Martinez Wines

35 The Grove, Ilkley, Leeds, W. Yorks LS29 9NJ (01943) 600000 **FAX** 0870 922 3940 **E-MAIL** julian-@martinez. co.uk **WEBSITE** www.martinez.co.uk **HOURS** Sun 12–6, Mon–Wed 10–8, Thurs–Fri 10–9, Sat 9.30–6 **CARDS** AmEx, MasterCard, Switch, Visa **DISCOUNTS** 5% on 6 bottles or more, 10% off orders over £150 **DELIVERY** Free local delivery, otherwise £10 per case mainland UK **EN PRIMEUR** Bordeaux, Burgundy. **C G M T**
✪ **Star attractions** *Starting at the beginning, Alsace and Beaujolais look spot-on. Bordeaux, Burgundy and Rhône are carefully chosen, and so I would trust their selections from other regions – sweeties and fortifieds are strong, too.*

- Jurançon Sec, Chant des Vignes, Domaine Cauhaupé, South-West France, £11.99
- 2003 Chianti Classico, Isole e Olena, Tuscany, Italy, £14.99
- 2000 Nine Popes, Charles Melton, Barossa Valley, South Australia, £18.99
- 1999 Geyserville Zinfandel blend, Ridge, Santa Cruz Mountains, California, USA, £49.99

Millésima

87 Quai de Paludate, BP 89, 33038 Bordeaux Cedex, France (00 33) 5 57 80 88 08 **FAX** (00 33) 5 57 80 88 19 Freephone 00800 26 73 32 89 or 0800 917 0352 **WEBSITE** www.millesima.com **HOURS** Mon–Fri 8–5.30 **CARDS** AmEx, Diners, MasterCard, Switch, Visa **DELIVERY** Free to single UK address **EN PRIMEUR** Bordeaux, Burgundy, Rhône. **C M T**
✪ **Star attractions** *Wines come direct from the châteaux to Millésima's cellars, where 3 million bottles are stored. A sprinkling of established names from other French regions.*

- 2002 Cap de Faugères, Côtes de Castillon, Bordeaux, France, £9.00
- 2000 Château Peyrabon, Haut-Médoc, Bordeaux, France, £15.00
- 2003 Château Bellefont-Belcier, St-Émilion Grand Cru, Bordeaux, France, £18.00
- 2001 Château de Myrat, Sauternes, Bordeaux, France, £27.00

Montrachet

MAIL ORDER 59 Kennington Road, London SE1 7PZ (020) 7928 1990 **FAX** (020) 7928 3415 **E-MAIL** charles@montrachetwine.com **WEBSITE** www.montrachetwine. com **HOURS** (Office and mail order) Mon–Fri 8.30–5.30 **CARDS** MasterCard, Switch, Visa **DELIVERY** England and Wales £12 including VAT, free for 3 or more cases; Scotland ring for details **MINIMUM ORDER** 1 unmixed

case **EN PRIMEUR** Bordeaux, Burgundy.
M T
✪ Star attractions *Impressive Burgundies, some very good Rhônes, and Bordeaux is excellent at all price levels. A short but starry set of German wines.*

- 2000 Vieux Château Gaubert, Graves Rouge, Bordeaux, France, £12.50
- 2002 Nuits St-Georges, Domaine Robert Arnoux, Burgundy, France, £24.25
- 2004 Corton Charlemagne, Domaine Vincent Girardin, Burgundy, France, £41.00
- 2003 Crozes-Hermitage, Cuvée Traditionelle, Domaine Yann Chave, Rhône Valley, France, £11.75

Moreno Wines

11 Marylands Road, London W9 2DU
(020) 7286 0678 **FAX** (020) 7286 0513
E-MAIL merchant@moreno-wines.co.uk
WEBSITE www.morenowinedirect.co.uk
HOURS Mon–Fri 4–9, Sat 12–10
CARDS AmEx, MasterCard, Switch, Visa
DISCOUNTS 10% 2 or more cases
DELIVERY Free locally, 3 or more cases within UK also free, otherwise £7.50.
M
✪ Star attractions *Fine and rare Spanish wines, but plenty of everyday drinking too, from upcoming regions like Aragon and Castilla y León. Then there's weird and wonderful stuff like Txomin from the Basque country, or Don P X Gran Reserva, a wonderful Christmas pudding of a wine from Montilla-Moriles in the sunny south. Also wines from South America.*

- NV Goya Moscatel, Camilo Castilla, Navarra, Spain, £5.99
- 1971 Don PX G.R., Bodegas Toro Albala, Montilla, Spain, £10.99 (half bottle)
- Tio Diego Amontillado, Valdespino, Jerez, Spain, £11.99
- 2001 Allende, Bodegas Allende, Rioja, Spain, £13.49

Moriarty Vintners

Unit 3, Penarth Road Retail Park, Penarth Road, Cardiff CF11 8TW
(02920) 705572 **FAX** (02920) 488300
E-MAIL david@moriarty-vintners.co.uk
WEBSITE www.moriarty-vintners.co.uk
HOURS Mon–Thurs 10–6, Fri–Sat 10–8, Sun 12–5 **DISCOUNTS** 15% off mixed case **DELIVERY** free locally, nationwide at cost **EN PRIMEUR** Italy, Port, Rhône.
C G M T
✪ Star attractions *This list concentrates on exciting gems from small producers. Italy is strong and other regions with good coverage include the Languedoc, Bordeaux, Australia and Spain.*

Wm Morrison Supermarkets

HEAD OFFICE Hilmore House, Gain Lane, Bradford, W. Yorks BD3 7DL (0845) 6111 5000 **FAX** (01274) 494831 **CUSTOMER SERVICE** (0845) 611 6111 360 licensed branches **WEBSITE** www.morrisons.co.uk
HOURS Variable, generally Mon–Sat 8–8, Sun 10–4 **CARDS** Amex, Delta, Maestro, MasterCard, Solo, Style, Visa Electron. **G T**
✪ Star attractions *Inexpensive, often tasty wines, with masses below £5. But if you're prepared to trade up a little*

there's some really good stuff here. A handful of clarets, too.
- **2005 Sauvignon Blanc, Misiones de Rengo, Maule Valley, Chile, £4.99**
- **2003 Rioja Club Privado, Baron de Ley, Spain, £6.99**
- **2003/5 Shiraz Reserve, Buckingham Estate, Western Australia, £7.99**
- **2002 Montagny Premier Cru, Caves des Vignerons de Buxy, Burgundy, France, £8.99**

James Nicholson

27a Killyleagh Street, Crossgar, Co. Down, N Ireland BT30 9DQ (028) 4483 0091 **FAX** (028) 4483 0028 **E-MAIL** shop@jnwine.com **WEBSITE** www.jnwine.com **HOURS** Mon–Sat 10–7 **CARDS** MasterCard, Switch, Visa **DISCOUNTS** 10% mixed case **DELIVERY** Free (1 case or more) in Eire and N Ireland; UK mainland £7.95, 2 cases £10.95 **EN PRIMEUR** Bordeaux, Burgundy, California, Rioja. **G M T**
✪ **Star attractions** *Everything is well chosen, mainly from small, committed growers around the world. Bordeaux, Rhône and southern France are slightly ahead of the field, and there's a good selection of affordable Burgundy – as affordable as decent Burgundy ever is, anyway. Spain has new-wave wines from the likes of Artadi and Martínez Bujanda, and there's excellent drinking from Germany.*
- **2005 Syrah Porcupine Ridge, Cape of Good Hope, South Africa, £7.75**
- **2004 Viñas de Gain, Artadi, Rioja, Spain, £11.75**

- **2005 Émotion de Terroirs, Domaine Vincent Girardin, Burgundy, France, £11.75**
- **2001 St-Joseph, Domaine Courbis, Rhône Valley, France, £14.35**

Nickolls & Perks

37 Lower High Street, Stourbridge, West Midlands DY8 1TA (01384) 394518 **FAX** (01384) 440786 **E-MAIL** sales@ nickollsandperks.co.uk **WEBSITE** www.nickollsandperks.co.uk **HOURS** Tues–Fri 10.30–5.30, Sat 10.30–5 **CARDS** MasterCard, Switch, Visa **DISCOUNTS** negotiable per case **DELIVERY** £10 per consignment **EN PRIMEUR** Bordeaux, Champagne, Port. **C G M T**
✪ **Star attractions** *Wine shippers since 1797, Nickolls & Perks has always been important in the en primeur Bordeaux market. The wide-ranging list – and terrific website – covers most areas and is particularly strong in France. Advice is available to clients wishing to develop their cellars or invest in wine.*
- **2000 Château La Tour-Carnet, Haut-Médoc, Bordeaux, France, £14.64**
- **2000 Fontalloro, Felsina, Tuscany, Italy, £19.00**
- **2000 Cuvée Papet, Clos du Mont Olivet, Châteauneuf-du-Pape, Rhône Valley, France, £33.62**
- **1997 Champagne Grande Année, Bollinger, Champagne, France, £41.28**

Nidderdale Fine Wines

2a High Street, Pateley Bridge, North Yorkshire HG3 5AW (01423) 711703

E-MAIL
info@southaustralianwines.com
WEBSITE www.southaustralianwines.com
HOURS Tue–Sat 10–6 **CARDS**
MasterCard, Switch, Visa **DISCOUNTS** 5%
case discount on shop purchases
DELIVERY £5 per case in England, Wales
and southern Scotland; rest of UK £25
per case. Single bottle delivery
negotiable. **G T**
✪ Star attractions *South Australia is the
speciality here, with 400 wines broken
down into regions, so if you want to see
what's available from Barossa,
Coonawarra, Adelaide Hills or Clare
Valley, you need look no further. Also 350
or so wines from other parts of Australia
and the rest of the world. Look out for
online offers and winemaker dinners.*
• **2003 Tryst, Nepenthe, Adelaide Hills,
South Australia, £6.99**
• **NV Jansz Brut, Jansz (Yalumba),
Tasmania, Australia, £9.99**
• **2002 Shiraz Klauber Block, Kies
Estate, Barossa Valley, South
Australia, £9.99**
• **2003 Polish Hill Riesling, Grosset,
Clare Valley, South Australia, £15.99**

Noble Rot Wine Warehouses

18 Market Street, Bromsgrove,
Worcestershire, B61 8JZ
(01527) 575606 **FAX** (01527) 833133
E-MAIL info@noble-rot.co.uk **WEBSITE**
www.noble-rot.co.uk
HOURS Mon–Fri 10–7, Sat 9.30–6.30
CARDS MasterCard, Switch, Visa
DISCOUNTS Various **DELIVERY** Free
within 10-mile radius. **G T**
✪ Star attractions *What Noble Rot's*

*customers want is good wine for
current drinking, mostly at £4 to £15 a
bottle. Australia, Italy, France and Spain
feature most strongly in a frequently
changing list of more than 400 wines.*
• **2005 Chardonnay, Andes Peaks,
Casablanca Valley, Chile, £3.82**
• **2004 Poachers' Blend, St Hallett,
Barossa Valley, South Australia,
£4.58**
• **2003 Crozes-Hermitage, Cave de Tain
l'Hermitage, Rhône Valley, France,
£6.88**
• **NV Sparkling Pinot Noir &
Chardonnay Brut, Brown Brothers,
Victoria, Australia, £7.65**

The Nobody Inn

Doddiscombsleigh, Nr Exeter, Devon
EX6 7PS (01647) 252394
FAX (01647) 252978 **E-MAIL**
info@nobodyinn.co.uk
WEBSITE www.nobodyinn.co.uk
HOURS Mon–Sun 12–3 & 6–11
(summer) **CARDS** AmEx, MasterCard,
Switch, Visa **DISCOUNTS** 5% per case
DELIVERY £7.99 for 1 case, free over
£150. **G M T**
• The Wine Company (01392) 477752
FAX (01392) 477759 **E-MAIL**
sales@thewinecompany.biz
WEBSITE www.thewinecompany.biz
HOURS Mon–Fri 9.30–6, 24-hr ordering
service **CARDS** AmEx, MasterCard,
Switch, Visa **DELIVERY** Free for orders
over £150.
✪ **Star attractions** *If you're going to
eat here I advise you to turn up 2 hours
early to browse through this
extraordinary list. Australia rules, but*

there's something exciting from just
about everywhere. Amazing range of
sweet wines: Loire, of course, but also
Greece's Samos Muscat and Anthemis.
The Wine Company is a mail order
venture for wines mostly priced at
£5–10.

- 2003 The Explorer Shiraz, Jonathan
  Maltus, Colonial Estate, Barossa
  Valley, South Australia, £13.99
- 1989 Coteaux du Layon, Château de
  La Roulerie, Loire Valley, France, £17.55
- 2000 Pinot Noir, Sanford, Santa
  Barbara County, California, USA,
  £23.30
- 20-year-old Malvasia Special Reserve
  Madeira, Barbeito, Madeira, Portugal,
  £35.72

Oddbins

HEAD OFFICE 31–33 Weir Road, London
SW19 8UG (020) 8944 4400 **FAX** (020)
8944 4411
MAIL ORDER Oddbins Direct 0800 328
2323 **FAX** 0800 328 3848;
260 shops nationwide
WEBSITE www.oddbins.com
HOURS Ask local branch for details
CARDS AmEx, MasterCard, Switch, Visa
DISCOUNTS regular offers on
Champagne and sparkling wine, and
general promotions **DELIVERY** (Stores)
free locally for orders over £100 **EN
PRIMEUR** Bordeaux. **G M T**
- **CALAIS STORE** Cité Europe, 139 Rue de
  Douvres, 62901, Coquelles Cedex,
  France (0033) 3 21 82 07 32 **FAX** (0033)
  3 21 82 05 83 **PRE-ORDER**
  www.oddbins.com/storefinder/
  calais.asp

✪ **Star attractions** New World pioneer
or champion of the classics? Both,
actually. Extensive Aussie selection,
well-chosen Chileans and Argentinians;
Spain, Italy, Greece, New Zealand, South
Africa, Burgundy and Rhône all look
good, and Languedoc is currently in the
limelight. Great deals on Champagne.
Now owned by French multinational
group Castel who are also owners of
the Nicolas chain of wine shops.

- 2003 Viognier Vin de Pays d'Oc,
  Domaine Virginie, Languedoc,
  France, £4.99
- 2005 Rias Baixas Albariño, Val de
  Sosego, Galicia, Spain, £6.99
- 2002 Cabernet Sauvignon,
  Peñalolen, Maipo Valley, Chile,
  £7.49
- 2004 Pinot Noir, Glen Carlou, Paarl,
  South Africa, £9.99

OZ WINES

MAIL ORDER Freepost Lon 17656,
London SW18 5BR, 0845 450 1261
FAX (020) 8870 8839
E-MAIL sales@ozwines.co.uk
WEBSITE www.ozwines.co.uk
HOURS Mon–Fri 9.30–7 **CARDS** Access,
Diners, MasterCard, Switch, Visa
DELIVERY Free. **MINIMUM ORDER**
1 mixed case. **M T**

✪ **Star attractions** Australian wines
made by small wineries and real
people, which means wines with the
kind of thrilling flavours that
Australians do better than anyone else.

- 2004 Shiraz, Water Wheel Vineyards,
  Bendigo, Victoria, Australia,
  £9.50

O^{dd}bins

wine merchant extraordinaire

Over 260 stores throughout the UK, Dublin and Calais with the biggest and the best range of wines on the High Street and knowledgeable staff with a real passion for everything from Albariño to Zinfandel.

Apart from over 1000 different wines at all prices, we also offer:

Oddbins Fine Wine
Rare and special wines from
all over the world.

Oddbins Direct
Our UK mail order and gift
service that can deliver anything from
single bottles to whole cases wherever
you need them to go.
Phone 0800 328 2323 or log on to
www.oddbins.com to order.

Oddbins Wholesale
Serving the On-Trade with everything
Oddbins does at wholesale prices.
Ask in your local store or phone
020 8944 4420/4422 for more details.

**Wedding services
& party planning**
Offering friendly advice, free delivery
(subject to minimum spend), ice and free
glass hire.

- 2004 Chardonnay, Diamond Valley, Yarra Valley, Victoria, Australia, £10.99
- 2005 Riesling Skilly Ridge, Inghams, Clare Valley, South Australia, £10.99
- 2004 Shiraz-Grenache DNA, Tim Smith Wines, Barossa Valley South Australia, £10.99

Penistone Court Wine Cellars

The Railway Station, Penistone, Sheffield, South Yorkshire S36 6HP
(01226) 766037 **FAX** (01226) 767310
E-MAIL chris@pcwine.plus.com **HOURS** Tues–Fri 10–6, Sat 10–3 **CARDS** MasterCard, Switch, Visa **DELIVERY** Free locally, rest of UK mainland charged at cost 1 case or more **MINIMUM ORDER** 1 case. **G M**

✪ **Star attractions** *A well-balanced list, with something from just about everywhere, mostly from familiar names. So, you've got Champagne (Pol Roger, Bollinger, Roederer and others), Burgundy, Beaujolais, Alsace, Loire, Rhône and a short list of clarets. Outside France, there's a good range from Italy, plus Austria, Spain, Chile, the USA, New Zealand and Australia.*

- 2004 Santa Digna Rosé, Miguel Torres, Chile, £5.13
- 2003 Rueda Verdejo, Marqués de Riscal, Castilla y León, Spain, £5.86
- 2003 Côtes du Rhône Belleruche, Chapoutier, Rhône Valley, France, £6.59
- 2000 Pelorus, Cloudy Bay, Marlborough, New Zealand, £14.50

Philglas & Swiggot

21 Northcote Road, Battersea, London SW11 1NG (020) 7924 4494 • 64 Hill Rise, Richmond, London TW10 6UB (020) 8332 6081 • 22 New Quebec Street, Marylebone, London W1H 7SB (020) 7402 0002 **E-MAIL** info@philglas-swiggot.co.uk **WEBSITE** www.philglas-swiggot. co.uk **HOURS** (Battersea) Mon–Sat 11–7, Sun 12–5 (Richmond) Tue–Sat 11–7, Sun 12–5 (Marylebone) Mon–Sat 11–7 **CARDS** AmEx, MasterCard, Switch, Visa **DISCOUNTS** 5% per case **DELIVERY** Free 1 case locally. **G M**
○ Star attractions *Excellent Aussie selection – subtle, interesting wines, not blockbuster brands. The same philosophy applies to wines they buy from elsewhere, so you'll find serious Italians and good French wines. Austria fits the bill nicely and dessert wines are good too.*
• **2003 Cabernet Sauvignon, Best's, Victoria, Australia, £8.15**
• **2004 La Segreta Bianco, Planeta, Sicily, Italy, £9.99**
• **NV Riesling Icewine, Mission Hill, British Columbia, Canada, £15.99**
• **2004 Grüner Veltliner, Ried Renner, Schloss Gobelsburg, Kamptal, Austria, £15.99**

Christopher Piper Wines

1 Silver Street, Ottery St Mary, Devon EX11 1DB (01404) 814139 **FAX** (01404) 812100 **E-MAIL** sales@christopherpiperwines.co.uk **WEBSITE** www.christopherpiperwines.co.uk **HOURS** Mon–Fri 8.30–5.30, Sat 9–4.30 **CARDS** MasterCard, Switch, Visa

DISCOUNTS 5% mixed case, 10% 3 or more cases **DELIVERY** Free for orders over £190, otherwise £7.05 per case **MINIMUM ORDER** (for mail order) 1 mixed case **EN PRIMEUR** Bordeaux, Burgundy, Rhône. **C G M T**
○ Star attractions *Huge range of well-chosen wines that reflect a sense of place and personality, with lots of information to help you make up your mind. The shop is open 6 days a week for single bottle sales.*
• **2002 Chardonnay Fût de Chêne, Vin de Pays Oc, Domaine St-Hilaire, Languedoc, France, £5.77**
• **1998 Miral Monte Crianza, Bodegas Frutos Villar, Toro, Castilla y León, Spain, £6.81**
• **2000 Madiran, Château Montus, South-West France, £10.91**
• **Crusted Port, Churchill, Douro, Portugal, £11.17**

Terry Platt Wine Merchants

Council Street West, Llandudno LL30 1ED (01492) 874099 **FAX** (01492) 874788 **E-MAIL** info@terryplattwines.co.uk **WEBSITE** www.terryplattwines.co.uk **HOURS** Mon–Fri 8.30–5.30 **CARDS** Access, MasterCard, Switch, Visa **DELIVERY** Free locally and UK mainland 5 cases or more **MINIMUM ORDER** 1 mixed case. **G M T**
○ Star attractions *A wide-ranging list with a sprinkling of good growers from most regions. New World coverage has increased recently: Terrazas de los Andes from Argentina; Casa Lapostolle and Montes from Chile; Grangehurst*

and Warwick Estate from South Africa; Water Wheel and Cape Mentelle from Australia.

- Minervois, Château la Grave, Languedoc, France, £5.51
- 2002 Rueda Blanco, Marqués de Riscal, Castilla y León, Spain, £5.89
- 2003 Alto Malbec 1067 Metres, Terrazas de Los Andes, Mendoza, Argentina, £5.99
- 2003 Sauvignon Blanc, Vergelegen, Stellenbosch, South Africa, £6.95

Playford Ros

Middle Park, Thirsk, Yorkshire YO7 3AH (01845) 526777 FAX (01845) 526888 E-MAIL sales@playfordros.com WEBSITE www.playfordros.com HOURS Mon–Fri 8–6 CARDS MasterCard, Visa DISCOUNTS negotiable DELIVERY Free Yorkshire, Derbyshire, Durham, Newcastle; elsewhere £10–15 or at courier cost MINIMUM ORDER 1 mixed case EN PRIMEUR Bordeaux, Burgundy.
C G M T
✪ Star attractions A carefully chosen list, with reassuringly recognizable representatives from Bordeaux and Burgundy, the Rhône and the Loire. Similar standards apply elsewhere, with Australia looking exceptional, and there is a good selection of wines at around the £5 to £6 mark.

- 2004 Stickleback Cabernet/ Shiraz/Grenache, Heartland Estate, South Australia, £5.35
- 2001 Lasendal Garnacha, Montsant, Cataluña, Spain, £7.25

- 2003 Barrel-Fermented Chardonnay, Felton Road, Central Otago, New Zealand, £14.95
- 2004 Moonambel Pinot Noir, Dalwhinnie, Pyrenees, Victoria, Australia, £14.95

Portland Wine Co

16 North Parade, off Norris Road, Sale, Cheshire M33 3JS (0161) 962 8752 FAX (0161) 905 1291 • 152a Ashley Road, Hale WA15 9SA (0161) 928 0357 • 82 Chester Road, Macclesfield SK11 8DL (01625) 616147 E-MAIL enquiries@ portlandwine.co.uk WEBSITE www.portlandwine.co.uk HOURS Mon–Sat 10–10, Sun 12–9.30 CARDS MasterCard, Switch, Visa DISCOUNTS 5% 2 cases or more, 10% 5 cases or more DELIVERY Free locally 1 case or more, £10 + VAT per consignment nationwide EN PRIMEUR Bordeaux. C T
✪ Star attractions Spain, Portugal and Burgundy are specialities; there is also a promising-looking list of lesser clarets, as well as more expensive, stunning older vintages. This consumer-friendly list has something at every price level from around the world.

- 2002 Vierlas, Vino de Mesa Ribera del Queiles, Guelbenzu, Navarra, Spain, £6.99
- 2002 Reserva Red, Esporão, Portugal, £9.99
- 2004 Sauvignon Blanc, Isabel Estate, Marlborough, New Zealand, £12.99
- 2004 Chablis Premier Cru Montmains, Brocard, Burgundy, France, £13.99

Quaff Fine Wine Merchant

139-141 Portland Road, Hove BN3 5QJ
(01273) 820320 **FAX** (01273) 820326
E-MAIL sales@quaffit.com **WEBSITE**
www.quaffit.com **HOURS** Mon–Thurs
10–7, Fri–Sat 10–8, Sun 12–7 **CARDS**
Access, MasterCard, Switch, Visa
DISCOUNTS 12% mixed case **DELIVERY**
£5.99 next day nationwide **C G M T**
✪ Star attractions *Interestingly, their
wine list is organized by grape variety
and style, rather than by country. I've
got no objections to that, especially
when the range is as extensive and
keenly priced as it is.*

- **2005 Hand Picked Riesling,
  Knappstein, Clare Valley, South
  Australia, £8.29**
- **2003 Tempranillo Navarro La Planta,
  Arzuaga, Ribera del Duero, Castilla y
  León, Spain, £8.99**
- **2004 Viognier Fairview, Paarl, South
  Africa, £10.50**
- **Malbec, Catena Zapata, Mendoza,
  Argentina, £12.75**

Raeburn Fine Wines

21–23 Comely Bank Road, Edinburgh
EH4 1DS (0131) 343 1159 **FAX** (0131) 332
5166 **E-MAIL**
sales@raeburnfinewines.com **WEBSITE**
www.raeburnfine
wines.com **HOURS** Mon–Sat 9.30–6,
Sun 12.30–1 **CARDS** AmEx, MasterCard,
Switch, Visa **DISCOUNTS** 5% unsplit
case, 2.5% mixed **DELIVERY** Free local
area 1 or more cases (usually);
elsewhere at cost **EN PRIMEUR**
Australia, Bordeaux, Burgundy,
California, Germany, Italy, Languedoc-

Roussillon, Loire, New Zealand, Rhône.
G M T
✪ Star attractions *Everything here is
carefully chosen, usually from small
growers: if you want obvious choices
you won't like this list, but if you want
to try interesting wines from an
impressive array of vintages you'll be
more than happy. Burgundy is
something of a speciality and from the
Loire there are oodles of Vouvrays from
Huet, in vintages going back to 1924.
Italy, North Spain and California all
look fabulous. Ports from Niepoort.*

- **1999 Late Bottled Vintage Port,
  Niepoort, Douro, Portugal, £11.99**
- **2002 Priorat Blanc de Botes, Clos
  Berenguer, Cataluña, Spain, £13.99**
- **1989 Vouvray Le Haut Lieu Moelleux,
  Domaine Huet, Loire Valley, France,
  £14.50**
- **2000 Gevrey-Chambertin Premier
  Cru, Denis Mortet, Burgundy, France,
  £25.99**

Real Wine Co.

1 Cannon Meadow, Bull Lane, Gerrards
Cross, Buckinghamshire SL9 8RE
(01753) 885619 **E-MAIL** mark@
therealwineco.co.uk **WEBSITE**
www.therealwineco.co.uk **CARDS**
Delta, Mastercard, Switch, Visa
DELIVERY Up to 2 cases £5, free for 3 or
more cases to single address; free to
postcodes SL9 and HP9 irrespective of
number of cases
MINIMUM ORDER 1 mixed case
✪ Star attractions *Owner Mark
Hughes has based his list entirely and
unapologetically on his personal taste.*

*Nothing wrong with that – check it out
and see if you agree with him.*

- **2003 Negro Amaro, Montebello,
  Puglia, Italy, £5.99**
- **Lambrusco Grasparossa di
  Castelvetro, Villa Cialdini, Emilia-
  Romagna, Italy, £6.99**
- **NV Champagne Brut, Carlin,
  Champagne, France, £13.99**
- **2003 Costières de Nîmes La Bolida,
  Château d'Or et de Gueles, Rhône
  Valley, France, £16.00**

Reid Wines

The Mill, Marsh Lane, Hallatrow,
Nr Bristol BS39 6EB (01761) 452645 **FAX**
(01761) 453642 **E-MAIL** reidwines@aol.
com **HOURS** Mon–Fri 9–5.30 **CARDS**
Access, MasterCard, Switch, Visa (3%
charge) **DELIVERY** Free within 25 miles of
Hallatrow (Bristol), and in central
London for orders over 2 cases **EN
PRIMEUR** Claret. **C G M T**

O Star attractions *Reid's is one of the lists
I look forward to reading most: it's full of
pithy comments alongside its fabulous
array of older vintages.* 'We seem to have
acquired a large number of these wines
[the '75s], many of which have, after a
very tannic youth, turned into rather
good, if slightly austere bottles. But
austerity is what proper Bordeaux is all
about. Who wants tarty, sweet, oaky
Merlot wines?' *A mix of great old wines,
some old duds and splendid current stuff.
Italy, USA, Australia, port and Madeira
look tremendous.*

- **2001 Riesling Kabinett Maximiner
  Grünhauser, Abtsberg, von Schubert,
  Mosel, Germany, £11.50**

- **2001 Barbera d'Alba Conca Tre Pile,
  Aldo Conterno, Piedmont, Italy,
  £16.00**
- **1999 Pinot Noir Isabelle, Au Bon
  Climat, Santa Barbara County,
  California, USA, £33.85**
- **1989 Château Léoville-Barton, St-
  Julien, Bordeaux, France, £55.00**

Richardson & Sons

26a Lowther Street, Whitehaven,
Cumbria CA28 7DG **FAX/TEL** (01946)
65334 **E-MAIL** mailwines@tiscali.co.uk
HOURS Mon–Sat 10–5.30 **CARDS** AmEx,
Delta, MasterCard, Switch, Visa
DELIVERY Free locally **M T**

O Star attractions *It's the only place in
Cumbria stocking Château Latour, but
in general Richardson & Sons select
from small producers, preferring 'little
hidden gems' to big names. They
specialize in reds from Australia,
Bordeaux and Burgundy. No actual list
– but if you get on their mailing list
they'll send you regular updates.*

- **2005 Sauvignon Blanc, Whitehaven,
  New Zealand, £9.99**
- **1995 Vintage Port Quinta da Roêda,
  Croft, Portugal, £19.00**
- **2001 Cabernet Sauvignon, Clarendon
  Hills, McLaren Vale, South Australia,
  £34.00**
- **1986 Château Cissac, Haut-Médoc,
  Bordeaux, France, £49.00**

Howard Ripley

25 Dingwall Road, London
SW18 3AZ (020) 8877 3065
FAX (020) 8877 0029 **E-MAIL**
info@howardripley.com

WEBSITE www.howardripley.com
HOURS Mon–Fri 9–8, Sat 9–1
CARDS MasterCard, Switch, Visa
DELIVERY Minimum charge £10.50 +
VAT, free UK mainland on orders over
£500 ex-VAT **MINIMUM ORDER** 1 mixed
case **EN PRIMEUR** Burgundy, Germany.
C M T
⊙ **Star attractions** *If you're serious
about Burgundy, this is one of perhaps
half a dozen lists that you need. Yes,
the wines are expensive – great
Burgundy is expensive – but they're not
excessive. The German range is also
excellent.*

- 2003 Graacher Domprobst Spätlese
  (No. 10), Willi Schafer, Mosel,
  Germany, £16.50
- 2003 Chambolle-Musigny, Domaine
  Roumier, Burgundy, France, £23.50
- 1996 Côte de Beaune-Villages,
  Maison Leroy, Vosne-Romanée,
  France, £25.50
- 2002 Chassagne-Montrachet
  Premier Cru, La Truffière, Colin-
  Deléger, Burgundy, France, £50.00

Roberson

348 Kensington High Street, London
W14 8NS (020) 7371 2121 **FAX** (020) 7371
4010
E-MAIL retail@roberson.co.uk
WEBSITE
www.robersonwinemerchant.co.uk
HOURS Mon–Sat 10–8 **CARDS** Access,
AmEx, Diners, MasterCard, Switch, Visa
DISCOUNTS MAIL ORDER 5% on
champagne and spirits, 10% or wine
cases **DELIVERY** Free delivery within
London, otherwise £15 per case **EN**

PRIMEUR Bordeaux, Port. **C G M T**
⊙ **Star attractions** *Fine and rare wines,
sold by the bottle. Plenty of clarets
from the great 1989 and 1990 vintages.
All of France is excellent; so is Italy and
port.*

- 2003 Côtes du Rhône Coudoulet
  Blanc, Château de Beaucastel, Rhône
  Valley, France, £16.95
- Cahors Prince Probus, Clos
  Triguedina, South-West France,
  £19.95
- 2001 Château Roc de Cambes, Côtes
  de Bourg, Bordeaux, France,
  £22.50
- NV Champagne Grand Rosé, Gosset,
  Champagne, France, £33.95

The RSJ Wine Company

33 Coin Street, London SE1 9NR (020)
7928 4554 **FAX** (020) 7928 9768
E-MAIL tom.king@rsj.uk.com
WEBSITE www.rsj.uk.com
HOURS Mon–Fri 9–6, answering
machine at other times **CARDS**
MasterCard, Switch, Amex, Visa
DELIVERY Free central London,
minimum 1 case; England and Wales
(per case), £14.10 1 case, £10.25 2 cases
or more. **G M T**
⊙ **Star attractions** *A roll-call of great
Loire names. From Savennières there is
Domaine aux Moines, from Chinon
Philippe Alliet, from Saumur Domaine
des Roches Neuves, to mention just a
few. And now there are a few Bordeaux
wines too.*

- 2004 Le Clos des Allées Vieilles
  Vignes, Domaine Luneau-Papin, Loire
  Valley, France, £6.95

- 2003 Anjou-Villages, Domaine Ogereau, Loire Valley, France, £8.75
- 2003 Saumur-Champigny Terres Chaudes, Domaine de Roches Neuves, Loire Valley, France, £10.65
- 2003 Chinon Vieilles Vignes, Philippe Alliet, Loire Valley, France, £11.95

Safeway

Now owned by Wm Morrison plc (see page 129)

Sainsbury's

HEAD OFFICE 33 Holborn, London EC1N 2HT (020) 7695 6000
CUSTOMER SERVICE 0800 636262; 720 stores
WEBSITE www. sainsburys.co.uk Click on Wines to your door for exciting and exclusive offers **HOURS** Variable, some 24 hrs, locals generally Mon–Sat 7–11, Sun 10 or 11–4 **CARDS** AmEx, MasterCard, Switch, Visa
DISCOUNTS 5% for 6 bottles or more **G M T · MAIL ORDER** 0800 917 4092 **FAX** 0800 917 4095 · **CALAIS STORE** Sainsbury's, Centre Commercial Auchan, Route de Boulogne, 62100 Calais, France (0033) 3 21 82 38 48 **FAX** (0033) 3 21 36 01 91 **PREORDER** www.sainsburys.co.uk/calais
○ **Star attractions** *Sainsbury's manages to cater for bargain hunters as well as appealing to lovers of good-value wine higher up the scale. They've expanded their Taste the Difference range and got some top producers on board. Very strong in Chile, a good*

range of fortified wines, and there's a short list of affordable clarets.
- 2005 SO Chilean Merlot (organic), Maipo Valley, Chile, £4.99
- 2005 Sauvignon Blanc-Semillon, Sainsbury's Taste the Difference (Capel Vale), Western Australia, £6.99
- 2005 Chablis Sainte Celine, Sainsbury's Taste the Difference (Jean-Marc Brocard), Burgundy, France, £7.99
- 2004 Pinot Noir Reserve, Las Brisas, Viña Leyda, Leyda Valley, Chile, £8.99

Savage Selection

The Ox House, Market Place, Northleach, Cheltenham, Glos GL54 3EG (01451) 860896 **FAX** (01451) 860996 · The Ox House Shop and Wine Bar at same address (01451) 860680 **E-MAIL** wine@savageselection.co.uk **WEBSITE** www.savageselection.co.uk
HOURS Office: Mon–Fri 9–6; shop: Tue–Wed 10–7.30, Thur–Fri 10–10, Sat 10–3 **CARDS** AmEx, MasterCard, Switch, Visa **DELIVERY** Free locally for orders over £100; elsewhere on UK mainland free for orders over £250: otherwise £11.75 per consignment **EN PRIMEUR** Bordeaux. **C G M T**
○ **Star attractions** *If ever you find yourself getting bored by standard wine fare and feel the need for a seachange of flavours, get in touch with Mark Savage. He takes the trouble to find wines for himself, seeking them out in Austria, Hungary, Greece and Idaho as well as Italy, Spain and*

Germany. France is also strong, with wines from Bordeaux, Burgundy and Provence, and Billecart-Salmon Champagne.

- **2004 Verdiso, Vincenzo Toffoli, Veneto, Italy, £5.95**
- **2002 Beerenauslese, Erwin Tinhof, Burgenland, Austria, £11.95 (37.5cl)**
- **Manzanilla La Gitana, Hidalgo, Jerez, Spain,£4.95 (50cl)**
- **2004 Syrah Domaine Astruc, Domain Paul Mas, Languedoc, France, £5.95**

Seckford Wines

Dock Lane, Melton, Suffolk IP12 1PE
(01394) 446622 **FAX** (01394) 446633
E-MAIL sales@seckfordwines.co.uk
WEBSITE www.seckfordwines.co.uk
CARDS MasterCard, Switch, Visa
DELIVERY £10 per consignment, UK mainland; elsewhere at cost.
MINIMUM ORDER 1 mixed case **EN PRIMEUR** Bordeaux, Burgundy. **C**
✪ Star attractions *Bordeaux, Burgundy and the Rhône are the stars of this list, and if you prefer older vintages, Seckford have got plenty of these. There's serious stuff from Italy, Spain and Austria, too.*

- **2002 Heysen Shiraz, Rolf Binder Wines, Barossa Valley, South Australia, £15.75**
- **1990 Château d'Angludet, Margaux, Bordeaux, France, £29.00**
- **1998 Château de Beaucastel, Châteauneuf-du-Pape, Rhône Valley, France, £39.00**
- **Meursault Clos de la Barre, Domaine des Comtes Lafon, Burgundy, France, £65.00**

Somerfield

HEAD OFFICE Somerfield House, Whitchurch Lane, Bristol BS14 0TJ
(0117) 935 9359 **FAX** (0117) 935 6669;
800 Somerfield stores and 500 Kwiksave stores nationwide
WEBSITE www.somerfield.co.uk
HOURS Mon–Sat 8–8, Sun 10–4 **CARDS** MasterCard, Switch, Visa **DISCOUNTS** 5% off 6 bottles **DELIVERY** Free local delivery for orders over £25 in selected stores. **M T**
✪ Star attractions *Somerfield have increased their £5–7 range this year, which is great news for wine lovers. Fizz is looking good at all price points.*

- **2004 Trio Merlot-Carmenère-Cabernet Sauvignon, Concha y Toro, Rapel Valley, Chile, £5.99**
- **NV Cava Brut rosé, Spain, £6.99**
- **2005 Sauvignon Blanc, Veramonte, Casablanca Valley, Chile, £7.03**
- **NV Champagne Brut, Prince William Premier Cru, Champagne, France, £14.99**

Sommelier Wine Co

23 St George's Esplanade, St Peter Port, Guernsey, Channel Islands, GY1 2BG
(01481) 721677 **FAX** (01481) 716818
HOURS Mon–Sat 9.15–5.30, except Fri 9.15–6 **CARDS** MasterCard, Switch, Visa
DISCOUNTS 5% 1 case or more **DELIVERY** Free locally 1 unmixed case. Customs legislation restricts the shipping of wine to the UK mainland. **G T**
✪ Star attractions *An excellent list, with interesting, unusual wines. It's a big selection, too: there are yards of lovely subtle Italian whites and well-*

made reds, and lots of Loires and Beaujolais. Burgundy, Bordeaux, the Rhône, Spain, Italy and South Africa all look good, though Australia outdoes them all.

- 2003 Goats do Roam in Villages Red, Fairview Estate, Stellenbosch, South Africa, £5.95
- Malbec, Bodegas Terrazas de Los Andes, Mendoza, Argentina, £6.95
- 2004 Is Argiolas Bianco, Argiolas, Sardinia, Italy, £8.45
- 2005 Pinot Gris, Tim Adams, Clare Valley, South Australia, £8.50

Frank Stainton Wines

3 Berry's Yard, Finkle Street, Kendal, Cumbria LA9 4AB (01539) 731886 FAX (01539) 730396 E-MAIL admin@stainton-wines.co.uk WEBSITE www.stainton-wines.co.uk HOURS Mon–Sat 9–5.30 CARDS MasterCard, Switch, Visa DISCOUNTS 5% mixed case DELIVERY Free Cumbria and North Lancashire; elsewhere (per case) £13 1 case, more than 1 case variable. G M T
✪ Star attractions *Some interesting Burgundy growers, but on the whole Bordeaux is better. The worldwide range includes leading names from Italy and from Chile the wines of Casa Silva, which have real character and subtlety. Three Choirs wines from England.*

- 2004 Carmenère Los Lingues Vineyard, Casa Silva, Colchagua Valley, Chile, £8.75
- 2000 I Capitelli Recioto, Roberto Anselmi, Veneto, Italy, £12.50
- 1999 Viña Ardanza Reserve, La Rioja Alta, Rioja, Spain, £16.50

- 2001 Cabernet Sauvignon Alta, Catena Zapata, Mendoza, Argentina, £25.50

Stevens Garnier

47 West Way, Botley, Oxford OX2 OJF (01865) 263303 FAX (01865) 791594 E-MAIL shop@stevens garnier.co.uk HOURS Mon–Wed 10–6, Thur–Fri 10–7, Sat 10–6 CARDS AmEx, MasterCard, Switch, Visa, Solo DISCOUNTS 5% on a mixed case DELIVERY Free locally; 'competitive rates' elsewhere. G T
✪ Star attractions *'Regional France' is a strength: this is one of the few places in the UK you can buy wine from Savoie. Portugal is from quality-conscious Sogrape. Pleasant surprises from the New World include Willow Bridge from Australia, Carmen from Chile and Chateau des Charmes from Canada.*

- 2004 Fitou Cuvée Pierre, Paul & Jacques, Les Vignerons de Mont Tauch, Languedoc-Roussillon, France, £5.45
- 2000 Late Harvest Riesling, Château des Charmes, Niagara, Ontario, Canada, £10.95 (37.5 cl)
- 2000 Winemaker's Maipo Reserve Red, Viña Carmen, Chile, £15.25
- 2004 Sancerre Rouge Belle Dame, Domaine Vacheron, Loire Valley, France, £23.25

Stone, Vine & Sun

No. 13 Humphrey Farms, Hazeley Road, Twyford, Winchester SO21 1QA (01962) 712351 FAX (01962) 717545 E-MAIL sales@stonevine.co.uk WEBSITE www.stonevine.co.uk HOURS Mon–Fri

9–6, Sat 9.30–4 **CARDS** Access, MasterCard, Switch, Visa **DISCOUNTS** 5% on an unmixed case **DELIVERY** £4.50 per case. Prices vary for Scottish highlands and islands and N Ireland. Free delivery for orders over £250 **G M T**

✪ Star attractions *Lovely list marked by enthusiasm and passion for the subject. Lots of interesting stuff from France, but also from Germany, South Africa, New Zealand and elsewhere – and they're determined to do it properly: whenever I'm nosing about the byways and backroads of France, who do I meet but someone from Stone, Vine & Sun doing the same thing?*

- **2003 Minervois, Domaine Piccinini, Languedoc, France, £5.95**
- **2004 Moscato, Gatti Piero, Piedmont, Italy, £7.95**
- **2003 Chardonnay Leyda, Falaris Hill Vineyard, Leyda Valley, Chile, £8.50**
- **2001 Vacqueyras, Domaine le Couroulu, Rhône Valley, France, £9.75**

Sunday Times Wine Club

New Aquitaine House, Exeter Way, Theale, Reading, Berks RG7 4PL **ORDER LINE** 0870 220 0010 **FAX** 0870 220 0030 **E-MAIL** orders@sundaytimeswineclub.co.uk **WEBSITE** www.sundaytimeswine club.co.uk **HOURS** 24-hr answering machine **CARDS** AmEx, Diners, MasterCard, Switch, Visa **DELIVERY** £5.99 per order **EN PRIMEUR** Australia, Bordeaux, Burgundy, Rhône. **C M T**

✪ Star attractions *Essentially the same list as Laithwaites (see page 186), though the special offers come round at different times. The membership fee is £10 per annum. The club runs tours and tasting events for its members.*

- **2004 Pedro Ximenez-Sauvignon Blanc, Viña Falernia, Elquí Valley, Chile, £6.00**
- **2002 Semillon, De Bortoli, New South Wales, Australia, £6.99**
- **2003 Primitivo Pillastro, Puglia, Italy, £7.00**
- **2003 Pinot Noir, Hunter's, Marlborough, New Zealand, £10.99**

T & W Wines

5 Station Way, Brandon, Suffolk IP27 0BH (01842) 814414 **FAX** (01842) 819967 **E-MAIL** contact@tw-wines.com **WEBSITE** www.tw-wines.com **HOURS** Mon–Fri. 9.30–5.30, occasional Sat 9.30–1 **CARDS** AmEx, MasterCard, Visa **DELIVERY** (most areas) 7–23 bottles £14.95 + VAT, 2 or more cases free **EN PRIMEUR** Burgundy. **C G M T**

✪ Star attractions *The list is a good one, particularly if you're looking for Burgundy, Rhône, Alsace or the Loire, but prices are not especially low, and when working out the final cost remember that they exclude VAT. There's an amazing list of over 240 half bottles, including the superb sweet wines of Willi Opitz, from Austria, and 25 biodynamic wines from France.*

- **2005 Gewurztraminer Beerenauslese, Willi Opitz, Austria, £15.10 (half)**

- 2003 Menetou-Salon, Clos des Blanchais, Domaine Henry Pellé, Lolire Valley, France, £16.39
- 1999 Riesling Cuvée Frédéric Émile, Trimbach, Alsace, France, £40.36
- 2003 Nuits-St-Georges, Les Grandes Vignes, Domaine Daniel Rion, Burgundy, France, £32.72

Tanners

26 Wyle Cop, Shrewsbury, Shropshire SY1 1XD (01743) 234500 FAX (01743) 234501 • 4 St Peter's Square, Hereford HR1 2PG (01432) 272044 FAX (01432) 263316 • 36 High Street, Bridgnorth WV16 4DB (01746) 763148 FAX (01746) 769798• Severn Farm Enterprise Park, Welshpool SY21 7DF (01938) 552542 FAX (01938) 556565 E-MAIL sales@tanners-wines.co.uk WEBSITE www.tanners-wines.co.uk HOURS Shrewsbury Mon–Sat 9–6, branches 9–5.30 CARDS AmEx, MasterCard, Switch, Visa DISCOUNTS 5% 1 mixed case, 7.5% 5 mixed cases (cash & collection); 2.5% for 3 mixed cases, 5% for 5, 7.5% for 10 (MAIL ORDER) DELIVERY Free 1 mixed case over £80, otherwise £7.50 MINIMUM ORDER £25 EN PRIMEUR Bordeaux, Burgundy, Rhône, Germany, Port. C G M T
✪ Star attractions *The sort of list from which it's extremely difficult to choose, because you simply want everything on it. There are lots of lovely Rhônes; Bordeaux and Burgundy are both terrific; Germany is outstanding, and there are even a couple of wines from Switzerland, Greece and Lebanon. Spain and Italy look very good, and Australia,*

South Africa, Chile, Argentina and California all show what these places can do.

- 2004 Three Choirs Estate Premium, Medium Dry, Three Choirs, Gloucestershire, England, £5.99
- 2004 Wehlener Sonnenuhr Riesling Spätlese, Heribert Kerpen, Mosel, Germany, £9.10
- 2003 Premier Cru Les Purozots-Dessus Meursault, Domaine Vincent Girardin, Burgundy, France, £29.60
- 1997 Château Latour, Pauillac, Bordeaux, France, £79.00

Tesco

HEAD OFFICE Tesco House, PO Box 18, Delamare Road, Cheshunt EN8 9SL (01992) 632222 FAX (01992) 630794, CUSTOMER SERVICE 0800 505555; 916 licensed branches E-MAIL customer.services@tesco.co.uk WEBSITE www.tesco.com HOURS Variable CARDS MasterCard, Switch, Visa DISCOUNT 5% on 6 bottles or more G M T
• CALAIS STORE Tesco Vin Plus, Cité Europe, 122 Boulevard du Kent, 62231 Coquelles, France (0033) 3 21 46 02 70 WEBSITE www.tesco.com/ vinplus; www.tesco-france.com HOURS Mon–Sat 8.30–10pm
✪ Star attractions *These days there's something for everyone at Tesco. They've just introduced a range of 50 very serious premium wines, mostly priced around £20, in between 90 and 190 stores. The Tesco Finest range reveals some true beauties, well worth the extra quid or two they'll cost.*

Tesco.com offers an even greater selection of wines by the case. And there are still lots of cheapies for when your budget is more of the baked beans on toast sort.

- **2005 Vieille Fontaine, Vin de Pays de Gers, Producteurs Vignoble de Gascogne, South-West France, £2.99**
- **2004 Semillon, Tim Adams, Clare Valley, South Australia, £8.99**
- **2004 Touriga Nacional, Tesco Finest (Jose Neiva), Estremadura, Portugal, £5.99**
- **NV Champagne Premier Cru Brut , Champagne, France, £14.79**

Thameside Wines

265 Putney Bridge Road, Putney, London, SW15 2PT (020) 8788 4752 **FAX** (020) 8789 5884 **E-MAIL** sales@thamesidewines.com **WEBSITE** www.thamesidewines.com
HOURS Mon–Sat 10–9, Sun 11–9 **CARDS** AmEx, MasterCard, Switch, Visa **DISCOUNTS** 10% mixed case, 10% on 6 bottles sparkling **DELIVERY** Free locally otherwise £12 per case, £6 each additional case. **G T**
✪ Star attractions *Stephen Skelton MW heads the wine-buying team here; he knows more about English wines than almost anyone else on the planet, so you can be confident in his selection of English still and sparkling wines. But there's far more to Thameside wines: the list is wide ranging and well chosen, and if you turn up at the shop you're likely to find the occasional bottle of mature Bordeaux at an excellent price.*

- **2003 Malbec Reserva, Familia Zuccardi, Mendoza, Argentina, £7.19**
- **2003 Madeleine Angevine, Sharpham, Devon, England, £9.86**
- **2004 Polish Hill Riesling, Grosset, Clare Valley, South Australia, £16.16**
- **2003 Célèbre, Ata Rangi, Martinborough, New Zealand, £16.65**

Thresher Group: Thresher Wine Shops and Wine Rack

HEAD OFFICE Enjoyment Hall, Bessemer Road, Welwyn Garden City, Herts AL7 1BL (01707) 387200 **FAX** (01707) 387350 **WEBSITE** www.threshergroup.com; 950 Thresher Wine Shops, 150 Wine Rack stores **HOURS** Mon–Sat 10–10 (some 10.30), Sun 11–10, Scotland 12.30–10.30 **CARDS** MasterCard, Switch, Visa **DELIVERY** Free locally, some branches. **G T**
✪ Star attractions *A major high street presence, Thresher wine shops are presumably a reflection of everyday wine drinking in Britain: there's certainly a good choice of Sauvignon Blanc. A lot of effort has gone into sourcing new wines over the past couple of years: Australia and France take the leading roles, with strong support from Spain, New Zealand and South America. Prices start at £3.99, but the 'buy any 2 bottles get the third bottle free' deal brings this down to £2.66 – it needn't be 3 of the same wine.*

- **2004 Campo de Borja Garnacha-Tempranillo, La Riada, Aragón, Spain, £4.99/£3.33**

Exploring the World couldn't be easier!

At Wine Rack and Threshers you'll find an exclusive range of great wines at over 1,000 stores across the UK. With around 600 wines from all over the world to choose from and a stack of wine awards under our belt, you'll be spoilt for choice.

Buy 2 get 3rd free
And we couldn't offer you better value with our ongoing Buy 2 get 3rd free offer available on all wines and champagnes every day, all year round. What else would you expect from The Drinks Business, 2006 Retailer of the Year.

Visit your local store or go to **www.threshergroup.com** to find your nearest Wine Rack or Thresher.

- 2005 Sauvignon Blanc, Old Vines, Doña Dominga, Colchagua Valley, Chile, £6.99/£4.66
- 2005 Sauvignon Blanc, Penmara, Orange, New South Wales, Australia, £8.99/£5.99
- NV Pelorus, Cloudy Bay, Marlborough, New Zealand, £17.99/£11.99

Turville Valley Wines

The Firs, Potter Row, Great Missenden, Bucks HP16 9LT (01494) 868818 FAX (01494) 868832 E-MAIL chris@turville-valley-wines.com WEBSITE www.turville-valley-wines.com HOURS Mon–Fri 9–5.30 CARDS None DELIVERY By arrangement MINIMUM ORDER £300/12 bottles. C M
✪ Star attractions *Serious wines for serious spenders. The Bordeaux is all classic, mostly mature stuff – no lesser wines here – and there are buckets of Domaine de la Romanée-Conti Burgundies. There are top names too from Spain, Italy, the Rhône, California (Screaming Eagle, Harlan Estate, Pahlmeyer), Australia (Grange, Duck Muck, Torbreck) and odds and ends from all over.*

- 1990 Dame de Montrose St-Estèphe, Château Montrose, Bordeaux, France, £50.00
- 1995 Grange, Penfolds, Australia, £115.00
- 1999 Échézeaux, Domaine de la Romanée-Conti, Burgundy, France, £210.00
- 1998 Maya Proprietary Blend, Dalla Valle, California, USA, £222.00

Valvona & Crolla

19 Elm Row, Edinburgh EH7 4AA (0131) 556 6066 FAX (0131) 556 1668 E-MAIL wine@valvonacrolla.co.uk WEBSITE www.valvonacrolla.com HOURS Mon–Sat 8–6.30, Sun 11–5 CARDS AmEx, MasterCard, Switch, Visa DISCOUNTS 7% 1–3 cases, 10% 4 or more DELIVERY Free on orders over £150, otherwise £9; Saturdays free on orders over £200, otherwise £15. G M T
✪ Star attractions *If you're fond of Italian wines you should be shopping here. The list has dozens and dozens of wines from Piedmont and Tuscany, and there are others from Lombardy, Basilicata, Calabria, the Marche, Sicily, Sardinia, the Veneto, and terrific dessert wines. It's a simply fabulous selection, and at all prices. There are wines from Australia, New Zealand, France, Argentina, Spain and Portugal and elsewhere, but they are not what V&C is really about.*

- 2004 Aglianico Beneventano, Campania, Italy, £7.99
- 2004 Nebbiolo Langhe, Produttori del Barbaresco, Piedmont, Italy, £9.99
- 2004 Morellino di Scansano, Le Pupille, Tuscany, Italy, £11.95
- 2002 Torcolato, Fausto Maculan, Veneto, Italy, £15.95

Villeneuve Wines

1 Venlaw Court, Peebles, Scotland EH45 8AE (01721) 722500 FAX (01721) 729922
- 82 High Street, Haddington EH41 3ET (01620) 822224
- 49A Broughton Street, Edinburgh

EH1 3RJ (0131) 558 8441
E-MAIL wines@villeneuvewines.com
WEBSITE www.villeneuvewines.com
HOURS (Peebles) Mon–Sat 9–8, Sun
12.30–5.30; (Haddington) Mon–Sat
9–7; (Edinburgh) Mon–Thurs 10–10,
Fri–Sat 9–10, Sun 12.30–10 **CARDS**
AmEx, MasterCard, Switch, Visa
DISCOUNTS 5% per case **DELIVERY** Free
locally, £8.50 per case elsewhere.
G M T
✪ Star attractions *Italy, California,
Australia and New Zealand are all
marvellous here. Italy has Pieropan,
Planeta, Aldo Conterno, Livio Felluga,
Jermann, Allegrini and many others.
From California there are wines from
Duckhorn, Cuvaison, Sanford and Ridge.
Australia includes Brokenwood, Cullen,
Mount Horrocks, Rockford and
Plantagenet and New Zealand has
Mount Difficulty, Cloudy Bay and Saint
Clair, among others. Spain is clearly an
enthusiasm too.*
• 2004 Sauvignon Blanc, Wairau
  Reserve, Saint Clair, Marlborough,
  New Zealand, £9.00
• 2004 Sharjs (Chardonnay-Ribolla
  Gialla), Livio Felluga, Friuli-Venezia
  Giulia, Italy, £15.00
• 2003 Plexus Shiraz-Grenache-
  Mourvedre, John Duval, Barossa
  Valley, South Australia, £18.00
• 2001 Pinot Noir, Sanford, Santa
  Barbara County, California, USA,
  £21.00

Vinceremos

74 Kirkgate, Leeds LS2 7DJ (0113)
244 0002 **FAX** (0113) 288 4566

E-MAIL info@vinceremos.co.uk
WEBSITE www.vinceremos.co.uk
HOURS Mon–Fri 8.30–5.30
CARDS AmEx, Delta, MasterCard,
Switch, Visa, **DISCOUNTS** 5% on 5 cases
or over, 10% on 10 cases or over
DELIVERY Free delivery 5 cases or more
MINIMUM ORDER 1 mixed case **M**
✪ Star attractions *Organic specialist,
with a wide-ranging list of wines: Guy
Bossard's Muscadet, Huet's Vouvray,
Sedlescombe in England, Millton in
New Zealand, Fetzer's Bonterra wines
from California and a whole page of
reds and whites from Morocco.*
• 2004 Primitivo, Era, Puglia, Italy,
  £4.59
• 2003 Dry White, Sedlescombe
  Vineyard, East Sussex, England,
  £8.29
• 2003 Riesling Opou Vineyard,
  Millton Vineyards, Gisborne, New
  Zealand, £8.99
• 2003 Vacqueyras, Montirius, Rhône
  Valley, France, £9.49

Vin du Van

MAIL ORDER Colthups, The Street,
Appledore, Kent TN26 2BX (01233)
758727 **FAX** (01233) 758389
HOURS Mon–Fri 9–5 **CARDS** Delta,
MasterCard, Switch, Visa **DELIVERY**
Free locally; elsewhere £5.95 for first
case, further cases free.
Highlands & islands ask for quote
MINIMUM ORDER 1 mixed case. **G M**
✪ Star attractions *Quirky, star-studded
Australian list, the kind of inspired
lunacy I'd take to read on the first
manned space trip to Mars.*

- 2004 Seven Sleepers/Siebenschlafer, Kurtz Family, Barossa Valley, South Australia, £8.95
- 2005 Semillon, Ashbrook, Margaret River, Western Australia, £10.75
- 2003 Zinfandel, Lowe, Mudgee, New South Wales, Australia, £12.95
- 2002 The Malleea Cabernet-Shiraz, Majella, Coonawarra, South Australia, £24.95

Vintage Roots

Farley Farms, Reading Road, Arborfield, Berkshire, RG2 9HT (0118) 976 1999 FAX (0118) 976 1998 HOURS Mon–Fri 8.30–5.30, Saturdays in December E-MAIL info@vintageroots.co.uk WEBSITE www.vintageroots.co.uk CARDS Delta, MasterCard, Switch, Visa DISCOUNTS 5% on 5 cases or over DELIVERY £5.95 for single case, £6.95 2–5 cases, free 6 cases or more. M T

✪ Star attractions *Everything on this list is organic and/or biodynamic, beginning with Champagnes and other fizz and ending with beers and cider. Chile looks good – as indeed it should – alongside France, Spain and Italy.*

- 2005 Valpolicella, Fasoli Gino, Veneto, Italy, £5.75
- 2005 Navarra Rosa de Azul y Garanza, Fernando Barrena, Spain, £6.50
- 2005 Grüner Veltliner Meinklang, Michlits Werner, Burgenland, Austria, £6.99
- 2004 Chenin Blanc, Te Arai Vineyard, Millton Vineyards, Gisborne, New Zealand, £11.99

Virgin Wines

MAIL ORDER The Loft, St James' Mill, Whitefriars, Norwich NR3 1TN 0870 164 9593 FAX (01603) 619277 CUSTOMER SERVICE 0870 164 9593 E-MAIL help@virginwines.com WEBSITE www.virginwines.com HOURS (office) Mon–Fri 8–7, Sat–Sun 10–5, Internet 24 hrs CARDS AmEx, MasterCard, Switch, Visa DISCOUNTS regular special offers DELIVERY £4.99 for UK, N Ireland and Scottish Highlands, £6.99 for Saturday delivery within M25 MINIMUM ORDER 1 case. G M

✪ Star attractions *Internet retailer with hundreds of reasonably priced wines from all around the world. The list is organized by style – Kiwi Sauvignon Blanc style, Fragrant but dry whites, Soft and juicy reds, Huge reds, etc – and encourages the buyer to branch out and try new wines.*

Waitrose

HEAD OFFICE Doncastle Road, Southern Industrial Area, Bracknell, Berks RG12 8YA CUSTOMER SERVICE 08456 049049, 166 licensed stores E-MAIL customerservice@waitrose. co.uk WEBSITE www.waitrose.com/wines HOURS Mon–Sat 8.30–7, 8 or 9, Sun 10–4 or 11–5 CARDS AmEx, Delta, MasterCard, Switch, Visa DISCOUNTS 5% for 6 bottles or more DELIVERY Home Delivery and Waitrose deliver for £3.95, Free for orders over £150 EN PRIMEUR Bordeaux, Port. G T

- WAITROSE WINE DIRECT order online

The spectacular Amalfi Coast, south of Naples,
has grown grapes since ancient times

at www.waitrose.com/winelist
E-MAIL winedirect@waitrose.co.uk
DISCOUNTS Vary monthly on featured
cases **DELIVERY** Free for orders of £75
or more throughout UK mainland and
Isle of Wight, otherwise £4.95 per
delivery address.

✪ Star attractions *Still ahead of the
other supermarkets in quality, value
and imagination. Waitrose brings you
the best from around the world. There
are some very good clarets – such as
the Côtes de Castillon Seigneurs
d'Aiguilhe at £7.99 (see page 126) – and
Burgundies, and some wonderful
discoveries from southern France, the
Rhône and the Loire. Italy, Germany,
Australia and New Zealand have wines
to suit every pocket. Despite its
reputation for being a tad expensive,
we found lots of really tasty stuff at
under £5. All Waitrose wines are
available from Waitrose Wine Direct.*

- **2005 Sauvignon-Semillon, Delors,
  Bordeaux, France, £3.99**
- **2005 Chiroubles, Georges Duboeuf,
  Beaujolais, France, £7.99**
- **2004 Clos de los Siete, Mendoza,
  Argentina, £10.99**
- **1999 Nyetimber Blanc de Blancs
  Première Cuvée, Nyetimber, West
  Sussex, England, £21.99**

Waterloo Wine Co

OFFICE AND WAREHOUSE 6 Vine Yard,
London SE1 1QL **SHOP** 59–61 Lant
Street, London SE1 1QL (020) 7403 7967
FAX (020) 7357 6976 **E-MAIL**
sales@waterloowine. co.uk **WEBSITE**
www.waterloowine. co.uk **HOURS**
Mon–Fri 10–6.30, Sat 10–5 **CARDS**
AmEx, MasterCard, Switch, Visa
DELIVERY Free 5 cases in central London
(otherwise £5); elsewhere, 1 case £10, 2
cases £7.50 each. **G T**

✪ Star attractions *Quirky, personal list,
strong in the Loire and making
something of a speciality of the wines of
the Waipara region of Canterbury, New
Zealand. Waterloo are the UK agents for
Minervois from Domaine La Tour Boisée
– and this is one of the few places you'll
find wines from Slovenia. Also a shortish
but interesting list of clarets.*

- **2004 Minervois, Cuvée Marielle et
  Frederique, Domaine la Tour-Boisée,
  Languedoc, France, £6.35**
- **2004 Chardonnay Two Terrace,
  Waipara West, Waipara, New
  Zealand, £7.99**
- **2004 Anjou Gamay, Domaine
  Richou, Loire Valley, France, £8.30**
- **2003 Grüner Veltliner,
  Schneiderberg, Weingut Weinrieder,
  Weinviertel, Austria, £8.99**

Whitesides of Clitheroe

Shawbridge Street, Clitheroe,
Lancs BB7 1NA (01200) 422281
FAX (01200) 427129 **E-MAIL**
whitesides.wine@btconnect.com
HOURS Mon–Fri 9–5.30, Sat 10–4
CARDS MasterCard, Switch, Visa
DISCOUNTS 5% per case **DELIVERY** Free
locally, elsewhere at cost. **G M T**

✪ Star attractions *Shortish list, half
New World, half Europe, with a
reasonable amount of interesting kit
hidden away among rather a lot of
sub-£5 stuff.*

- 2004 Rioja Livor (organic), Viña Ijalba, Spain, £4.97
- 2004 Cabernet Sauvignon rosé, Santa Digna, Miguel Torres, Chile, £5.51
- 2003 Memsie, Water Wheel Vineyards, Bendigo, Victoria, Australia, £6.61
- 1999 Mercurey Blanc, Château de Chamirey, Antonin Rodet, Burgundy, France, £14.84

Wimbledon Wine Cellar

1 Gladstone Road, Wimbledon, London SW19 1QU (020) 8540 9979 **FAX** (020) 8540 9399
• 84 Chiswick High Road, London W4 1SY (020) 8994 7989 **FAX** (020) 8994 3683
• 4 The Boulevard, Imperial Wharf, Chelsea, London SW6 2UB (020) 7736 2191 **E-MAIL** enquiries@ wimbledonwinecellar.com, chiswick@wimbledonwinecellar.com or chelsea@wimbledonwinecellar.com **WEBSITE** www.wimbledonwinecellar.com **HOURS** Mon–Sat 10–9, Sun 11–7 (all stores) **CARDS** AmEx, MasterCard, Switch, Visa **DISCOUNTS** 10% off 1 case (with a few exceptions), 20% off case of Champagne **DELIVERY** Free local delivery. Courier charges elsewhere. **EN PRIMEUR** Burgundy, Bordeaux, Tuscany, Rhône. **C G M T**
✪ **Star attractions** *Top names from Italy, Burgundy, Bordeaux, Rhône, Loire – and some of the best of the New World, especially Australia, South Africa and California. They don't issue a list,*

WATERLOO WINE CO

61 Lant Street
London
SE1 1QL

Tel: 020 7403 7967

Email: sales@waterloowine.co.uk
www.waterloowine.co.uk

Agents for
independent producers from around
the world, including Waipara West.

www.waiparawest.com

as stock changes so frequently, so you'll just have to go along to one of the shops and dig out your own treasure or look at their website.
- 2003 Alto Malbec, Terrazas de los Andes, Mendoza, Argentina, £6.49
- 2000 Salice Salentino Riserva, Candido, Puglia, Italy, £7.99
- 2001 Prazo de Roriz, Quinta de Roriz, Douro, Portugal, £8.99
- 2003 Eden Valley Viognier, Yalumba, Eden Valley, South Australia, £9.99

Wine & Beer World (Majestic)

HEAD OFFICE Majestic House, Otterspool Way, Watford, Herts WD25 8WW (01923) 298200 **FAX** (01923) 819105 **PRE-ORDER** (01923) 298297 • Rue du Judée, Zone Marcel

Doret, Calais 62100, France (0033) 3 21 97 63 00

• Centre Commercial Carrefour, Quai L'Entrepôt, Cherbourg 50100, France (0033) 2 33 22 23 22

• Unit 3A, Zone La Française, Coquelles 62331, France (0033) 3 21 82 93 64 **E-MAIL** info@wineandbeer.co.uk **WEBSITE** www.wineandbeer.co.uk **HOURS** (Calais) 7 days 7–10 (Cherbourg) Mon–Sat 8.30–8 (Coquelles) 7 days 8–8. There is a free ferry crossing from Dover to Calais when your pre-order is over £300. All stores open bank holidays at the usual times **CARDS** MasterCard, Switch, Visa. **T**
✪ **Star attractions** *Savings of up to 50% on UK prices. The French arm of Majestic, handy for trips across the Channel: Calais is the largest branch, Coquelles the nearest to the Channel Tunnel terminal, while Cherbourg has a more limited range of wines. English-speaking staff.*

• **2003 Fitou Les Hauts de Montluzy, Les Producteurs du Mont Tauch, Languedoc-Roussillon, France, £2.79**
• **Viña Sol, Torres, Penedés, Cataluña, Spain, £3.49**
• **Pinot Noir, Cono Sur, Rapel Valley, Chile, £3.99**
• **NV Champagne Black Label, Lanson, Champagne, France, £14.99**

Winemark

3 Duncrue Place, Belfast BT3 9BU, 028 9074 6274 **FAX** 028 9074 8022 71 branches **E-MAIL** info@ winemark.com **WEBSITE** www.winemark.com **HOURS** Branches vary, but in general Mon–Sat 10–10, Sun 12–8 **CARDS** Delta, MasterCard, Switch, Visa **DISCOUNTS** 5% on 6–11 bottles, 10% on 12 bottles or more. **G M T**
✪ **Star attractions** *Winemark is strong in the New World, with plenty of everyday drinking from the likes of Peter Lehmann in Australia, or you could trade up to Chateau Reynella or Hardys Eileen Shiraz at £49.99; also wines from New Zealand (Esk Valley, Villa Maria), California (Geyser Peak), Chile (Errázuriz Wild Ferment Chardonnay), and there's a shortish but good list of Bordeaux from older vintages.*

• **Crianza, Campillo, Rioja, Spain, £9.99**
• **Wild Ferment Chardonnay, Errázuriz, Aconcagua, Chile, £9.99**
• **Sauvignon Blanc Clifford Bay, Villa Maria, New Zealand, £10.99**
• **Stonewell Shiraz, Peter Lehmann, Barossa Valley, Australia, £29.99**

wine-pages-shop.com

(0141) 576 4958 **FAX** (0141) 576 4958 **E-MAIL** info@wine-pages. com **WEBSITE** www.wine-pages.com
Now, this sounds like a great idea, it's a website set up by wine writer Tom Cannavan, and offers mixed cases selected by Tom (with tasting notes to help you choose) and supplied direct from UK retailers. Tom has negotiated some exclusive discounts and persuaded the retailers to waive their delivery charges, so there are some truly amazing savings to be made.

Wine Rack

See Thresher Group.

The Wine Society

Gunnels Wood Road, Stevenage, Herts
SG1 2BG (01438) 741177 FAX (01438)
761167 ORDER LINE (01438) 740222
E-MAIL memberservices@
thewinesociety.com WEBSITE
www.thewinesociety.com
HOURS Mon–Fri 8.30–9, Sat 9–5;
showroom: Mon–Thurs 10–6, Fri 10–7,
Sat 9.30–5.30 CARDS AmEx,
MasterCard, Switch, Visa DISCOUNTS
(per case) £3 per collection DELIVERY
Free 1 case or more UK mainland and
N Ireland. Collection facility at
Montreuil, France, at French rates of
duty and VAT EN PRIMEUR Bordeaux,
Burgundy, Germany, Port, Rhône.
✪ Star attractions *The Wine Society has
an inspired wine-buying team and this is
an outstanding list. Bordeaux is
excellent, with masses of well-chosen
affordable wines as well as big names;
Burgundy ditto; Rhône ditto; Loire, Italy,
Spain, Portugal, all ditto, and lovely,
classy New World wines. If you close your
eyes and choose wines from this list with
a pin, you'll always get something
wonderful. The own label wines are as
good as ever. You have to be a member to
buy wine, but it costs only £40 for life
and although it is necessary to be
proposed by an existing member to join,
the secretary of the society will propose
you if you don't know any members.*
• **2004 The Society's Chilean Cabernet
  Sauvignon, Concha y Toro, Maipo
  Valley, Chile, £5.50**
• **2005 Sauvignon Blanc Ventolera,
  Viña Litoral, Leyda Valley, Chile,
  £8.50**
• **2003 Château Pey la Tour, Bordeaux
  Supérieur, Dourthe, Bordeaux,
  France, £8.75**
• **NV The Society's Exhibition
  Champagne Blanc de Blancs, Alfred
  Gratien, Champagne, France,
  £25.00**

Wine Treasury

MAIL ORDER 69–71 Bondway,
London SW8 1SQ (020) 7793
9999 FAX (020) 7793 8080
E-MAIL bottled@winetreasury.com
WEBSITE www.winetreasury.com
HOURS Mon–Fri 9.30–6 CARDS
MasterCard, Switch, Visa DISCOUNTS
10% for unmixed dozens DELIVERY £10
per case, free 2 or more cases over
£200, England and Wales; Scotland
phone for more details MINIMUM
ORDER 1 mixed case. M T
✪ Star attractions *California is a
speciality here. There are the stunning
Cabernet Sauvignons and Chardonnays
from Stag's Leap Wine Cellars,
Zinfandel from Cline Cellars, lots of
tasty stuff from Joseph Phelps and
much, much more. Italy looks just as
good, with stars such as Roberto
Voerzio from Piedmont and Tuscany's
Castello di Ama. But these top names
don't come cheap.*
• **2005 Moscato Bricco Quaglia, La
  Spinetta, Piedmont, Italy, £9.75**
• **2002 Alsace Gewurztraminer,
  Domaine Rieflé, Alsace, France,
  £11.95**

- 2004 Big Break Zinfandel, Cline, Sonoma Valley, California, USA, £13.45
- 2004 Conundrum, Caymus Vineyards, Napa Valley, California, USA, £16.90

The Winery

4 Clifton Road, London W9 1SS (020) 7286 6475 **FAX** (020) 7286 2733 **E-MAIL** info@thewineryuk.com **WEBSITE** www.thewineryuk.com
- The Winery at Liberty, Tudor Building, Second Floor, Liberty, Regent Street, London W1B 5AH (020) 7734 3239 **E-MAIL** liberty@thewineryuk.com **HOURS** Mon–Sat 11–9.30, Sun and public holidays 12–8 **CARDS** MasterCard, Switch, Visa **DISCOUNTS** 5% on a mixed case **DELIVERY** Free locally or for 3 cases or more, otherwise £10 per case. **G M T**
✪ **Star attractions** *Burgundy, Rhône, Italy and California are the specialities, and there's a range of grower Champagnes. The company sources its own wines, so it's a list to linger over – and a shop to linger in, especially when they're holding one of their regular tastings.*
- 2004 Rueda, Blanco Nieva Verdejo, Viñedos de Nieva, Spain, £8.99
- 2004 Salento Rosso, Armentino, Schola Sarmenti, Puglia, Italy, £11.50
- 2002 Zinfandel, Chiles Mill Vineyard, Green & Red, Napa Valley, California, USA, £21.99
- NV Champagne Grand Cru Cuvée Delos, Pierre Moncuit, Champagne, France, £22.50

Wines of Westhorpe

136a Doncaster Rd, Mexborough, South Yorks S64 0JW (01709) 584863 **FAX** (01709) 584863 **E-MAIL** wines@westhorpe.co.uk **WEBSITE** www.westhorpe.co.uk **HOURS** Mon–Thu 9–9, Fri–Sat 9–6 **DISCOUNTS** Variable on 2 dozen or more **DELIVERY** Free UK mainland (except northern Scotland) **MINIMUM ORDER** 1 mixed case. **M**
✪ **Star attractions** *An excellent list for devotees of Eastern European wines – especially Hungarian and Romanian – all at reasonable prices. From Hungary there's Kékfrankos, Kékoportó and Tokaji, as well as Szekszárdi Cabernet Franc and Budai Sauvignon Blanc. The smaller selection from Chile is good this year.*
- 2005 Chardonnay Budai, Nyakas, Buda, Hungary, £4.92
- 2002 Carmenère Reserve, Peteroa, Central Valley, Chile, £5.77
- 2004 Kékfrankos, Tamas Gere & Zsolt, Villany, Hungary, £5.93
- 2000 Chateau Vincent Extra Brut, Hungary, £7.43

Wright Wine Co

The Old Smithy, Raikes Road, Skipton, N. Yorks BD23 1NP (01756) 700886 (01756) 794175 **FAX** (01756) 798580 **E-MAIL** bob@wineand whisky.co.uk **WEBSITE** www.wine andwhisky.co.uk **HOURS** Mon–Fri 9–6; Sat 10–5:30; open Sundays in December 10.30–4 **CARDS** MasterCard, Switch, Visa **DISCOUNTS** 10% unsplit case, 5% mixed case **DELIVERY** Free within 30 miles, elsewhere at cost. **G**

✪ Star attractions *Looking equally
good in both Old World and New
World, this is a pretty comprehensive
list, packed with good stuff at keen
prices. Wide choice of half bottles.*

- 2005 Unoaked Chardonnay, Jordan,
Stellenbosch, South Africa, £7.50
- 2003 Bourgogne Blanc, Cuvée St-
Vincent, Domaine Vincent Girardin,
Burgundy, France, £11.85
- 2002 Rufus Stone Shiraz, Tyrrell's,
Heathcote, Victoria, Australia £12.85
- 2000 Dão, Touriga Nacional, Quinta
dos Roques, Dão, Portugal, £18.75

Peter Wylie Fine Wines

Plymtree Manor, Plymtree,
Cullompton, Devon EX15 2LE (01884)
277555 **FAX** (01884) 277557
E-MAIL peter@wylie-fine-wines.
demon.co.uk **WEBSITE** www.wylie
finewines.co.uk **HOURS** Mon–Fri 9–6
CARDS None **DISCOUNTS** Unsplit cases
DELIVERY Up to 3 cases £20, 4 or more
cases at cost. **C M**
✪ Star attractions *Fascinating list of
very old wines. Bordeaux from
throughout the 20th century (the
current lists begins with 1914) and a
decent selection of serious wines from
every top vintage. Red and white
Bordeaux are the top performers on
this list, but there are also a few
Rhônes and Burgundies, plus ports
going back to 1904, Madeiras to 1860.*

- 1989 Château Canon-la-Gaffelière
St-Émilion Grand Cru Classé,
Bordeaux, France, £50.00
- 1970 Vintage Port, Fonseca, Douro,
Portugal, £65.00

- 1940 Sercial Madeira, Blandy,
Madeira, Portugal, £95.00
- 1982 Château Léoville-Barton, St-
Julien, Bordeaux, France, £530
(double magnum)

Yapp Brothers

The Old Brewery, Mere, Wilts BA12 6DY
(01747) 860423 **FAX** (01747) 860929
E-MAIL sales@yapp.co.uk
WEBSITE www.yapp.co.uk **HOURS**
Mon–Sat 9–6 **CARDS** MasterCard,
Switch, Visa **DISCOUNTS** £5 per case on
collection **DELIVERY** £5 one case, 2 or
more cases free. **C G M T**
✪ Star attractions *Rhône and Loire
specialists who really know their way
around these regions. They also have
some of the hard-to-find wines of
Provence (Bunan/Château de la
Rouvière, Richeaume, Trévallon), Savoie
and Corsica – oh, and two interlopers
from Australia (Jasper Hill and Neagles
Rock).*

- 2004 Saumur-Champigny, Domaine
Filliatreau, Loire Valley, France, £8.50
- 2005 Sancerre Les Perriers, André
Vatan, Loire Valley, France, £10.95
- 2004 Crozes-Hermitage, Alain
Graillot, Rhône Valley, France, £13.50
- 2003 Châteauneuf-du-Pape, Le Vieux
Donjon, Rhône Valley, France, £26.00

Noel Young Wines

56 High Street, Trumpington,
Cambridge CB2 2LS (01223) 844744
FAX (01223) 844736 **E-MAIL**
admin@nywines.co.uk
WEBSITE www.nywines.co.uk
HOURS Mon–Sat 10–8, Sun 12–2 **CARDS**

AmEx, MasterCard, Switch, Visa
DISCOUNTS 5% for orders over £500
DELIVERY Free over 12 bottles unless
discounted **EN PRIMEUR** Australia,
Burgundy, Italy, Rhône. **G M T**
✪ **Star attractions** *Fantastic wines
from just about everywhere. Think of a
region and you'll find the best wines on
Noel Young's list. Australia is a
particular passion. There's a famously
good Austrian list, some terrific
Germans, plus beautiful Burgundies,
Italians and dessert wines.*

- **2004 Chablis Premier Cru Vaillons,
  Christian Moreau, Burgundy, France,
  £15.99**
- **1999 Welschriesling TBA No. 8
  Zwischen Den Seen
  Trockenbeerenauslese, Kracher,
  Austria, £28.99**
- **2005 Nantua Les Deux, Giaconda,
  Beechworth, Victoria, Australia,
  £32.99**
- **Escherndorfer Lump Riesling
  Trockenbeerenauslese, Horst Sauer,
  Franken, Germany, £37.00**

Who's where

COUNTRYWIDE/ MAIL ORDER ONLY
Adnams
Aldi
ASDA
L'Assemblage
Australian Wine Club
H & H Bancroft Wines
Bibendum Wine
Bordeaux Index
ChateauOnline
Co-op
Nick Dobson Wines
Domaine Direct
Fine Wines of New Zealand
Roger Harris Wines
Jeroboams
Justerini & Brooks
Laithwaites
Lay & Wheeler
Laytons
Liberty Wines
O W Loeb
Majestic
Marks & Spencer
Millésima
Montrachet
Morrisons
Oddbins
OZ WINES
Real Wine Co
Howard Ripley
Sainsbury's
Somerfield
Stone, Vine & Sun
Sunday Times Wine Club
Tesco
Thresher
Vin du Van
Vintage Roots
Virgin Wines
Waitrose
wine-pages-shop.com
Wine Rack
The Wine Society
Wine Treasury
Wines of Westhorpe
Peter Wylie Fine Wines
Yapp Brothers
Noel Young Wines

LONDON
Armit
Balls Brothers
H & H Bancroft Wines
Berkmann Wine Cellars
Berry Bros. & Rudd
Budgens
Corney & Barrow
Farr Vintners
Fortnum & Mason
Friarwood
Goedhuis & Co
Green & Blue
Handford Wines
Harvey Nichols
Haynes Hanson & Clark
Jeroboams
Lea & Sandeman
Moreno Wines
Philglas & Swiggot
Roberson
RSJ Wine Company
Thameside Wines

Waterloo Wine Co
Wimbledon Wine Cellar
The Winery

SOUTH-EAST AND HOME COUNTIES
A&B Vintners
Bacchus Wine
Berry Bros. & Rudd
Budgens
Butlers Wine Cellar
Cape Wine and Food
Les Caves de Pyrene
Flagship Wines
Le Fleming Wines
The Flying Corkscrew
Hedley Wright
Maison du Vin
Quaff Fine Wine Merchant
Turville Valley Wines

WEST AND SOUTH-WEST
Averys Wine Merchants
Bennetts Fine Wines
Berkmann Wine Cellars
Great Western Wine
Haynes Hanson & Clark
Hicks & Don
Laymont & Shaw
The Nobody Inn

Christopher Piper Wines
Reid Wines
Savage Selection
Peter Wylie Fine Wines
Yapp Brothers

EAST ANGLIA
Adnams
Amey's Wines
Budgens
Anthony Byrne
Corney & Barrow
Hicks & Don
Seckford Wines
T & W Wines
Noel Young Wines

MIDLANDS
Bat & Bottle
Connolly's
Croque-en-Bouche
deFINE
Gauntleys
Harvey Nichols
S H Jones
Nickolls & Perks
Noble Rot Wine Warehouses
Portland Wine Co
Stevens Garnier
Tanners

WALES
Ballantynes Wine Merchants
Devigne Wines
Irma Fingal-Rock
Moriarty Vintners
Terry Platt Wine Merchants
Tanners

NORTH

Berkmann Wine
  Cellars
Booths
D Byrne
Great Northern
  Wine
Halifax Wine Co
Harvey Nichols
Martinez Wines
Nidderdale Fine
  Fines
Penistone Court
  Wine Cellars
Playford Ros
Richardson &
  Sons
Frank Stainton
  Wines
Vinceremos
Whitesides of
  Clitheroe
Wright Wine Co

SCOTLAND

Berkmann Wine
  Cellars
Cockburns of Leith
Corney & Barrow
Friarwood
Peter Green & Co
Harvey Nichols
Linlithgow Wines
Raeburn Fine
  Wines
Valvona & Crolla
Vill   ve Wines

NORTHERN IRELAND

Direct Wine
  Shipments
James Nicholson
Winemark

CHANNEL ISLANDS

Sommelier Wine Co

FRANCE

Millésima
Oddbins
Sainsbury's
Tesco Vin Plus
Wine & Beer
  World

Acknowledgments

The publishers would like to thank all the retailers, agents and individuals who have helped to source wine labels and bottle photographs.

Photo credits

Cephas: Mick Rock/Cephas 3, 21, 49, 64, 86, 102, 105, 112, 128, 172–3, 214–5
Stephen Bartholomew 134–5
Nigel James 111
Marc de Tienda 1, 2, 4, 15
Adrian Webster 6